DOCUMENTS THAT CHANGED THE WAY WE LIVE

DOCUMENTS THAT CHANGED THE WAY WE LIVE

JOSEPH JANES

ROWMAN & LITTLEFIELD
Lanham • Boulder • New York • London

Published by Rowman & Littlefield
A wholly owned subsidiary of The Rowman & Littlefield Publishing Group, Inc.
4501 Forbes Boulevard, Suite 200, Lanham, Maryland 20706
www.rowman.com

Unit A, Whitacre Mews, 26-34 Stannary Street, London SE11 4AB

British Library Cataloguing in Publication Information Available

Library of Congress Cataloging-in-Publication Data Available

ISBN 978-1-5381-0033-2 (cloth : alk. paper)
ISBN 978-1-5381-0034-9 (electronic)

∞™ The paper used in this publication meets the minimum requirements of American National Standard for Information Sciences—Permanence of Paper for Printed Library Materials, ANSI/NISO Z39.48-1992.

Printed in the United States of America

for Terry,
who makes the songs make sense

CONTENTS

My office is a mess. Not just in a "Gee, somebody really ought to dust in here" way, either. There are papers and books and folders and such everywhere, ancient long-faded Post-it notes indicating what goes on what shelf or in what pile. (File drawers are for dead things.) You get the idea. It's not a mess to me, naturally, because I know where everything is. I put it there, with the most recently used or consulted things nearest by, so as a result, they're handy.

So when I say I know about documents, I know about documents. I swim in them daily. I also have professional credentials, with training and experience both as a librarian and as an information scientist and a few decades of educating and preparing people for careers of all kinds in the information world. Fundamentally, I am interested in and fascinated by the stuff itself; all the forms and genres of information that we've created over the centuries to record, well, just about everything, how those have been developed and evolved, how they work, and how it's all changing. In that light, a project like this seems not only like a great fit, it seems practically inevitable.

That means I approach these documents and their stories as an information scientist and as a librarian. I'm not a historian—at least I wasn't trained that way—or an archivist, or a sociologist or journalist. Having spent my entire life immersed in the study of information and information objects, that's how I see the world; as my friend and mentor Mike Eisenberg invariably puts it, I look at the world through information-colored glasses. So while most people would see the Rosetta Stone as a monumental object that has survived the centuries to represent its culture, I want to know what it *says*, how it got written, and what happened to it. People visit the Vietnam Veterans Memorial on the National Mall and grieve for a generation or more of young men and women lost in a ghastly and largely purposeless war. I do too, and I also want to know how those thousands of names got there, who decided who was listed and not. Those information stories are here, and many more besides.

What you see here is the printed and illustrated version of a podcast series I started in 2012 called *Documents That Changed the World*. I began that as a way of telling stories about documents, the various kinds of things we create, intentionally and otherwise, to record and remember. Lots of those things are obvious, so there's a birth certificate here, and a will, a map, a telegram, a presidential proclamation, a couple of letters, and quite a few books, the sorts of things everybody is used to thinking of as "documents."

There are also a few things that stretch that definition a bit: a home movie, for example, which if it were not taken in Dallas on a certain November afternoon in 1963 would be completely unremembered. A ticker tape. A ballot. A test. A quilt and a wall meant to memorialize people lost. None exactly leaps to mind when you think "document," though with a moment's thought, they make sense. There are also some objects that aren't what they seem: forgeries, frauds, fakes, a poster everybody recognizes but almost nobody knows. And creatures even more exotic: a sketch that can't be found, a law that has to be read out loud to work, a list that never was, a critical paragraph deleted, a conversation that became a void, the Constitution that I'll almost guarantee you isn't where you think it is.

I purposely decided to stretch that definition of "document" for a couple of reasons.

One of my not terribly well-concealed motives here is to help people understand the breadth and reach of what documents are and can be and are becoming, and the power they have in our lives individually and as communities and societies. Many things are created for the purpose of documenting, such as an invoice or a class photo. Just about anything, though, *can* document, based on the meaning somebody assigns to it. There are a handful of tiny pieces of white—now yellowed—paper I keep in a special place. They're a little less than an inch square and have no marking whatsoever, and if anybody else ran across them, they'd likely be seen as scrap paper or something equally meaningless. To me, though, they represent a powerful connection; they were used to simulate snow during the Opening Ceremony of the Winter Olympics in Vancouver, British Columbia, in 2010, which we got to attend, and every time I see those little scraps of paper, I go right back to that night and always will. There is power in every chapter here, and I wanted to expose that.

Where there's power, there's controversy, and that's here too. With a couple of obvious exceptions, I don't take sides—or at least I try my best not to—and tell these stories fair-mindedly and even-handedly, even though it's probably not all that hard to work out what I think in more than a few places. In general, I'm on the side of the documents, and like Bishop James Ussher in chapter 6, I do the best I can with the tools I have at hand.

After a quick glance at the table of contents, you might notice that some things you'd expect to find are missing. Where's Magna Carta? Or the Bill of Rights, the Bible, the Qur'an, the Bhagavad-Gita, the Emancipation Proclamation, the Communist Manifesto, the Code of Hammurabi? Those are all on the lists of the Most Important Documents in History, so to be honest, they've been written about thousands of times, and those stories aren't hard to find. I'm more interested in the ones that are somewhat less familiar, a bit off the beaten track, even a little odd. (And the list of topics I haven't yet done fill several pages in my battered black notebook, now its own document—the Bayeux Tapestry, "Steamboat Willie," the Q Source, the Tiriti o Waitangi, the first viral video, Sequoyah's syllabary, the first spreadsheet, the *Damnatio memoriae,* the *Kama Sutra,* Wikileaks, the Apple "1984" commercial, the Motion Picture Production Code, *My Name is Bill W.,* "Video Killed the Radio Star," Grimm's Fairy Tales, and on and on.) The list of what *is* here is admittedly idiosyncratic; as I began this project, I did what interested me, and now several dozen documents later, I hope it interests you as well.

What will you learn here? Who can say? Though I can tell you what you'll find:

- Why the Roman Catholic Church is "Roman"
- Why we only use Roman numerals for Super Bowls, royalty, and Olympiads
- Why, if you're American, you spell "color" with only five letters
- Why there are so many kinds of football
- Why every kitchen store sells measuring cups and spoons
- Why you can't prove your way out of a conspiracy
- Why about 5 percent of all the research reports you hear about aren't necessarily what they seem to be
- Why the Internet works the way it does
- Why an attempt to help more people to vote more easily in one community may have swung the entire history of a nation
- Why race is still . . .

And now, it's all changing. With a few exceptions, just about every document and format you see represented here has, or could have, some digital counterpart, and in many cases those digital versions might be more authentic or faithful or useful than the analog ones. That's certainly the case that the creators of the Nupedia made, which gave rise to the Wikipedia. Real-time stock market reports and texts are quicker than waiting for a ticker or telegram; a money-sharing app is more efficient than writing out and depositing a check; modern imaging techniques are substantially more effective and safer than taking and developing X-ray films; Googling a word is much faster than looking it up in a dictionary. All true, though then we'd be deprived the ornate script of the check that purchased Alaska, the haunting image of the first X-ray, or the homespun beauty of Catherine Elizabeth Brewer's diploma.

Four millennia of such progress are on display here, stories of faith and belief, science and investigation, learning, commerce, art, law, politics, war, revolution, hate, love, hope, death, birth, loss, memory, error, triumph—the great and noble and the simple and small. And food. It's the stories of us all, of our eternal, necessarily human quest to make sense of the world around us and make it work a little better.

We will begin with two men, separated by a few hundred miles and about half a dozen generations, a pope and a printer, and the two pieces of paper they generated that completely transformed their world and our world, and still do.

ACKNOWLEDGMENTS

Everybody knows—at least everybody who reads the acknowledgment sections of books—that things like these don't get done by anybody on their own. I have many debts of gratitude to repay for helping bring this book to fruition.

First, to my students, all the students I've had over the years at various schools and institutions, and in particular to those I've worked with on this project. This all started several years ago with one of my typically wacky ideas—wouldn't it be fun to do a podcast series about the stories and impacts of important documents? Andrew Brink, a master's student at the time, thought so too, and so we spent a quarter exploring the Gregorian Calendar and the Cholera Map (Andrew picked the gross one), figuring out what a podcast was, how to make it, how to make it interesting, how to write the scripts, how to do the research, and all the other various bits and pieces of the process. We indeed had great fun and the results came out pretty well, so I owe him a lot for helping to get this whole thing started. His work is here, as is the work of another of my graduate students, Eli Gandour-Rood, and several undergraduates who were part of freshman seminars I led about this project, so thanks also to Jill Fenno, Kelsey Gibbons, and Andrew Kyrios and all their colleagues for their questions, interest, and hard work. I'm proud to have their efforts included here.

I am also grateful to many generous people at the University of Washington Information School. Few people in academia are fortunate enough to have as large and collegial a community as we have, and so many of them have been interested in and supportive of my work. Allyson Carlyle, Katie Davis, Eliza Dresang, Megan Finn, Nancy Gershenfeld, Ricardo Gomez, Dave Hendry, Batya Friedman, Trent Hill, Ian King, Cortney Leach, Liz Mills, Marie Potter, Matt Saxton, David Stearns, Jevin West, and Jake Wobbruck, and especially Cheryl Metoyer, Mike Eisenberg, and Harry Bruce suggested topic ideas, answered ridiculous questions, listened patiently to me go on at great length about obscure aspects of documents they'd never heard of, talked me in off a few ledges, and in general have just been terrific colleagues and friends. Being a part of the iSchool community has been one of the great privileges of my professional life. Special thanks also to Nancy Huling and Mary Whisner and others at the University of Washington libraries for their help in tracking down the exotica I couldn't find on my own.

I'm particularly indebted to several people who were greatly instrumental in getting the podcast series heard and noted: Lori Dugdale and Michele Norris of the Information School, and the redoubtable Peter Kelley of the UW Office of News and Information. Each of them saw something in my work that they believed in and thought would be of greater and wider interest, yielding interviews, opportunities, and way more stories on the university's news website than I could ever have dreamed possible. Kindred spirits all, and friends to boot.

The book you see here is, I assure you, insanely complicated. It all looks easy—some breezily intriguing stories and a few pictures to liven things up, and the whole thing has in fact been a labor of love. That also means, though, that it's been a labor, and two people in particular made the labor much lighter and more manageable. I was so lucky to get help in the preparation and production of the manuscript from two outstanding graduate students: first Katie Mayer, who got the process off to such a solid and promising beginning before graduating and starting off on her career, and then the extraordinary Tim Blankemeyer, who has gone so far above and beyond what I could have expected from him. He has wrangled dozens of images and the nightmarish process of rights and permissions to use them, wrestled with all the text files, gotten everything into the correct formats and layouts and done it all with a calm and genial attitude that I find truly remarkable—all of which while he was taking too many credits and doing lots of other stuff besides. He quite literally saved my bacon, and I know he will go on to do great things from here on. Whoever is lucky enough to hire him will never regret it for a moment.

Tim also has thanks to pass along: Agnete Wisti Lassen, associate curator of the Yale Babylonian Collection, for help tracking down and verifying that a tablet among forty thousand in the YBC collection did indeed have an excerpt from the Exaltation of Inanna on it. Cathy Coxey Snow, director of Alumnae Affairs at Wesleyan College, for her kind assistance in acquiring the high-resolution image of Catherine Elizabeth Brewer Benson's 1840 diploma. David Mandapat, director of public relations for Space Needle LLC, for help locating a high-resolution image of the Space Needle sketch. Anthony "Indy" Magnoli, owner of Magnoli Props, for providing the image of his wonderful replica Letters of Transit. Patrick Fahy, archives technician at the Franklin D. Roosevelt Presidential Library, for his flexibility in assisting the project in acquiring both the Einstein letter to FDR and FDR's Thanksgiving Proclamation.

Now, finally, to the two people who really made this happen. First, my long-suffering publisher (aren't all publishers long-suffering?) and cherished friend, Charles Harmon, who may not quite have fully appreciated what we were all getting ourselves in for here, but who always cajoles and nudges and pushes and prods and occasionally scolds me in the nicest possible way into producing work I'm proud of and I hope he is too. This would never have seen the light of day as a book without his vision and confidence in me and, as ever, he has my undying gratitude.

Nor would it have happened if not for my husband, Terry Price. Always my loudest cheerleader, always my greatest supporter, always willing to tell me the truth when something doesn't sound quite right or needs to be better, always the first person to listen to a new podcast episode or read a new script, and the last word I turn to for guidance. He is the love of my life and makes the good days better and the bad days better and has been with me every step of the way with this and I wouldn't have it any other way.

1
Gregorian Calendar/Gutenberg Indulgence

a papal bull, known by the name *Inter gravissimas*
issued by Pope Gregory XIII in Rome
now housed in the Vatican Secret Archives

1582

an indulgence
printed in Mainz, Germany, almost certainly in the
print shop of Johannes Gutenberg
now housed at the University of Manchester

1454

What day is it?

That's a simple and common enough question, with a simple enough answer. As I write this, it's Wednesday; your mileage may vary. We all lose track of what day of the week it is from time to time, ditto with the day of the month. It's much less common not to know what month it is, let alone the year—if somebody asks you that seriously, it's a good sign they've just emerged from a coma or you're in a time-travel movie.

Here's a trickier question, which you may not ever have considered: "*Why* is today's date today's date?" This also has a simple answer: "Because the calendar/my phone/my computer/everybody says so," and for most purposes that's sufficient. There's a much deeper reason, though, which dictates why the calendar says so and who got to say what the calendar says and how.

Today, we know that a year has 365 days, sort of. Thousands of years ago, though, knowing how long a year was, when the sun would rise over a particular hill, when a star would be in the right position, really mattered, so that you knew when it was time to plant or bundle up for the winter or carry out a particular ritual.

The length of a modern month is a little trickier; some are 30 days, some are 31, February's indecisive, but in ancient times, this was actually easier. Particularly with the degree of imprecision in all of the examples I've just described. You can see a month right up in the sky, as the moon waxes and wanes over the course of 29 days or so. In fact, there's a prehistoric bone fragment etched with what might be a lunar cycle, potentially one of the earliest examples of purposeful writing we have. Days are simpler still; although the hours of sunlight vary in length over the course of a year and that effect is more pronounced the farther you get from the equator, the earth rotates on its axis regularly once every 23 hours, 56 minutes, and 4.1 seconds. Give or take.

The problem is, even though we can reckon the days and the months and the years independently from observation, trying to make them work together in a coordinated, structured way, is really hard. The year isn't exactly 365 days; it's more like 365¼—more precisely, 365 days, 5 hours, 48 minutes, and 46 seconds. And the lunar cycle of 29 days, which is really closer to 29½ and changes over the course of the year, doesn't divide evenly into either 365 or 365¼. The moon and the sun don't play all that well together, calendrically speaking, which leads to some serious challenges if you're trying to build a way of recording time that takes account of both the moon and the sun. Today, we take for granted that all this has been sorted out, but it's a subtle, difficult, and important problem, potentially as important as your eternal soul, and the question is: Who gets to decide?

Trying to figure out a way to make sense of the years and the months goes back to the dawn of human history. The Egyptians had a functioning calendar at least 6,000 years ago, and Ptolemy III added a leap day every four years in 238 BCE; the current Mayan calendar is at least 2,000 years old. Julius Caesar took a crack at solving the calendar problem and got it very nearly right, in the process giving us several month names that have persisted for two millennia, modestly naming July for himself.

That calendar worked just fine for quite a while, though over the centuries, a growing sense emerged, among people who paid attention to such things, that something about it wasn't quite right. There were a number of attempts to understand and fix this over the centuries in the West, but as learning and science faded during the Dark Ages, those got weaker and feebler, while others, particularly the Islamic world, continued to make progress.

In Christian Europe, the primary motivator for fixing the calendar was figuring out the right date for Easter. Caesar's calendar, good as it was, assumed a year that was just a shade too long, by about 11 minutes. That doesn't sound like much, but as the decades march on, it adds up, to the tune of about a day every 130 years. Easter, ever since the Council of Nicaea in 325, has been celebrated on the first Sunday after the first full moon after the vernal equinox, which is complicated enough, but if your year is too long, eventually the vernal equinox starts to creep earlier and earlier. Get the equinox wrong and Easter is wrong, and celebrating Easter on the wrong day, as people were increasingly concerned could happen, could imperil your chances for salvation.

The process by which this got resolved is a fascinating mélange of the medieval and the modern. Things were finally coming to a head in the late 16th century, as Pope Gregory XIII, who devoted much of his papacy to reforming the church, sending missionaries far and wide and furthering the Catholic faith, realized that something had to be done. The modern part, sounding very familiar to our ears, was the commission he convened in the 1570s to come up with a solution. They made a report with a series of recommendations to correct the drift that had accumulated over sixteen centuries and to prevent the calendar from going astray in the future. Those recommendations were sent to universities and the crowned heads of Europe for commentary. Which they got—dozens and dozens of responses came in, many simply signing off on the proposals, some suggesting revisions, and others thundering disapproval on grounds both scientific and religious.

One idea that got some traction was a calendar that would simply count the consecutive days from a fixed historical point, eliminating any concern for months or years. Straightforward, if impractical for everyday life, this Julian date calendar has been adopted by astronomers and some computer operating systems for its ease of use, counting from noon on January 1, 4713 BCE. If you want to be ready in case this catches on popularly, the Julian date for January 1, 2020, will be 2458849.

A fresco showing Pope Gregory XIII and his advisers discussing calendar reforms. Alamy Stock.

In any event, the feedback was collected, tweaks were made, and here's where the medieval part comes in. On February 24, 1582, Gregory XIII, Pontifex Maximus, one imagines in all his regal splendor, signed a bull—from the Latin *bulla*, the clay or lead seal attached to a document to authenticate it. Similar devices go back to the very beginnings of writing and recording. Papal bulls by tradition take their titles from the first two words in Latin, in this case "*Inter gravissimas*," "among the most serious tasks of our pastoral office. . . ." It was posted on the doors of St. Peter's on March 1, then around the city, with copies also sent to every Catholic country by papal ambassadors. Even more medievally, it prohibited unauthorized publication of the calendar or associated documents on pain of fine or excommunication.

It established the system we still use today, now called the Gregorian calendar, with a year of 365 days, a leap year with an extra day every four years, except those years that are multiples of 100 not also divisible by 400, so 1900 wasn't a leap year, and 2100 won't be, but 2000 was. It realigned the calendar; established January 1 as the first day of the year (it had previously been the vernal equinox); and, most critically, corrected the overshoot of the previous calendar by decreeing that October 4, 1582, would be followed by October 15, eliminating, almost literally with the stroke of a pen, 10 days.

Picture for a moment the kind of confusion that move would produce today. What would be done about deadlines, taxes, interest payments, shipping schedules? Birthdays? Prison sentences? Saints' days? A riot erupted in Frankfurt, based on the belief that the pope was trying to steal days away from people's lives.

The new calendar was not an immediate, universal hit. To be blunt, the papacy wasn't what it used to be, so what might have been accomplished by unquestioned fiat just a century or so previously now took some work to achieve. A few reliably Catholic countries—Spain, Portugal, Poland, Italy—went along more or less immediately. Others moved a little more deliberately; France and Hungary took a few years longer. Then it started to lose momentum and languished; most of Germany didn't adopt the Gregorian system until about 1700, England not until 1752, and other parts of the world much later, including Russia in 1917 and China not fully until Mao in 1949. For that matter, Judaism and Islam have never used solar calendars. The Jewish calendar employs 12 months of 29 or 30 days, adding a leap month when needed (such a year is called Shanah Me'uberet, literally "pregnant year") to at least partially align with the solar year. The Islamic year is purely lunar, consisting of about 354 days, and thus continually floats against the Gregorian year, explaining why the holy month of Ramadan comes a few days earlier in the Gregorian system each year.

Setting aside the rest of the world, this seems like a curiously long time for such a change to become established in Europe. To be sure, communication in those days was substantially slower than today, able to rely on nothing faster than the horse or carrier pigeons, so it's not as though Gregory could just send this out as a PDF attachment by e-mail. And yes, this was a major change with ramifications for many aspects of everyday life for people, governments, and institutions of all kinds, which would require time and effort to implement. But still—why does it take over a century to make its way to places like England, Sweden, and Germany?

To answer that, we need to consider another document from an even more well-known source, though not the most well-known document from that source. Let's travel from 1582 Rome to Mainz, in the Rhine Valley, in 1452, when it is a free city of the Holy Roman Empire. More importantly for our story, at this time, it's a place of second chances.

I imagine we've all wanted a real get-out-of-jail-free card at one point or another after we've done something we regret or gotten ourselves into a situation we'd just as soon undo. (A document with its own history: the actual "Get Out of Jail Free" card comes from the board game Monopoly, first marketed by Parker Brothers in 1935, with roots back to The Landlord's Game developed in 1903 by Elizabeth Magie as a teaching tool on the evils of monopolization. Centuries earlier, though, the first British lottery in 1567 offered all ticketholders "freedom from arrest for all crimes other than murder, felonies, piracy, or treason.") People are often willing to forgive and sometimes to forget, but the idea of a magic ticket that could wipe the slate clean is very attractive indeed. In the right circumstances, in fact, this isn't out of the question. You've got to mean it, you've got to do something to earn it, and you've got to be Catholic, but there is a way to get a redo, and for a long time a simple piece of paper, or parchment, would do the trick. Something like that not only can buy you out of a heap of sinning; in sufficient quantities it can also lead to the transformation of an entire continent. And here we introduce one of the great names of the last millennium: Johannes Gutenberg.

Gutenberg. Bible. We're so used to hearing those together, that many people likely haven't thought much about what else he might have been up to. Yes, he invented printing using movable type in Europe, everybody knows that; maybe somewhat fewer know he pioneered oil-based inks or the wooden screw printing press.

Gutenberg himself is, in large part, a cipher. There are large chunks of his life we know nothing about, leading some to wonder if it was really him at the wheel, so to speak. We know his father worked at a mint and he had experience as a goldsmith; we also know that he was either a terrible businessman or incredibly unlucky. Or both. He and others wanted to make money by selling mirrors for use in a holy festival, only to have it postponed by a year because of flood or perhaps plague. Whatever the reason, stuck with a bunch of unsellable mirrors, he now says he has a great idea—and it's not clear to this day where that idea came from—that will turn around their fortunes. In effect, then, the development of printing using movable type in Europe, one of the most profound innovations in Western history, which still reverberates to this very day—was for all intents and purposes, Plan B.

He started work on the Bible in 1452, amid a series of loans from one Johann Fust (who later sued him, claiming no interest was paid and the money misused), who bankrolled the scheme. Within three years, the time it would take to produce one Bible by hand, the work is done. A total of 180 were printed, of which 48 complete examples are known to have survived. They're trophies for collectors and institutions; even having a single page, or "leaf," is a point of pride. (Word to the wise: This sort of collection envy can be quite serious. According to a census of locations of Gutenberg Bibles, while there are four on the island of Manhattan, there are none in Canada, and some Canadian bibliophiles and antiquarians can get a bit cranky about that, as I learned once the hard way. Best not to bring it up.)

It appears that two presses were used in Gutenberg's workshop, with different sets of type, as many as 100,000 separate pieces in all, along with paper and the skins of 3,200 animals for the 40 vellum copies. They were even customizable; if you bought one, you could have your own decoration added in spaces intentionally left blank for just that purpose.

Except there's more to the story. The Bible is universally known as his masterwork, but while that was in the works, there was badly needed cash to be made in the meantime to help keep the place going, producing schoolbooks, calendars, and especially, in the lucrative business of printing indulgences. These had been around for centuries in manuscript form, an opportunity for the faithful to atone and have their sins remitted by, say, good works, making a pilgrimage, fasting, going on Crusade . . . or a little gold. The indulgence itself is just a form, boilerplate we'd say today, with spaces for the name, date, and seller. Take that to your confessor, in a state of grace, and you've gotten yourself or a loved one out of Purgatory. This was big business for everybody involved, for the printers certainly, but mainly for the church; print runs ran into the thousands. In one case at least 190,000 were printed.

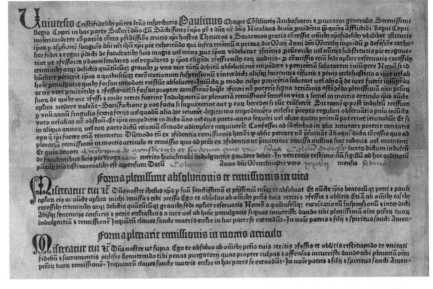

The *Indulgentia*, or Letter of Indulgence, commissioned by the Catholic Church, printed by Johannes Gutenberg, and issued February 27, 1455. This particular indulgence is for contributions to a war against the Turks. Copyright of the University of Manchester.

There is some evidence that Gutenberg produced indulgences as early as 1452, though the earliest one to survive is from a series printed in 1454—the earliest Western printed document with a date. That one was created to raise money for the defense of Cyprus from the Turks, who had just taken Constantinople the previous year. Gutenberg's legacy is obvious and well rehearsed—the printing processes he pioneered spread across the continent within decades, helping to nourish the emerging Renaissance and Enlightenment that led Europe out of the Middle Ages.

Both the indulgence and the Bible were printed with type that make them look very much like their handwritten, manuscript predecessors; today, it's referred to as blackletter printing, connoting its weight and density. That decision makes sense; if you want something new to be adopted, making it look familiar, as much like an old and established version or product as possible, can be very helpful. This is an example of a "skeuomorph," and they're still around. That's why word processors still use "cut" and "paste" metaphors, and why cell phone cameras often make a clicking sound like a shutter when there's no mechanism at work at all. Or why electronic books, so far, try so hard to resemble their print counterparts.

It wasn't long before new type styles and formats and illustrations made an appearance. Those first Bibles also have no page numbers, indentations, or paragraphs; these devices we take so for granted in books today were yet to be widely adopted. Books printed in the 15th century are called *incunabula*, from the Latin for "cradle," which is most apt. Gutenberg and the other early printers were responsible for more than the birth of a new way of making copies faster. They were at the very beginning of a long road of figuring out what a printed book or a printed anything would be and what it would look like, and over the centuries, those have developed in ways that medieval copyists couldn't have imagined. Printing also led to higher levels of education and literacy, movements to censor uncomfortable works, and the development of national literatures and cultures.

Some 60 years later, though, and about 300 miles to the northeast in Wittenberg, a German priest and theologian got fed up with the latest abuses of the indulgence system, now made so easy by the new technology. This time it was to raise money for the building of St. Peter's. He was fed up enough to compose a letter outlining his points, all 95 of them, to his bishop. Those "theses," we think intended for private discussion, went viral. They quickly got printed and disseminated, though we don't know how or by whom. So were later demands for change in sermons and broadsides—a format that helped to lead to the development of newspapers—as well as Bibles in German, which helped to coalesce the evolving language. Oh, yeah, and it kick-started the Reformation, making Martin Luther another central figure of the previous millennium.

So by 1582, another 65 years later, as Gregory tries to get his calendar reform edict on track, the Counter-Reformation is moving into high gear less than 20 years after the Council of Trent condemned Protestantism as heresy. This didn't help matters in trying to get, say, Lutheran Germany to go along with anything the pope wanted, much less slicing days away from people's lives. As a result, this became a highly political and politicized document, not well taken in Protestant Europe. That first sentence, from which *Inter gravissimas* comes, in particular, was a problem, since those "most serious duties" it refers to are explicitly following up on the dictates of the Council of Trent.

In thinking about all this, one muses, who could accomplish this today? There are proposals out there, earnest and well meaning, that would give us, say, thirteen months of 28 days each, with an extra holiday day to make 365. Or the World Calendar, four quarters of 91 days, each one starting on a Sunday, with additional days as necessary that aren't days of a week ("Worldsday" for one, a yearend holiday that follows Saturday, December 30, and is followed by Sunday, January 1.)

What single person could, by virtue of their position, establish a new calendar with any hopes that it would be broadly or universally adopted? Certainly not the pope, and there's no proper emperors around anymore, so who else is in a position to effect that kind of sweeping change beyond the boundaries of a single nation? It feels as though it would have to come from an international organization, the UN and one of its obscurely named agencies, or a global conference, but it would have to be the result of broad consensus and national approvals, and even then, inevitably a wide swath of the world wouldn't be happy about it no matter how rational or necessary it was. The idea that a single person, any single person, could, with that proverbial stroke of a pen, achieve such a monumental transformation, seems completely impossible to us today. It's simply not that sort of top-down world any more.

At first glance, this is a straightforward historical account, the pope and the printer and the priest, and how their stories and actions intertwined in ways largely unintentional and coincidental. Without Gutenberg's innovations, Luther's ideas would have had a great deal more difficulty spreading nearly that widely, quickly, or effectively, and thus no Reformation, so Gregory's calendar reforms would have been embraced and implemented with fewer obstacles. Yes, entirely different pathways and actors might have produced similar, or widely different, outcomes; such is the fun of alternative histories.

Look again, though, and you see the mechanisms by which it all transpired: documents, genres, formats, and the processes by which they got developed and used. By my count, the story above mentions at least twenty specific documents or kinds of documents, from the papal bull to the broadside to the letter. Each of them could be dismissed as "just a piece of paper" (not including the electronic book or PDF unless it was printed out), but each of them was designed and created to perform some kind of work, to fulfill a role or function, both generically and specifically.

These stories, intertwined by coincidence, are a small sampling of what you'll find in this book. These two in particular illustrate how documents of all kinds facilitate various kinds of work and how that work is changing, and there are others: from the Riot Act to the rules of soccer to Alfred Nobel's will to the "butterfly ballot" from the 2000 Palm Beach County election. You'll also find stories here of documents and ideas that spread much more widely than their creators might have imagined: the *Liber Abaci*, "The Star-Spangled

Banner," *The Protocols of the Elders of Zion* and the *Quotations of Chairman Mao.* The self-assured creators Noah Webster and Fannie Farmer and Joseph Smith and Henry Martyn Robert and for that matter Larry Sanger and Jimmy Wales, confident enough in their own ideas and in themselves that they took the risk of publishing and won the day.

You'll find things to surprise here, not just in the details of how these came to be (Who would have guessed that Albert Einstein thought he'd have difficulty in getting a letter to Franklin Roosevelt, or that a chemist imagined what became the airplane black box when he was sort of bored in a meeting?) but also perhaps in the forms and types of objects that are here. Everybody's used to "documents" like birth certificates and checks and letters and pamphlets; there are less obvious forms too, such as the AIDS Quilt and Vietnam Veterans Memorial, the Zapruder Film, the first X-ray image, the IQ test. You will also encounter documents that are not what they appear to be: forgeries, frauds, secrets. Travel documents that are entirely fictional. 18½ minutes of missing conversation that inflamed a nation and helped bring down a president. A poster who isn't who you think she is. A sketch that is likely lost. A passage from one of our most cherished founding documents, removed, and the price we continue to pay. Even a list that never existed.

A large number of these documents are the product of faith and belief: the hymn Exaltation of Inanna—one of the oldest recorded works, written by perhaps the first known author—the Rosetta Stone, the Donation of Constantine and the Book of Mormon, among others. There are also many that are the product of science and empirical investigation: the *Philosophical Transactions* and John Snow's cholera map, the rise of statistical significance and the diagnoses of mental disorders.

Those may seem diametrically opposed, or at least very differently intended, but they're really not; in fact, to me they share a great deal in common. In particular, they are all attempts to figure it out, to understand the world around us and the worlds inside us, and you can make an argument that everything described here is a product of precisely that, our ongoing and never-ending yearning to know, to question, and to record, so that what we learn and what we do and how we do is passed down for those yet to come. This, then, is the story of these records, where they come from, why we have them, what happens to them, why they are the way they are, and thus the societies that give rise to them and the societies they produce. It's also the story of how this is all changing and what that might mean for our future.

SOURCES

Baum, Cardinal William Wakefield. "The Gift of the Indulgence." The Holy See, January 29, 2000. Accessed August 10, 2012. http://www.vatican.va/roman_curia/tribunals/apost_penit/docu ments/rc_trib_appen_pro_20000129_indulgence_en.html.

Duncan, David Ewing. *Calendar: Humanity's Epic Struggle to Determine a True and Accurate Year*. New York: Bard, 1999.

Füssel, Stephan. *Gutenberg and the Impact of Printing*. English ed. Aldershot, UK: Ashgate, 2005.

John Rylands University Library. "The Two Mainz Indulgences of 1454 and 1455." University of Manchester. Accessed December 7, 2016. http://www.library.manchester.ac.uk/firstimpres sions/assets/downloads/01-The-two-Mainz-indulgences-of-1454-and-1455.pdf.

Kapr, Albert, and Douglas Martin. *Johann Gutenberg: The Man and His Invention*. Aldershot, UK: Scolar Press, 1996.

Lux in Arcana. "The Calendar Reform." Accessed July 16, 2012. http://www.luxinarcana.org/en/ documenti/curiosita/la-riforma-del-calendario/.

Man, John. *Gutenberg: How One Man Remade the World with Words*. New York: John Wiley & Sons, 2002.

Spencer, Bill. "Inter Gravissimas." Blue Water Arts. Last modified March 20, 2002. http://www.blue waterarts.com/calendar/NewInterGravissimas.htm.

World Calendar Association. Home Page. Accessed October 4, 2016. http://www.theworldcalendar .org/.

2
Exaltation of Inanna
a hymn composed by the high priestess Enheduanna
in the Sumerian city-state of Ur
c. 2300 BCE

What does it mean to be an author? That probably sounds like a ridiculous question, particularly from someone writing a book about written objects among other things. Get an idea, put a bunch of words together in some order that makes some sense—though I bet we've all read stuff from "authors" who fell somewhat short on that score—maybe find a way to get somebody else to listen or read, and bingo bango bongo, you're an author. More seriously, "authorship" also typically connotes creativity, productivity, inventiveness, and originality.

My fellow-travelers in the library field, the intrepid catalogers who design precise tools to find just the right work in an ever-growing, if not wine-dark, sea of the human record, prefer the term "statement of responsibility" to denote authorship, and while that sounds bureaucratic and a bit obtuse, it does make sense. An author is responsible for a work, and if you think about it, in two different ways: responsible for it being created, and responsible for what it says, no matter how long it survives.

One author did even more. She not only was responsible for a series of works, which have survived a very long time, she may also be responsible for the idea of being responsible. She may be the origin of the idea of authorship itself.

Here we're going way back, about as far back as we can go. Enheduanna's father was Sargon, whom one source referred to as a "charismatic usurper" and who united a number of city-states into the first Mesopotamian Empire. This didn't go over universally well, since not everybody appreciates a "usurper," so in a savvy move, he appointed his daughter to be a high priestess, to calm the waters and solidify his position. Whatever she did, it worked, and the high priestess job stayed with princesses of the blood for another 500 years. And her job became her name; "en" means high priestess, and Nanna was the moon god.

A disk of white calcite, circa 2300 BCE; on the side shown here a scene of sacrifice is carved in relief, on the other is carved an inscription of Enheduanna. Courtesy of Penn Museum, image #150424.

It's remarkable that we know this much about a woman who lived over 4,000 years ago in what is present-day southern Iraq, at the same time as the Old Kingdom in Egypt and the rise of maize and pottery in Mesoamerica, at roughly the middle of the Bronze Age in Europe. It's even more remarkable why we know so much about her, which is primarily through her writings. She produced a quite impressive body of work, including a series of hymns dedicated to temples, a number of other works known to us in fragments, and the piece for which she is best known, a 153-line hymn that has no known title of its own, which has been designated by modern scholars as the "Exaltation of Inanna." Inanna was the Sumerian Queen of Heaven and goddess of love, related to the Akkadian Ishtar, and in the hymn, Enheduanna praises her, and then asks for her help and, moreover, vengeance, in reclaiming her position and home after being exiled due to some unknown political disturbance. It ends triumphantly with her return. It's quite affecting, even today. Here's a sample:

When mankind comes before you
In fear and trembling at your tempestuous radiance
They receive from you their just deserts.

This has come to us in multiple versions; the major translation in 1968 lists at least 50 distinct extant manuscripts on clay tablets, including some from several hundred years after its composition, so it seems that this hymn survived and was important for a long time. We also know her from a limestone disc relief showing her in worship, which also bears her name, now at the University of Pennsylvania Museum.

Let's put this in a bit of context; the origins of writing are a bit murky, but it's safe to say that people were writing purposefully by about 3000 BCE, and the oldest "literature" is about 2600 BCE. This puts the Exaltation among the very first works we know, a little earlier than the first parts of the *Epic of Gilgamesh*, 500 or so years before the Code of Hammurabi and the Rig Veda, 700 years before the Egyptian Book of the Dead, more than 1,000 years before the I Ching, and 1,500 years before the *Iliad* and *Odyssey*, and the Hebrew Bible. In other words, this is really old, among the oldest things we actually have.

A tablet showing an excerpt, lines 31–66, from the Exaltation of Inanna. YBC 4671, Yale Babylonian Collection.

Many sources describe Enheduanna as the "earliest known author," and also coincidentally one of the earliest women in history whose name has survived, though without any citation or definitive—dare one say authoritative—source, and then move on to tell her story, of her political/social/religious impact and importance, describe the works, and so on. What I find stunning is how that completely breezes past the most extraordinary aspect: the *first known author*. Even if she's not, which is nigh impossible to be conclusive about (not to mention new archeological evidence could always come along to dislodge her claim), let's not bury the lede here. Somebody had to be first one to think of recording "I wrote this" and she may well have been that person.

The idea of writing, of taking credit, of authorship, is so deeply ingrained, so common now, it's difficult to fully appreciate how profound its development is. As I said, authorship comes with responsibility, for the writing itself and also the ideas and the results of those ideas. In the contemporary world, authorship also brings rights in the form of copyright and the opportunity to protect the ways in which expressions of ideas can be copied, shared, and used, including potential monetary reward. More deeply, there is credit, and blame, to be had, for works noble and toxic and everywhere in between.

And, names matter; we use authors' names in many settings such as libraries and bookstores, to bring together a body of work, because that's often what people are looking for; works that are anonymous or pseud-onymous often engender curiosity about who "really" wrote it, which can even migrate to contempt when a well-known author like Stephen King or J. K. Rowling writes under another name, as though somehow that's not fair or appropriate.

Three very important, and very common, forces converge here. Enheduanna wrote this, apparently, after some sort of power struggle, turning to her goddess for help and then expressing gratitude that her prayers were answered. She is in the position she's in as high priestess due to a nakedly political move on the part of her father in consolidating his power base in a time of great upheaval. And she's using a couple of newish technologies, in this case writing and the baking of clay to shape that writing, in order to record and preserve her actions and ideas. So we have, for one of the first times, the coordination of faith, politics, and communication, mutually reinforcing each other, all in the service of power. This too is a story that will be told over and over throughout the millennia.

A couple of last notable aspects here. One is the overt nature of the creative process in the Exaltation. There's a section of the hymn that explicitly describes its own composition, in a maternal way:

> I have given birth,
> oh exalted lady, to this song for you.

Which seems somehow very contemporary. As does this:

> I am placed in the lepers' ward
> the light is obscured about me
> The shadows approach the light of day,
> My mellifluous mouth is cast into confusion
> My choicest features are turned to dust.

Who hasn't been fired, or heartbroken, or feel like the world was out to get you? And so you want to even the score:

> "This city—
> May it be cursed . . .
> May its plaintive child not be placated by his mother!"

After something like 200 generations, her bitterness, pain, and satisfaction in her ultimate victory ring very true to modern ears.

Throughout the poem, Enheduanna uses the first person, and twice refers to herself by name. In the process of speaking to her goddess, she speaks also to us, in her own voice from a time so long ago we can barely imagine it. By impressing marks in tablets of clay first wet, then baked, she recorded her faith, her hopes, her fears, herself. For dozens of centuries those tablets went unread and unremembered until they were rediscovered and translated, and so Enheduanna speaks to us again, and still.

SOURCES

Electronic Text Corpus of Sumerian Literature. "The Exaltation of Inana (Inana B)." Accessed May 29, 2014. http://etcsl.orinst.ox.ac.uk/cgi-bin/etcsl.cgi?text=t.4.07.2#.

Feldman, Marian H. "Enheduanna (c. 2300 B.C.E.)." In *The Oxford Encyclopedia of Women in World History*, edited by Bonnie G. Smith. New York: Oxford University Press, 2008.

Feminist Theory Website. "Enheduanna." Center for Digital Discourse and Culture. Accessed May 29, 2014. http://www.cddc.vt.edu/feminism/Enheduanna.html.

Hallo, William W., and J. J. A. van Dijk. *The Exaltation of Inanna*. New Haven, CT: Yale University Press, 1968.

Leith, Mary J. W. "Gender and Religion: Gender and Ancient Near Eastern Religions." In *Encyclopedia of Religion*, edited by Lindsay Jones. Detroit: Macmillan Reference USA, 2005.

Melville, Sarah C. "Royal Women and the Exercise of Power in the Ancient Near East." In *A Companion to the Ancient Near East*, edited by Daniel C. Snell, 219–28. Oxford: Blackwell Publishing Ltd, 2005.

Salisbury, Joyce E. *Encyclopedia of Women in the Ancient World*. Santa Barbara, CA: ABC-CLIO, 2001.

Wikipedia. "Enheduanna." May 21, 2014. https://en.wikipedia.org/w/index.php?title=Enheduanna &oldid=609474720.

3
The Rosetta Stone
**a fragment of a stela, engraved with what is called
the Decree of Memphis in three languages**
now known as the Rosetta Stone
and housed in the British Museum
196 BCE

If you had something really important you wanted to record, and you wanted it to last for a long time, how would you go about it? That likely depends on how important it was, and how long you were thinking it should endure. The longer the term, the sturdier you'd want your medium to be. We don't have that much experience with digital media, so we don't quite know how durable those are, not to mention whether there will still be a device around that can read it; it doesn't matter if a zip drive or eight-track tape is still intact and workable if there's nothing to stick it in to make it work. We do have really old documents on vellum or parchment, both made from animal skin, harder to get at Office Depot these days, and even older ones in baked clay, though that's a bit out of fashion as well.

If you're seriously in it for the long haul, though, it's hard to do better than stone. Stone lasts. It can be worn away by weather or pollution or be damaged, yes, but . . . stone lasts. A message for the ages deserves a medium for the ages, though sometimes the medium can outlast the message. That's the case for one of the most famous messages in the world, which I bet you would instantly recognize and I also bet you have no idea what it says, or why, or about whom—which tells us something about durability as well as the various twists and turns a document can take.

Now *this* is a document; just shy of nine square feet in surface area, about 1,700 pounds, and about 2,200 years old. The basic story of the Rosetta Stone is well known: an ancient record, written in three languages, and how those multiple versions of the same text led to cracking the code of Egyptian hiero-glyphics and thus an entrée into their long-forgotten civilization. All quite familiar, yet as is so often the case, there's considerably more to the story. For instance, Jean-Francois Champollion, the teacher who eventually cracked the

The Rosetta Stone on display at the British Museum. Justin Ennis (flickr user: averain).

code, worked from a reproduction, and never saw the real thing. Each linguistic version of the text was intended for a different audience: hieroglyphics for tradition's sake (that language had been dead for centuries and only a few priests could even read it), demotic for your run-of-the-mill literate Egyptian, and Greek for the Macedonians who had actually been in charge of the kingdom for the last century or so. There are really four languages on it if you include "Captured in Egypt by the British Army in 1801" and "Presented by King George III," neither entirely true, helpfully painted along the sides—yesterday's vandalism is today's historical detail. And for many decades, it's been the most popular, and most lucratively marketed, object in the British Museum.

Even less well known is what it says, and why it was created. It's a verbose decree to shore up and reinforce the rule of the pharaoh Ptolemy V. Imagine you're a boy king, succeeding to the throne at age five after both of your parents are murdered by conspirators, including your father's mistress, who then rule as your regents as you grow up, until they in turn get lynched by a mob in a revolt. Nine years later, you're in a tenuous position in a time fraught with peril, dissension, and upheaval. If you knew what was good for you, you'd lower taxes as well as free political prisoners and kiss up to the temple priests, after polishing off some rebel leaders by impaling them on the stake. In return, the priests magnanimously proclaim your legitimacy and greatness, add your birthday to the holiday list, erect statues, and put up stelae all over the place to announce this glorious decision. All of this is lovingly recorded in what we now know as the Rosetta Stone. It was likely originally leaned upright against a wall outside a temple, where it probably sat for several centuries until about a third of the top was hacked off at some point, likely when it was reused as a building stone for a fort, near Rashid, or Rosetta, hence the modern name.

It's been in the British Museum, object number EA 24, since 1802, apart from underground storage during wartime and a nervy month's loan to France in 1972 for the 150th anniversary of the decoding, when some feared the French might try to keep it. It's so heavy that an extension had to be built with reinforced floors to support it. At some point, chalk was imbedded in the lettering to make it more readable and wax was added to protect it from grubby fingers (any of which would make a modern conservator faint dead away); it wound up so dark it was misclassified as black basalt until it was cleaned and revealed to be much lighter granodiorite. And they intend to keep it.

This thing was created in the age of Hannibal and Cato, the Punic Wars, and the expansion of Rome, just after the Great Wall of China and the Terracotta Army, as the Mayans are starting to write and when the Olmecs have come and gone. The Egyptians who erected it had every reason to believe the stone would stand forever; their society had already lasted over 3,000 years. So when the decree ends by saying it will stand "alongside the state of the king who lives forever," they're not kidding.

Many sources, historians, and Egyptologists wax eloquent about the Stone (always capitalized) as a gateway to the past, an emblem of discovery and redis-covery, a symbol of our desire to know and understand, and as part of the telling of history as much as a historical object itself, if not more so. Granted, museum folks focus on the provenance, tapping into the larger matter of ownership of cultural objects, increasingly an issue in recent years as more nations and peoples request—or demand—repatriation of things so casually appropriated in days gone by.

For me, though, as an information scientist, the most fascinating bit is this object's journey as a document. It begins as a rock, and happily remains that way for untold gazillions of years before it's quarried up near Aswan, sailed down the Nile, and then shaped and carved with markings that meant something to the people who put them there. (More or less—the spelling errors in the Greek section imply that the carvers either weren't paying attention or didn't understand it.) Then it's put up outside temples to be seen and remembered, at least by the people who could read one of its scripts; to everyone else it's just so many squiggles. Then Ptolemy V dies, is succeeded by his infant son, time passes, and the purpose for the decree fades, though the stone remained, a bit like a Millard Fillmore presidential proclamation that means little to us today. After a couple of centuries, the dynasty falls, eventually the civilization and language and culture follow suit, and it's put to new use as building material. Still carved, still meaningful . . . sort of, but underground and unseen for maybe a millennium. It's eventually dug up by the French, who quickly lost it to the English, who plunked it in the British Museum, and many people studied the squiggles again, trying to make sense of them until they figured it out. It's one of the great document stories of all time, which might account for some of its popular fascination.

I used this once as an example with a group of college freshmen; I asked them whether or not this object was "information" when it was first displayed at the temple, freshly carved. And quite easily, they said yes. How about when Champollion decoded it? Yes. Today, as a museum artifact, representative of the ancient Egyptian culture? Sure. What about when it was dug back up but nobody could yet understand the hieroglyphics? Somewhat more hesitant here, but again, yes. Then—what about when it was under the fort? Still carved, still intact, though buried, used as building foundation, forgotten, unread, unread-able? The strong consensus here was no, so I asked why, what made it different then. One young woman, with the wisdom only inherent in 18-year-olds, said, "It has to *try*." I love that.

The Stone was intended, and made, to last. It didn't go quite as planned, though, surviving more by accident than design, and its original intent has long since been superseded by its role as a key to unlocking ancient long-forgotten Egyptian writing, language, and culture. Today? You may well be reading this as an electronic book, and I use a cloud server to store my research and materials. We take digital information media for granted for its ease and convenience, though in terms of endurance, they're the antithesis of the Stone.

When civilizations fall and fade away, what gets left behind is what's remembered. If there are museums in 2,000 years, what object from our time will occupy a similar place in a glass case and in the popular imagination? Will there ever be another document so robust, and so vividly engaged with? How will we be remembered? And where—and what—will the Rosetta Stone be on its journey then?

SOURCES

Parkinson, R. B., and British Museum. *The Rosetta Stone.* British Museum Objects in Focus. London: British Museum Press, 2005.

Ray, J. D. *The Rosetta Stone and the Rebirth of Ancient Egypt.* Wonders of the World. Cambridge, MA: Harvard University Press, 2007.

Solé, Robert, Dominique Valbelle, and Steven Rendall. *The Rosetta Stone.* New York: Four Walls Eight Windows, 2002.

Wikipedia. "Rosetta Stone." Accessed August 31, 2013. http://en.wikipedia.org/w/index.php?title= Rosetta_Stone&oldid=571002455.

4
Donation of Constantine

the *Constitutum Constantini;* in English, the Donation of Constantine
largely based on the *Actus Silvestri*
of uncertain origin
*apparent oldest version in a ninth-century manuscript now in
Bibliothèque Nationale de France in Paris*
around 750

For most of us, in most situations, we don't look all that hard at a receipt or contract or $20 bill to determine if it's real or bogus. Unless you're a border guard, you see a passport and assume it's valid. Unless you're a college registrar, you see a transcript and assume it's good. Sure, you know there are ways to figure this out, devices that can be used, like watermarks, holograms, seals, and whatever, but by and large, nobody pays attention. We just sort of give them the benefit of the doubt, take them for granted, take them . . . on faith.

For one document, though, "taking it on faith" had profound implications for that faith, for the people who profess it, and for the rest of the Western world, because any faith in that document was badly misplaced.

Whatever this is and whoever wrote it and when and why and how, all of which is unclear and in dispute, the bottom line is it worked. It was plausible, believable, believed, and adopted, and as a result the Roman Catholic Church is Roman. The so-called "Donation of Constantine" is often cited as the most famous forgery in history, and if it's a bit off the radar now, that's not for any lack of the impact it has had for a dozen centuries. As the name suggests, it's written in the name of the Emperor Constantine, who, in 313, upon his baptism, recovery from leprosy, and conversion to Christianity, sees the proverbial light. In return, he grants the pope, then Sylvester I, and all his successors, quite the prize package: primacy over the Eastern churches; a number of properties, including the Lateran Palace, still to this day the seat of the papal cathedra; imperial dignity and insignia; and a jeweled tiara—indeed, there is a lot of discussion of clothing and symbols throughout. Moreover, the pope is given domain over Rome "and all the provinces, districts and cities of Italy or of the western regions."

23

A 13th-century fresco showing the Emperor Constantine presenting the Donation to Pope Sylvester I. Alamy Stock.

Finally, because the pope and the papacy are now so exalted, the emperor declares he is no longer worthy to remain in Rome, so he will vacate his imperial seat to the yet-to-be-built Constantinople. To make it all official, the document says the decree is irrevocable, "uninjured and unshaken until the end of the world," and anyone doubting its validity is subject to eternal damnation. It ends with a statement that the decree was personally placed by the emperor above the body of St. Peter, and then given to the pope. As thank-you gifts go, this is right up there.

While it's an impressive gesture, it's also a fake; a forgery, in fact, derived largely from a fifth-century biography of Pope Sylvester. It may be that the decree was first used in 754 by Pope Stephen II to strengthen his hand in dealing with King Pepin in a mutually beneficial deal that wound up with Pepin establishing the Carolingian dynasty and the pope ruling much of central Italy for a millennium or so. As a result, suspicion is placed on Stephen's court or chancery as the source of the forgery for that purpose.

This gives us a rough creation date of 750, as Gregorian church music is on the rise, the Tang dynasty is falling in China, and the Abbasid dynasty is forming in the Middle East—within the decade they will adopt the Indian numerals we use today—and in remote Ireland, the magnificent Book of Kells is about to be created. There are a number of competing theories as to when and where it was created, and a number of potential goals cited for it: supporting Stephen and his Carolingian ambitions, yes, but perhaps also adding a devotional veneer to a political history and philosophy of the way in which Rome ascended, and thus maintaining the continued subjugation of Constantinople. Later popes, including Leo IX in the 11th century, drew on the Donation for a variety of purposes, and the Bishop of Paris wrote in 869 that a copy could be found in almost every church in Gaul.

At least one pope, Otto III, at the turn of the second millennium, declared it a fraud, but that didn't take. It wasn't until centuries later, and the development of more sophisticated techniques of documentary validation and textual criticism, that it was conclusively demonstrated, most notably and forcefully by Lorenzo Valla in 1440, to be forged. Valla's work took decades to be printed and widely disseminated, however, and for his troubles the Church placed it on its index of prohibited works in 1559. Not until the 19th century did the Church admit it was faked. By that point, of course, the deed was done and it was far too late to undo it. The popes ruled chunks of Italy for centuries, doled out parcels in the New World as they saw fit during the Age of Exploration, and remained in Rome.

Forgery is, and was, a crime. It's a felony under current federal law, which lists a couple of dozen different flavors, mostly regarding securities and financial

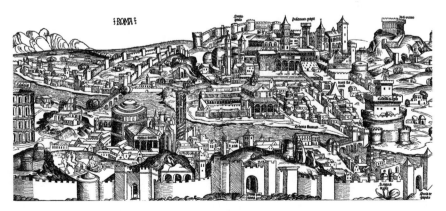

A view of Rome, around 1490, from Hartmann Schedel's *Schedelsche Weltchronik*, which was published in 1493. Wikimedia Commons (accessed at https://commons.wikimedia.org/wiki/File:Roma1493.png).

papers, but also contracts, powers of attorney, money orders, postage stamps, departmental seals, ship's papers, and even coins. Most of these will get you between 10 and 25 years; though only three for forging a penny or nickel, but seriously, why bother?

Legally, "forgery" is the "act of fraudulently making a false document or altering a real one, to be used as if genuine" and necessarily requires the intent to deceive. So something faked or invented or copied isn't necessarily a problem, if you don't try to pass it off as something it isn't. To work, it not only has to be created, it has to be accepted as genuine, and to truly come full circle, it must someday be discovered, exposed, and disproven. In law, there's even the concept of a "double forgery": a check with both signature and endorsement faked, for example. In Colonial America, a forger could wind up in the pillory or with an "F" branded on his cheek; medieval punishments could include fines, mutilation, or even death, as forgery of a royal document could be treated as a form of treason against the crown.

In ordinary language, we might say that a forgery creates a document that isn't what it purports to be, or even more simply, not what it says it is. It makes a document lie. So what sets apart a forgery from a copy, or reproduction, or facsimile is the intent to make it lie, and to be believed. Lots of this is penny-ante stuff, the canonical college fake ID, for example, though forgeries of art or manuscripts can fetch a pretty penny of their own. A newly "discovered" Emily Dickinson poem was sold by Sotheby's auction house in 1997 for over $20,000; it was later found to be the product of well-known forger Mark Hofmann, who specialized in faking things about the history of the Church of Jesus Christ of Latter-day Saints, and who, when the authorities and experts started to close in, started making car bombs to bump them off. He pleaded guilty to two counts of murder in 1988.

In the early Middle Ages, forgeries, of a sort, were common, in no small part because life was hard and documentation uncertain, so things like land titles were created to represent a reality everybody knew but nobody had yet written down. Eventually, the need to determine true from false documents increased, so a practice now known as "diplomatics" arose, which used a number of charac-teristics of documents to determine their validity: the materials they were made from, the language used, the styles of writing, abbreviations, seals, forms and contents, dates and how they're represented, and so on. The Anglo-Saxons devel-oped a technique called chirography; two versions of the same text were written on one piece of vellum with the word *chyrographum* (handwriting) written in the space between. They would cut through that word irregularly so only if the two pieces fit together perfectly would each version verify the other. These aren't exclusive to medieval documents; for over a decade now, work to adopt old techniques and create new ones has been pursued in digital diplomatics.

And it's worth saying that forgery, good forgery at least, is a creative act, an art in its own way. Counterfeiting attempts to make an undetectable copy of a genuine thing; forgery, though, often makes something new, invents something plausible and acceptable, and eventually, with the passage of enough time, becomes an object of interest in itself.

Of course, the most successful forgeries are the ones we don't know about. There must be untold numbers of documents of all kinds in libraries, museums, bank vaults, corporate archives, and shoe boxes around the world, waiting to be discovered and exposed, or perhaps not, lying through their carefully constructed teeth, doing their fraudulent thing, waiting for someone to come along and see them for what they truly are, and what they aren't.

SOURCES

Associated Press. "'Original' Dickinson Poem Is Another Hofmann Forgery." *Deseret News*, August 29, 1997. Accessed May 19, 2014. http://www.deseretnews.com/article/579889/Original -Dickinson-poem-is-another-Hofmann-forgery.html.

Counterfeiting and Forgery, 18 U.S.C. § 470-514 (2015).

Fastiggi, Robert L. *New Catholic Encyclopedia. Supplement 2010*. Detroit: Gale, Cengage Learning; Washington, DC: Catholic University of America, 2010.

Garner, Bryan A. *Black's Law Dictionary*. 9th ed. St. Paul, MN: West, 2009.

Guyotjeannin, Olivier. "Donation of Constantine." In *The Papacy: An Encyclopedia*, edited by Phillipe Levillain. New York: Routledge, 2002.

Herde, Peter. "Diplomatics: Study of Documents." In *Encyclopedia Britannica*. Accessed May 19, 2014. https://www.britannica.com/topic/diplomatics.

Hiatt, Alfred. *The Making of Medieval Forgeries: False Documents in Fifteenth-Century England*. London: British Library and University of Toronto Press, 2004.

Levinson, David. *Encyclopedia of Crime and Punishment*. Thousand Oaks, CA: Sage Publications, 2002.

"Medieval Sourcebook: The Donation of Constantine (c. 750–800)." *Internet Medieval Sourcebook*. Last modified November 23, 1996. Accessed May 17, 2014. http://www.fordham.edu/Halsall/ source/donatconst.asp.

Liber Abaci (Arabic numerals)

often translated "The Book of Calculation"
written by Leonardo of Pisa, also known as Fibonacci

1202

Quick—what's 872 times 594? Worse still, what's 872 divided by 594? You probably have an app on your smartphone or computer, or even your watch, that will calculate that for you; you might even have an actual calculator lying around somewhere. If all else failed, you could take the old school approach and work those out by hand, though who does that anymore?

Counting is prehistoric; a 35,000-year-old bone fragment with notches scratched into it might well reflect the recording of the days of the lunar cycle. Those are called tallies, and they might have led us to Roman numerals (think of the I, then the V, then the X as two V's point to point). Which are fine for addition and subtraction, and look impressive for royalty, Olympiads, and Super Bowls, but they're a pain for multiplication, let alone division, decimals, negative numbers, and so on.

People like to refer to our times as the digital age, which has been a long time coming. About 800 years, in fact, since an Italian mathematician and world traveler brought the gift of digits to Europe, from India, through Arabia, and taught the West how to count, and calculate, and figure it all out.

Some years fairly burst with the weight of history and instantly evoke their events without any words: 1066, 1492, 1789, 1941. But 1202 is not one of those years, so Fibonacci has the stage largely to himself, which makes it that much more of a shame that we know so very little about him and that most of what we do know comes from his own writings. We're not even sure of his name; he refers to himself as Leonardo Pisano, of Pisa, "filius Bonacci," from which we got "Fibonacci" from a 19th-century historian, but that's not his father's name. He tells us that he traveled with his father, a customs official, from Pisa to Egypt, Syria, Greece, Provence, and it was on those travels that he was exposed to the number system we know today as "Arabic" numerals, but which had originated in India several centuries before. That system had started to make its way to Europe a couple of centuries earlier, again via the Arabs in Spain, but it wasn't

A page from *Liber Abaci*, showing what is now known as the Fibonacci number sequence in the right-hand margin. Biblioteca Nazionale Centrale di Firenze (accessed at https://commons.wikimedia.org/wiki/File:Liber_abbaci_magliab_f124r.jpg).

widely known or used. Rather, calculation was typically undertaken by way of an abacus, a device used by the ancient Greeks and Romans as well as the Chinese and other cultures using beads on rods or stones on a table or the like.

The book itself has no explicit title, which was typical for the time. "Liber abaci" comes from the first sentence, "Here begins the book of calculation." There are also no titles per se of the fifteen chapters, though each is described, and in the very brief prologue he says, "I separated this book into xv chapters," because of course "15 chapters" wouldn't make any sense until you had read the book. The first chapter begins thus: "The nine Indian figures are: 9 8 7 6 5 4 3 2 1. With these nine figures and with the sign 0 which the Arabs call zephir any number whatsoever is written." Then follows 600+ pages of calculation problems, spiced up with some at least marginally diverting examples to keep the reader engaged, though by and large it's just page after page working problem after problem to help get his points across. It has sections on commerce, barter, currency and weight conversion, simple and compound interest, the alloying of money, along with problems and proofs in geometry and algebra, which also came from the Arab world, from the Arabic for "reunion of broken parts." For good measure, he introduces the practice of dividing large numbers into groups of threes, as we still do using commas, and lays out an extensive process of calculation using various finger and hand positions.

The Indian system was developed by about 700 CE, likely using base 10, 10 digits, because most of us have 10 digits, though that wasn't the only option; the Babylonian base-60 system still survives on every clock face and the latitude/longitude system. This included a zero, which seems to have originated independently in various cultures as far back as the symbol for the heart in 18th-century BCE Egyptian accounting, by a space in Babylon, and by several various grotesque numeral figures by the Mayans, who used base 20. The zero was rigorously if not entirely accurately defined by the Indian mathematician Brahmagupta in 628. It's widely believed that part of the delay in establishing zero as a number, rather than just a placeholder as was the case in many early systems, was a fear of what it represented: the unknown, the void, nonexistence, as one book about the history of zero called it: The Nothing That Is.

And over those centuries, the concept, and word, took on other meanings. The *OED* lists numerous senses of "zero" from mathematics, linguistics, geography, chemistry, business, physics, the military "zero hour," even radio and agriculture, and most recently such terms as "zero tolerance" policies and "zero day" software attacks, not to mention referring to a person who is a nobody.

Among the many examples in his book was the "rabbit problem"—you can guess how that goes—which gives rise to a sequence of what are now known as Fibonacci numbers. Start with 2 1's, and then each subsequent number is the sum of the previous two: 1, 1, 2, 3, 5, 8, 13, 21, 34, 55, and so on. They're a curiosity, one of those things you learn about in math class and then forget all about, though they seem to crop up in a variety of natural contexts like leaf petal and pine cone patterns, and can also be of use in other mathematical settings. There's even an association and journal, *The Fibonacci Quarterly*, so his name lives on in at least one way.

The first version of the Liber Abaci was written in 1202, though no copies of that survive; we have three almost complete examples and more fragments of a second version from 1228, all in manuscript copies from at least 50 years later. Remarkably, it apparently wasn't printed until 1857 and wasn't translated into English until 2002. It was very popular in its day; it was used for at least three centuries in the teaching of mathematics and sparked the production of around a thousand other texts on mathematics in Italy. Indeed, these secondary texts were so successful that within a few generations, it was forgotten and his name largely disappears from mathematical writings. The last we know of him was an audience with Frederick II, the Holy Roman Emperor, to demonstrate his abilities

Romanesco broccoli, an edible flower bud of the species *Brassica oleracea*, is one of many natural displays of Fibonacci numbers. iStock.

to solve challenge problems, a test that he passed with ease, and shortly thereafter we lose him; we don't even have a record of his death or where he is buried.

I said at the beginning that not much happened in 1202. That's not entirely true—lots of things happened; we just don't know much about them because so few records survive. However, somewhere around 1200, Tahitian Polynesians settle what is now New Zealand, the Icelandic family sagas begin, and the collection of poems known as *Carmina Burana* is written. Within the next several years, the Fourth Crusade will take Jerusalem, the Franciscan Order will be founded, and the warrior Temujin will unite the nomadic Mongol tribes and style himself Genghis Khan.

And in a lovely bit of circularity, without Liber Abaci, we wouldn't call it 1202, particularly the 0 part. We could refer to it as MCCII, or some other way, though it's difficult to imagine progress would have proceeded along the same pathways using Roman numerals. Fibonacci and his book paved the way for the foundation of almost every form of progress you can imagine, and that work is still played out every minute of every day and likely always will. Not bad for a quiet year.

Time to check your math; 872 divided by 594 is 1.468, and I didn't use a calculator or even pencil and paper. I googled it. Not many people know that Google can do calculations, including conversions and such; type in "half a cup in teaspoons" and see what you get, for example. Few people also know that "Google" is a play on the word "googol," invented around 1940 by the nine-year-old nephew of a mathematician when he was asked what to call 1 followed by 100 zeroes. A googolplex is 1 followed by a googol of zeroes. Which is a very big number. So a zero isn't really nothing after all.

SOURCES

Aczel, Amir. "The Origin of the Number Zero." *Smithsonian Magazine* (December 2014). Accessed November 24, 2015. http://www.smithsonianmag.com/history/origin-number-zero-180953392/.
Bragg, Melvyn. "Zero." *In Our Time*. BBC Radio 4, May 13, 2004. Accessed February 29, 2016. http://www.bbc.co.uk/programmes/p004y254.
Casselman, Bill. "All for Nought." American Mathematical Society. February 2007. Accessed November 24, 2015. http://www.ams.org/samplings/feature-column/fcarc-india-zero.
Devlin, Keith J. *The Man of Numbers: Fibonacci's Arithmetic Revolution*. New York: Walker & Co., 2011.
Fibonacci, Leonardo, and L. E. Sigler. *Fibonacci's Liber Abaci: A Translation into Modern English of Leonardo Pisano's Book of Calculation*. Sources and Studies in the History of Mathematics and Physical Sciences. New York: Springer, 2002.
Google. "Our History in Depth." Accessed March 1, 2016. https://www.google.com/about/company/history/.
Kaplan, Robert. *The Nothing That Is: A Natural History of Zero*. Oxford: Oxford University Press, 2000.
National Public Radio. "Fibonacci's 'Numbers': The Man Behind The Math." July 16, 2011. Accessed November 24, 2015. http://www.npr.org/2011/07/16/137845241/fibonaccis-numbers-the-man-behind-the-math.
O'Connor, J. J., and E. F. Robertson. "A History of Zero." *MacTutor History of Mathematics Archive*. November 2000. Accessed November 24, 2015. http://www-history.mcs.st-and.ac.uk/HistTopics/Zero.html.
Oxford English Dictionary. "googol, n." Oxford University Press. Accessed November 1, 2016. http://www.oed.com/view/Entry/80013.
———. "zero, n." Oxford University Press. Accessed November 1, 2016. http://www.oed.com/view/Entry/232803.
Seife, Charles. *Zero: The Biography of a Dangerous Idea*. New York: Viking, 2000.
Wallin, Nils-Bertil. "The History of Zero." *YaleGlobal Online*, November 19, 2002. Accessed November 24, 2015. http://yaleglobal.yale.edu/about/zero.jsp.
Wells, D. G. *The Penguin Dictionary of Curious and Interesting Numbers*. Harmondsworth, UK: Penguin Books, 1986.
Wikipedia. "0 (number)." Accessed November 16, 2015. https://en.wikipedia.org/w/index.php?title=0_(number)&oldid=690979504.

Annals of the World

**in the original Latin *Annales Veteris Testamenti*,
a chronology compiled by Bishop James Ussher**
published in London

1650

We're always told that good stories have a beginning, a middle, and an end. "Begin at the beginning," the King of Hearts tells the White Rabbit, "and go on till you come to the end: then stop." There has to be a beginning, a first scene, a first page, a first note—a first day. But what about *the* beginning, the beginning of everything? The definitive First Day?

Most ancient cultures didn't acknowledge any such thing; the Babylonians, the Greeks, the Hindus, all thought that the universe is eternal and cyclical, perhaps mirroring the movement of heavenly bodies. Recall, if you will, that whole Mayan calendar cycle thing in 2012, which we all seem to have survived unscathed, if you don't count the horrible John Cusack disaster porn movie.

One tradition, however, firmly believed that there was a specific start to the universe, and moreover that it wasn't all that long ago, which we find in the Old Testament. Figuring out when that was, as methodically and precisely as possible, became the life work of an Irish bishop and scholar who gave us a date and, for that matter, a time that held sway for a couple of centuries, and for many people, still does.

James Ussher had an unusual upbringing. Besides the story of somehow being taught to read by two blind aunts, he was raised Protestant in heavily Catholic Ireland, was one of the first scholars at Trinity College Dublin at age 13, was given a special dispensation to be ordained at 20, younger than the canonically required age, and was appointed as a professor six years later. He was deeply involved in the development of the Church of Ireland, made a bishop in 1621 and primate four years later. His career included work both sacred and secular, becoming a member of the Irish Privy Council, and helping to articulate the original tenets of his church. He was widely acknowledged for his thorough and impartial scholarship, based on scrupulous work with as many primary sources as possible; as early as 1624 he was invited to preach before

Portrait of James Ussher. © National Portrait Gallery, London.

King James I. His writings covered a range of topics historical and theological, and over time he drifted away from pastoral work and administration and toward scholarship as his primary activity.

Ussher made numerous trips to England, to visit, research, and obtain books for the Trinity library; the last was in 1640, when he got stuck, never to return, after an Irish Catholic uprising the following year. This left him homeless, penniless, and dependent on the charity of his friend and benefactor the Dowager Countess of Peterborough. He was a fervent royalist at a time when that wasn't always healthy; several versions are recounted of his witnessing Charles I's 1649 execution from the roof of the Countess's home and either fainting or weeping or just silently turning away. The regard in which he was held was, however, high enough that Cromwell paid for most of his state funeral in 1656 and allowed him to be buried in Westminster Abbey.

His masterwork, and the one for which he is remembered today, is a massive chronology, laying out the dates of important events both biblical and historical, and incidentally specifying the date and time of the creation of the universe: nightfall on Saturday, October 22, 4004 BCE. This was the *Annales Veteris Testamenti*, 20 years in the writing, though there are suggestions he was thinking about it since childhood, published originally in Latin in 1650, around the time of the chartering of Harvard College, the death of Descartes, the emergence of the overture in music and of tea drinking in England, and the building of the Taj Mahal. It appeared in English translation as *Annals of the World* eight years later. The work ran to 1,300 pages with 14,000 footnotes, each paragraph numbered and indexed for handy reference.

While Ussher is widely credited for pinning down Creation 6,000 years ago, he wasn't the only one to attempt that, or even the first; indeed, that rough cosmological age was, in effect, common knowledge in the 17th century.

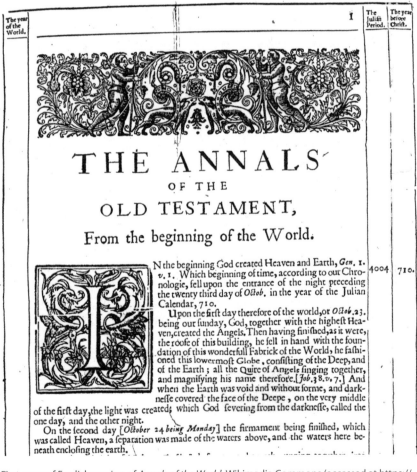

First page of English version of *Annals of the World*. Wikimedia Commons (accessed at https://commons.wikimedia.org/wiki/File:Annals_of_the_World_page_1.jpg).

Augustine's *City of God* had firmly established a definite creation in the Christian mind-set nearly 1,500 years before, and it stuck. It also echoed scripture: 2 Peter 3:8 says, "One day is with the Lord as a thousand years" so six days of Creation might imply the Earth would exist for roughly 6,000 years. There were numerous estimates already around, including from the Venerable Bede, Luther, Kepler, and even Newton, who pegged it at precisely 4000 BCE. Each of them, though, had derived different dates, so which one was right?

Ussher set about to find out. He scoured libraries and bookstores for different versions of the bible, each of which would have its own slightly different chronologies and genealogies, as well as other historical texts and artifacts, including a wide range of sources from a variety of societies, civilizations, and faiths. Using all of those, he worked backwards from the birth of Christ, which he placed at 5 BCE based on the writings of the Roman historian Josephus, tracing life spans, kingly reigns, and whatever else he could. He places the Exodus in 1491 BCE, Abraham's birth at 1996 BCE and the Flood at 2348 BCE, eventually reaching back to the beginning with a capital B on that fateful Saturday evening a little more than six millennia ago.

That date and time can seem oddly specific to modern ears, but let's remember that they are based on a desire to get it right, as right as he possibly could, paying attention to astronomical and religious sources in determining what the season of the year, day of the week and time had to be; for example, he believed it had to be in the autumn, since that was the beginning of the Jewish calendar year, and it had to be on a Sabbath, hence, on a Saturday evening.

The original printing sold well. Had things gone differently, his chronology would have been noted for a time and then forgotten as so many others were, if it were not for Thomas Guy, a London bookseller who saw a market opportunity for a Bible in 1675 with lots of bells and whistles, including engravings of, ahem, bare-breasted women, along with . . . voila, a handy chronology in the margin. The Church of England nudged matters along as well in 1701, when the bishop of Worcester authorized printing another edition of the Bible incorporating it.

Ussher, and his *Annals*, is rather too cavalierly dismissed today as a crackpot, or alternately embraced, equally mindlessly, as a stalwart symbol of what's now known as Young Earth Creationism, though I think neither is really justified. He deserves to be more than just a rim shot or caricature. He was a careful and thoughtful man, well schooled in his faith and in history, and as many have pointed out, including paleontologist Stephen Jay Gould, he was trying to do the best he could with the tools and knowledge available to him at the time.

Over the last few decades, new tools have been introduced to the search for the beginning, from geological to astronomical, which have pushed the temporal boundaries further and further back. As always, though, old ideas die hard, and Ussher's chronology and dates still resonate today. One website deplores that people have "started trusting in the latest secular findings based on fallible dating methods, instead of the only absolutely reliable method—consulting the history book provided by the Eyewitness account (the infallible Word of God)."

Public opinion surveys over the last several decades have consistently found that about three-quarters of Americans believe that God played some role in human development, and just under half believe the age of the earth and of humanity to be between 6,000 and 10,000 years. Separate surveys also show that a quarter believe the sun goes around the Earth, and a third that the mother's gene determines the gender of a child.

Modern archaeological scholarship places the 40th century BCE in what's known as the Copper Age, between the Stone and Bronze Ages in Europe, the Uruk period in Mesopotamia, and the El Omari culture in predynastic Egypt, as the horse and water buffalo are becoming domesticated, the plow is coming into use, and beer is starting to be brewed. I'm not sure what Bishop Ussher would make of contemporary estimates: the age of humanity at something over 200,000 years, of the earth at about 4.5 billion, and the universe at around 13.75 billion years. I'd like to think he'd have a mind as open as the breadth of his vision and scholarship.

So now one has to ask oneself: are *we* doing the best *we* can with the tools at *our* disposal? The answer, as is so often the case, depends on where you stand, and where you begin.

SOURCES

Barr, James. "Why the World Was Created in 4004 BC: Archbishop Ussher and Biblical Chronology." *Bulletin of the John Rylands Library* 67, no. 2 (1985): 575–608.

Ford, Alan. "Ussher, James (1581–1656)." *Oxford Dictionary of National Biography.* Oxford University Press, 2004 (online edition, October 2009). http://www.oxforddnb.com/view/article/28034.

Gorst, Martin. *Measuring Eternity: The Search for the Beginning of Time.* New York: Broadway Books, 2001.

Keim, Brandon. "Oct. 22, 4004 B.C.: Universe Usshered In." *Wired*, October 22, 2010. http://www.wired.com/2010/10/1022creation-4004bc-ussher/.

National Science Foundation. "Science and Engineering Indicators 2014." Last modified February 2014. http://www.nsf.gov/statistics/seind14/.

NBC News. "4 in 10 Americans Believe God Created Earth 10,000 Years Ago." June 6, 2014. http://www.nbcnews.com/science/science-news/4-10-americans-believe-god-created-earth-10-000-years-n124701.

Newport, Frank. "In U.S., 46% Hold Creationist View of Human Origins." *Gallup*, June 1, 2012. http://www.gallup.com/poll/155003/Hold-Creationist-View-Human-Origins.aspx.

Reynolds, Neil. "The Man Who Dated Creation at Oct. 23, 4004 BC." *Globe and Mail*, December 28, 2010. http://www.theglobeandmail.com/globe-debate/the-man-who-dated-creation-at-oct -23-4004-bc/article4084451/.

Pierce, Larry. "The World: Born in 4004 BC?" *Answers in Genesis*. Last modified October 23, 2007. https://answersingenesis.org/bible-timeline/the-world-born-in-4004-bc/.

Wikipedia. "40th century BC." March 8, 2015. http://en.wikipedia.org/w/index.php?title=40th _century_BC&oldid=650388081.

———. "James Ussher." April 2, 2015. http://en.wikipedia.org/w/index.php?title=James_Ussher &oldid=654686754.

———. "Ussher Chronology." March 25, 2015. http://en.wikipedia.org/w/index.php?title=Ussher _chronology&oldid=653391999.

7

Philosophical Transactions

a scholarly journal
still published under the auspices of the Royal Society in London

1665

Hardly a day goes by, it seems, without news of some new research study, and we learn that, say, heavy metal music improves concentration or caffeine is linked to immortality. (If only.) Most of us probably just rely on reports from the media or the Internet, with a vague sense that results like these were published in some organized way, somewhere, by somebody . . . scientists, right? And if you really wanted to, you could track down the original article and see all the details.

Perhaps. The ways in which the outcomes of scholarly inquiry are distributed are changing and differentiating fast, yet they all stem from a single source that was intended to be an easier and more timely way for a new class of investigators to hear about each other's work and that wound up helping to produce a fundamental shift in research itself—which might be happening all over again, in uncertain ways.

We should at least get the name right once, as it appeared on the title page of the first issue: "*Philosophical Transactions, Giving Some Accompt of the Present Undertakings, Studies and Labors of the Ingenious in Many Considerable Parts of the World.*" It's often credited with being the first scientific journal, even though it was squeaked out by two months and a day by the *Journal des Sçavans*, published in Paris, with similar but much more generic and literary aims and a spottier publication record. The *Transactions* have been published, more or less consistently, since its founding three and a half centuries ago, on March 6, 1665, the same year that Robert Hooke's *Micrographia* came out with the first published reference to a "cell," the first census was taken of what is now Quebec, and the first Native American, Caleb Cheeshahteaumuck, graduated from Harvard.

The first editor was Henry Oldenburg, the secretary of the then five-year-old Royal Society, founded to more broadly disseminate the findings of the newly emerging world of science and discovery. At first, the Society kept the journal at arms' length, perhaps for financial reasons—and with some found, which would polish as finely as Glass, and *reflect* as much light, as glass *transmits*, and the art of communicating to it a *Parabolick* figure be also attained. But there seemed very great difficulties, and I have almost thought them insuperable, when I further considered, that every irregularity in a reflecting superficies makes the rays stray 5 or 6 times more out of their due course, than the like irregularities in a refracting one : So that a much greater curiosity would be here requisite, than in figuring glasses for Refraction.

Amidst these thoughts I was forced from *Cambridge* by the Intervening Plague, and it was more then two years, before I proceeded further. But then having thought on a tender way of polishing, proper for metall, whereby, as I imagined, the figure also would be corrected to the last ; I began to try, what might be effected in this kind, and by degrees so far perfected an Instrument (in the essential parts of it like that I sent to *London*,) by which I could discern Jupiters 4 Concomitants, and shewed them divers times to two others of my acquaintance. I could also discern the Moon-like phase of *Venus*, but not very distinctly, nor without some niceness in disposing the Instrument.

From that time I was interrupted till this last Autumn, when I made the other. And as that was sensibly better then the first (especially for Day-Objects,) so I doubt not, but they will be still brought to a much greater perfection by their endeavours, who, as you inform me, are taking care about it at *London*.

I have sometimes thought to make a *Microscope*, which in like manner should have, instead of an Object-glass, a Reflecting piece of metall. And this I hope they will also take into consideration. For those Instruments seem as capable of improvement as *Telescopes*, and perhaps more, because but one reflective piece of metall is requisite in them, as you may perceive by the annexed diagram, where A B representeth the object metall, C D the eye glass, F their common Focus, and O the other focus of the metall, in which the object is placed.

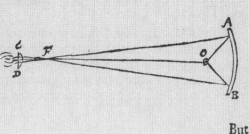

But

A page from Isaac Newton's article "New Theory about Lights and Colors," published in *Philosophical Transactions* in January 1671. © The Royal Society.

justification; Oldenburg hoped to yield £150 a year, but got closer to £40, barely enough to pay his rent. Early publication was erratic; intended to be monthly, it almost never was, what with financial difficulties, not to mention the last great plague to hit London in that first year. Perhaps 1,000 copies were printed of early issues, though that varied too. He also found it to be perilous business; Issue 27 is especially notorious as the one he didn't edit because he was locked in the Tower of London on suspicion of espionage due to all the correspondence he was carrying on with foreign scholars.

By this point, a number of forces and developments had arrayed themselves to enable what we now think of as the scholarly journal to arise. Of course, in the very beginning, transmission of knowledge was oral: how to make glass, how to build a pyramid, that sort of thing. It was passed on from generation to generation and required substantial memorization techniques once common but now no longer necessary and thus lost to us, which is why if your cell phone loses all your numbers, you're hosed. Then writing develops, and publishing in Europe in the 15th century, followed by a general rise in literacy, secular thinking, and economic stability, all of which helped to provide a fertile environment for what we now call the Scientific Revolution, based on direct observation and questioning ancient authorities rather than reprinting and parroting them. Francis Bacon, early in the 17th century, is often given credit for coalescing what would become the experiment and thus the scientific method, and indeed, it's the format of that method that dictated the order and structure for many scholarly articles then and now: lay out a problem or question, discuss what has been written about it before, design a method for investigating it, describe your results, and interpret them in drawing your conclusions.

Those results must be shared and validated by one's peers, and in the early days that was a one-to-one business, by conversation, attendance at scientific meetings, or personal correspondence. The Royal Society recognized this from its very beginning; a 1661 letter from Robert Moray, one of its founders, to the Dutch mathematician and astronomer Christiaan Huygens, said the Society intended "from time to time . . . [to] print what passes among ourselves, at least everything that may be published." Indeed, even today, titles of journals betray this heritage; for example, one of the most highly respected journals in physics is *Physical Review Letters*. The *Philosophical Transactions* enabled scientists (then referred to as "natural philosophers," hence the title) to disseminate their work much more widely, efficiently, and quickly, and not coincidentally to shore up the claim of priority for who published something first and thus gets the credit. Lest you think that was trivial, then or now, it's possible that Carlo Rubbia was awarded a share of the 1984 Nobel Prize in Physics because he rushed publication of a manuscript. Isaac Newton and Gottfried Leibniz and their surrogates and supporters waged a decades-long running battle over who should get credit for inventing calculus, which they developed independently.

That first issue is remarkable. After a couple of fawning pages aimed at the king and his patronage, we get down to business with an article on optics, then the first of several about the Great Comet of 1664, Boyle's summary of his experiments with cold, a report of a "very odd monstrous calf" born in Hampshire with a triple tongue among other deformities, and a sort of obituary of the great French mathematician Fermat. The second issue already has commentary on articles in the first, and as the first year draws to a close, we start to see book reviews, and even an index at the end, all features familiar to users of journals ever since.

As you look through that first year you can almost feel them working it out—evolving not only the way they're communicating results of their new science, but the science and the process of the science itself. The *Transactions* was a general-purpose vehicle; quickly, though, journals started to arise for specific disciplines. Today there are journals in every field and sub-field and sub-sub-field you can imagine and then some; tens of thousands of them, publishing what must be well over a million articles a year, not to mention the fields of endeavor that rely more on books, book chapters, conference proceedings, technical reports, and even posters to disseminate their scholarly and creative work.

The world of scholarly communication has gotten a lot more complicated in the last few decades. Things develop, naturally, but your average printed article, even today, would not look all that odd to a 17th- or 18th-century scholar. Behind the scenes and under the surface, however, things have been afoot. Corporate mergers and acquisitions have meant that more and more journals are in fewer and greedier hands. Add to this the critical nature of reputation and reward and the demands of the funding and tenure systems, and that means that individual high-status can't-not-have journals, single journals, can cost upwards of tens of thousands of dollars a year to subscribe to. It's not unusual for a major research or university library to spend millions of dollars a year just for subscriptions, and prices have risen by double-digit percentages, year after year, for decades. And those subscriptions typically only get you access to the digital works; back in the day if you dropped a journal you at least had the old print issues you received. Now, if the tap is turned off, you're left with nothing but happy memories.

At the same time, we've seen the rise of venues like digital and open-source journals, which often dispense with copyright and the profit motivation, so that they're available to all. Somebody's got to pay for the work that goes into it, such as editing and reviewing, so authors often foot the bill, which is

Photograph showing bound copies of the *Transactions of the Medical Society of Virginia*. Taber Andrew Bain (flickr user: andrewbain).

easy if you're a chemist with a research grant, less so if you're a literary scholar with a laptop. Since most of these venues are new and thus don't have a long track record, their attractiveness is somewhat dimmed, especially for younger scholars, by a lack of reputation and status, and they can also be the devil to find since they rarely get covered by large and established journal databases.

My generation of scholars grew up knowing we'd publish in print, mostly text, and might have to fight to include tables or figures, let alone photographs or (gasp) color. Now, my doctoral students easily envision "publishing" digitally, with text, certainly, but also, say, video clips, software simulations, or real-time commentary from readers, and increasingly providing access to the raw data their conclusions are based on. Maybe that'll be a journal, or a scholarly blog, or something far more exotic. Freed from the constraints of the journal article, they'll be able to construct new and different works and eventually ask new and different questions that never would have even been imaginable before.

Put these all together and you start to call into question the endurance and stability the scholarly community—indeed the scholarly enterprise—values and requires. Since scholarship relies so heavily on the continuity of the record of what has gone before, the ability to consult that, to find what has been written, yesterday, today, and tomorrow, is a critical component in making it work. Thus, we're going to have to figure out ways to preserve and maintain that record, in all its myriad and diversifying forms, representing what we know, how we know it, and what we don't know.

SOURCES

Bonitz, Manfred. "Notes on the Development of Secondary Periodicals: From the *Journal Des Sçavans* to the *Pharmaceutisches Central-Blatt.*" *International Forum on Information and Documentation* 2, no. 1 (1977): 26–31.

Harmon, Joseph E. "The Literature of Enlightenment: Technical Periodicals and Proceedings in the 17th and 18th Centuries." *Journal of Technical Writing and Communication* 17, no. 4 (1987): 397–405.

Kronick, David A. *"Devant le Deluge" and Other Essays on Early Modern Scientific Communication.* Lanham, MD: Scarecrow Press, 2004.

Lavoie, Brian F., Eric Childress, Ricky Erway, Ixchel M. Faniel, Constance Malpas, Jennifer Schaffner, and Titia van der Werf. *The Evolving Scholarly Record.* Dublin, OH: OCLC Research, 2014. Accessed August 29, 2016. http://www.oclc.org/content/dam/research/publications/library/2014/oclcresearch-evolving-scholarly-record-2014.pdf.

McKie, Douglas. "The Scientific Periodical from 1665 to 1798." In *Natural Philosophy through the 18th Century and Allied Topics,* edited by Alan Ferguson, 122–32. London: Taylor and Francis, 1972.

Osburn, Charles B. "The Place of the Journal in the Scholarly Communications System." *Library Resources and Technical Services* 28, no. 4 (1984): 315–24.

Royal Society, Richard Pearson, George Shaw, and Charles Hutton. *The Philosophical Transactions of the Royal Society of London, from Their Commencement, in 1665, to the Year 1800: Abridged, with Notes and Biographical Illustrations.* 18 vols. London: Printed by and for C. and R. Baldwin, 1809.

Schaffner, Ann C. "The Future of Scientific Journals: Lessons from the Past." *Information Technology and Libraries* 13, no. 4 (1994): 239–47.

8
The Riot Act

"An Act for preventing Tumults and Riotous Assemblies, and for the more speedy and effectual punishing the Rioters," better known as the Riot Act
enacted by the Parliament of Great Britain
now housed in the Parliamentary Archives, Public Act, 1 George I Statute 2, c. 5

1714

"Just say the word." It's a common phrase used to indicate you're expecting or waiting for an instruction or permission: Just say the word and I'll help out, or pick up dinner, or help you bury that body. Those instructions can be trivial or profound, depending on the circumstances, and even when there's more than just one word involved, the meaning remains clear—merely speaking, and hearing, the words is all that's needed to carry out somebody's wishes.

About three centuries ago, in a time and place of turmoil and upheaval, a law was passed, now largely forgotten except in the common expression it gave rise to, where saying the right words at the right time was meant to bring order—on pain of death for those who chose to ignore them.

The early 18th century was not an easy time in a Britain newly united. By the time the Hanoverian George I ascended to the joint throne of England and Scotland in 1714 after the death of the childless Queen Anne, there had been over a century and half of squabbling over succession all the way back to Mary and Elizabeth, a Civil War, a republic, the restoration of the monarchy, and the seemingly never-ending struggle for supremacy between Catholicism and Anglicanism. The Glorious Revolution in 1688 firmed up the Protestant character of the throne, and then the supporters of Catholic claimant James II rose up in what is now called the Jacobite Rebellion.

Perhaps not surprisingly after all that, a series of riots between competing groups of Tories and Whigs starting in 1710 were the last straw, and in 1714, the same year Parliament created a prize for the first person to figure out longitude and thus make ship navigation safer, they passed an act to put a stop the disorder in the country once and for all, to take effect the following year: the Riot Act.

Illustration from *Master Humphrey's Clock*, by Charles Dickens, that depicts the 1780 Gordon Riots in London. University of California Libraries; Internet archive.

The act itself allowed local officials, including sheriffs, mayors, and justices of the peace, to decide that any gathering of more than twelve people was "unlawfully, riotously, and tumultuously assembled together," and thus to proclaim them as a "riot." This distinguishes them from a "rout," which is an attempt to commit a riot, or "unlawful assembly," which common law helpfully defined as . . . an assembly of people to do something unlawful.

In any event, once that declaration was made, the rioters would then have an hour to disperse or face being charged with a felony, punishable by death. A tool as powerful as that has great allure, so its eventual use for political purposes comes as no surprise. In addition, the act allowed authorities to use force in dispersing a riotous crowd, and for good measure, any bystanders who helped out and perhaps, say, hurt or killed anybody in the process would face no charges of their own.

Here's the thing, though. The sheriff or mayor can't just make this decision and rely on people knowing about the law, or wave a copy of it at them. He has to say it. Out loud. "[A]mong the said rioters, or as near to them as he can safely come, with a loud voice," as the act says. There's an obvious hitch here; your average rioter, even in genteel, tea-and-sandwiches Britain, is not exactly amenable to being stopped mid-rumpus to be told to knock it off. And, as later court decisions would declare, the entire operative paragraph in the act, consisting of all of 53 words, had to be read and heard. Leave any bit of it out, including the closing "God Save the King!," and it's not valid. Here's the full text:

> Our sovereign Lord the King chargeth and commandeth all persons, being assembled, immediately to disperse themselves, and peaceably to depart to their habitations, or to their lawful business, upon the pains contained in the act made in the first year of King George, for preventing tumults and riotous assemblies. God save the King.

Rolled parchments containing acts of the Parliament of the United Kingdom at the Parliamentary Archives in London. Jeroen van Luin (flickr user: -jvl-).

By 1837, the penalty was reduced to transportation for life (to Australia, mostly); the last time it was used was apparently in Glasgow in 1919, before being repealed in 1973. Versions continue to be active in other places, including several Australian states, Canada (where it was read out following the Vancouver Stanley Cup riots in 2011), and the United States, starting in 1792 and persisting to this day. Americans, though, require only three people to make up a riot; I guess because we're just better at it.

It's tempting to think of this as an oral document—but it's not; it's written down and everything. It's more correct to say that this is a document that has to be oral to work. It's somewhat different from a written speech or play or, for that matter, music. The experience of hearing each of those is obviously different and unique each time, but they can all be read and understood on their own terms. It shares more in common with things like oaths, which we still make people recite and swear out loud, one of a number of vestiges of a legal system that was once largely oral in nature.

For that matter, it feels as though it most closely resembles an incantation or magic spell, whose mere presence doesn't work until read out loud, or a religious service such as the Mass. All of those have a ceremonial or ritual aspect, a time, place, circumstance; without the ceremony, without the words spoken by an ordained priest, it's an unleavened wafer—with all of that, it's the literal and physical body of Christ.

These are all examples of what linguists call "speech acts," things we say that cause something to happen, or to change, or to be. Think of a promise, an excuse, an invitation, thanks, apologies, congratulations. Several categories of these have been identified, including "commissives," which commit to a future act, like an oath to tell the truth. The Riot Act seems to be an example of both a "directive" act, like "Come here," which cause the hearer to do—or stop doing—something, and a "declaration," which somehow changes the state of the world—as when a judge "pronounces" a sentence or that a couple is married. One could say that speech acts have been around for a very long time. Have a look at Genesis 1: "Let there be light." A group isn't a "riot" until the sheriff says so and they hear him—the words had to be heard to take effect as well—and then they are. Because he said so, and the law says he can. If anybody else tried, it wouldn't work.

Times and circumstances are now different, as are tactics for quelling riots—water cannons and pepper spray seem to be more in vogue than a good stern talking to. "Reading the riot act" persists almost entirely rhetorically, meaning a scolding. But of course, rhetoric is all it ever was—words written to be spoken and heard, taking on the power they were given until no longer needed, and then eventually taking on a new meaning of their own.

SOURCES

Binder, Denis, and Dan Kahan. "Riots: Legal Aspects." *Encyclopedia of Crime and Justice*. New York: Macmillan Reference USA, 2002.

Brown, Keith, ed. *Encyclopedia of Language and Linguistics*. 2nd ed. Boston: Elsevier, 2006.

Damer, Seán. "The Last Reading of the Riot Act." *BBC*, January 30, 2009. Accessed July 18, 2016. http://news.bbc.co.uk/2/hi/uk_news/scotland/glasgow_and_west/7859192.stm.

Darity, William A., ed. *International Encyclopedia of the Social Sciences*. 2nd ed. 9 vols. Macmillan Social Science Library. Detroit: Macmillan Reference USA, 2008.

Legal Information Institute (LII). 10 U.S. Code Chapter 15—Insurrection. Accessed July 19, 2016. https://www.law.cornell.edu/uscode/text/10/subtitle-A/part-I/chapter-15.

The Riot Act, 2005. Accessed July 18, 2016. http://www.gutenberg.org/ebooks/8142?msg=welcome_stranger.

Searle, John R. *Expression and Meaning: Studies in the Theory of Speech Acts*. Cambridge: Cambridge University Press, 1979.

———. *Speech Acts: An Essay in the Philosophy of Language*. London: Cambridge University Press, 1969.

Wikipedia. "Riot Act." Last modified August 14, 2016. https://en.wikipedia.org/w/index.php?title=Riot_Act&oldid=734447033.

Declaration of Independence deleted passage

a passage, beginning with "He has waged cruel war"
deleted by the Second Continental Congress from
the American Declaration of Independence
original rough draft now housed in the Library of Congress

1776

How do you read something that isn't there? Well, you can't, unless somehow you know it used to be there. There are lots of examples of the creative process at work in all its messy, myriad varieties—in multiple drafts of novels, plays, scientific articles and so on, showing us how works have been tweaked and pruned and sometimes taken apart and put back together again.

A good example is lawmaking, where the stakes can be very high, so in a contemporary legislature, meticulous minutes are kept recording proposed amendments, speeches made, votes taken, and so on so that the public, and future generations can, if they care, know how it all happened and, moreover, who to thank or blame.

This wasn't always the case, and one of our most cherished and fundamental documents underwent a series of such edits and revisions from the trivial to the profound. We are largely in the dark as to how and why, and one piece in particular, taken out in one of the most pivotal decisions in our early history, resounds, even—especially—in its absence, today.

The year 1776 is so ingrained in the American consciousness with the Declaration of Independence that it sort of blots out everything else that happened that year. The first volume of Gibbon's *Decline and Fall of the Roman Empire* was published, as was *The Wealth of Nations*. Catherine the Great is in the middle of her reign, Louis XVI in the third year of his, and the Phi Beta Kappa society is founded at the College of William and Mary that winter. But pride of place goes to the document drafted by Thomas Jefferson in a second-floor rented apartment on the corner of Seventh and Market Streets in Philadelphia on behalf of a committee of five members of Congress.

First page of Thomas Jefferson's Rough Draft of the Declaration of Independence. Library of Congress.

There are many, many stories about the Declaration, including the early printed copy I nearly sneezed on one winter's morning at the Library of Congress, but those will have to wait for another day. The basics: Jefferson was much more interested in helping to prepare Virginia's new constitution and only somewhat reluctantly took on the task of drafting some sort of statement expressing and crystallizing the reasons why the American colonies were breaking away from the British Crown and stating as fact that they had; John Adams later claimed he talked him into it. In a time when anonymous political writing was commonplace (Poor Richard, Publius, *The Federalist* Papers to come), his authorship wasn't widely acknowledged at the time. Jefferson borrowed freely from numerous sources, and his initial effort went first to the rest of the committee, including Adams and Benjamin Franklin, who then made some 47 changes, mostly minor, adding several paragraphs.

There are seven versions and fragments in Jefferson's hand, including what's known as the "original Rough draught," which looks like exactly that. It's got crossouts, additions, boxes, even a pasted-on flap, showing how the text evolved, if not the reasons or people responsible. For example, somehow we got from "We hold these truths to be sacred and undeniable" to "self-evident." Who did that? Franklin, Adams, Jefferson? We don't know. To this day, research goes on about the writing and editing processes, including recent sophisticated imaging studies of Jefferson's drafts.

Congress debated the committee's submission over three days, making a further 39 edits, which seriously annoyed Jefferson, who by now was feeling more than a little protective of the prose, later calling his colleagues "pusillanimous" in trying not to offend the British people too grievously. It was adopted, as amended, on July 4. The original resolution on declaring independence was passed on July 2, but nobody remembers that. How important were these words? Just note that the date of the adoption of the Declaration on July 4 is celebrated as the American national holiday of independence rather than, as John Adams had predicted, the date the decision was actually made.

Anyway, adopted it was, and the committee took it that night to John Dunlap, their official printer, to have copies made. Twenty-six of these "Dunlap broadsides" are known to survive; one discovered hidden in a flea market picture frame in 1991 fetched $2.5 million at auction. The handwritten engrossed version was signed, first by John Hancock, beginning on August 2. That version has had a journey of its own, being moved at least 20 times, including sitting in the sun for about 35 years in the Patent Office, in a State Department library room with an open fireplace for another 17, and a trip to Fort Knox to wait out World War II. It has resided since 1952 in the National Archives, now in the rotunda, protected by a monitoring system designed by the Jet Propulsion

Laboratory, and not at all susceptible to being rolled up and stolen like you saw in *National Treasure*, which I can't believe they sell the DVD of in the Archives' gift shop. Seriously.

The Declaration has been inspirational, not only for its words and ideas, but as an idea unto itself. Visit the Alamo in San Antonio, and you're treated to considerable discussions about the Declaration of Independence—of Texas— signed in 1836. It's explicitly referenced in South Carolina's 1860 declaration of secession as well. In 1777, only a few months on, a "Petition for Freedom" from "A Great Number of Blackes" was submitted to the Massachusetts legislature. Declarations of independence have been composed over the decades by labor groups, farmers, women, socialists, and others. Frederick Douglass asked pointedly, in an 1852 speech to the Rochester Ladies' Anti-Slavery Society, "What to the Slave Is the Fourth of July?"

One of the most consequential amendments removed a section of some 168 words, laying out one of the litany of charges and accusations against George III, piling up the indictments and thus justifying the quite novel idea of colonies breaking away. It's typically known by its opening words as the "He has waged cruel war" passage, and it accuses the king of perpetuating the slave trade and by inference slavery itself. Adams said in 1822 he never thought it would get through unscathed, though his otherwise comprehensive diaries of the relevant days are silent on what happened. Jefferson also was sanguine if a bit snippy about it, saying it was "struck out in complaisance to South Carolina & Georgia, who had never attempted to restrain the importation of slaves.... Our Northern brethren also I believe felt a little tender ... for tho' their people have very few slaves themselves yet they had been pretty considerable carriers of them to others."

The rudimentary congressional journal is of no help on what actually happened; it simply records that there was discussion and debate, as a committee of the whole, and approval, but that's it. The next order of business concerned the hiring of a boat from a Mr. Walker.

Much has been written about Jefferson's deeply conflicted position as slaveholder and as defender of individual rights. At the time of the Declaration's drafting, he owned 180 slaves, rising to 267 by 1822. He had six children by Sally Hemmings, who was his slave and also his dead wife's half-sister, and he did not, as was often the practice, free his slaves upon his death. There are few clean hands here; at least a third of the signers were slave owners, and even in northern states abolition was gradual; New York didn't outlaw slavery until 1827, the 1840 census lists seven slaves in Rhode Island, and in at least a few Union states full abolition wasn't achieved until 1865. And lest we get too smug about all this, estimates put the current number of people in forced labor or human trafficking worldwide today at between 20 and 35 million.

This edit can be seen as the result of ordinary and unremarkable deliberative mechanics: provisions are drafted, revised, taken out, added, re-revised, and so on, all part of the process of discussion and coming to agreement. That original draft was eventually subjected to no less than 86 edits in all, eventually reducing its length by roughly a quarter of its words.

For many, though, this is the American national mark of Cain; the proverbial can that has been kicked down our proverbial road for nearly a quarter of a millennium. Yes, it's true, as well as cliché, to say that progress has been made—including the Fourteenth and Nineteenth Amendments (to a Constitution that countenances slavery without ever soiling its hands by using the word outright). You could also point to civil rights legislation, Supreme Court decisions from *Brown* to *Obergefell*, the Americans with Disabilities Act, and so on. And yet, well, you know.

Reynolds's political map of the United States, published approximately 1856. (Printed on map: "Designed to exhibit the comparative area of the free and slave states and the territory open to slavery or freedom by the repeal of the Missouri compromise. With a comparison of the principal statistics of the free and slave states, from the census of 1850.") University of Houston Digital Library.

Any writer will tell you that less can be more. Sometimes, however, more is more—more words, more ideas, more voices, more people. Alloys are stronger for a reason.

This decision has been second-guessed, criticized, and defended since, it seems, day one if not even before; many believe the Declaration and the new nation would never have worked otherwise. Quite possibly—though that doesn't remove the inherent sting. It's hard not to think of this as a missed turning, an opportunity lost.

So, we finish where we started: How *do* you read something that isn't there? There's a difference between something that isn't there and never was and something that's been removed intentionally, purposefully. Perhaps knowing how that happened and why and by whom would be useful or make a difference; perhaps not. Without a more comprehensive record, we shall never know. Ultimately, this is a story about grand and noble language and ideas that have stirred souls for generations—and, within, a silence, which nonetheless speaks volumes, still.

SOURCES

Allen, Danielle S. *Our Declaration: A Reading of the Declaration of Independence in Defense of Equality*. New York: Liveright Publishing Corporation, a Division of W. W. Norton & Company, 2014.

BlackPast.org. "The Deleted Passage of the Declaration of Independence (1776)." Accessed August 18, 2015. http://www.blackpast.org/primary/declaration-independence-and-debate-over-slavery.

Boyd, Julian. "Jefferson's 'original Rough draught' of the Declaration of Independence." Library of Congress. Accessed August 18, 2015. http://www.loc.gov/exhibits/declara/ruffdrft.html.

Boyd, Julian P., and Gerard W. Gawalt. *The Declaration of Independence: The Evolution of the Text*. Rev. ed. Washington, DC: Library of Congress in Association with the Thomas Jefferson Memorial Foundation; Distributed by University Press of New England, 1999.

Dershowitz, Alan M., and Rogers D. Spotswood Collection. *America Declares Independence*. Turning Points. Hoboken, NJ: John Wiley & Sons, 2003.

Dyer, Justin Buckley. *American Soul: The Contested Legacy of the Declaration of Independence*. Lanham, MD: Rowman & Littlefield Publishers, 2012.

Foner, Philip Sheldon. *We, the Other People: Alternative Declarations of Independence by Labor Groups, Farmers, Woman's Rights Advocates, Socialists, and Blacks, 1829–1975*. Urbana: University of Illinois Press, 1976.

Gawalt, Gerald W. "Jefferson and the Declaration." *Library of Congress Information Bulletin* 58, no. 7 (July 1999). http://www.loc.gov/loc/lcib/9907/jeffdec.html.

Hazelton, John H. *The Declaration of Independence: Its History*. New York: Da Capo Press, 1970.

International Labour Organisation. "Statistics and Indicators on Forced Labour and Trafficking." Accessed August 20, 2015. http://www.ilo.org/global/topics/forced-labour/policy-areas/statistics/lang--en/index.htm.

Jayne, Allen. *Jefferson's Declaration of Independence: Origins, Philosophy, and Theology*. Lexington: University Press of Kentucky, 1998.

———. *Lincoln and the American Manifesto*. Amherst, NY: Prometheus Books, 2007.

Library of Congress. "Declaring Independence: Drafting the Documents." Accessed September 29, 2015. http://www.loc.gov/exhibits/declara/declara3.html.

———. "Hyperspectral Imaging by Library of Congress Reveals Change Made by Thomas Jefferson in Original Declaration of Independence Draft." July 2, 2010. http://www.loc.gov/today/pr/2010/10-161.html.

McCullough, David G., Pauline Maier, Robert G. Parkinson, Robert M. S. McDonald, David Armitage, Sandra Day O'Connor, Christian Yves Dupont, and Peter S. Onuf, *Declaring Independence: The Origin and Influence of America's Founding Document: Featuring the Albert H. Small Declaration of Independence Collection*. Charlottesville: University of Virginia Library, 2008.

National Archives and Records Administration (NARA). "The Declaration of Independence: A History." Accessed August 18, 2015. http://www.archives.gov/exhibits/charters/declaration_history.html.

Shain, Barry Alan. *The Declaration of Independence in Historical Context: American State Papers, Petitions, Proclamations & Letters of the Delegates to the First National Congresses*. New Haven, CT: Yale University Press, 2014.

Spalding, Matthew. "How to Understand Slavery and the American Founding." The Heritage Foundation. Accessed August 18, 2015. http://www.heritage.org/research/reports/2002/08/how-to-understand-slavery-and-americas.

Tsesis, Alexander. *For Liberty and Equality: The Life and Times of the Declaration of Independence*. New York: Oxford University Press, 2012.

United States Continental Congress. *Journals of the American Congress: From 1774–1788*: In Four Volumes. Washington, DC: Way and Gideon, 1823.

The Walk Free Foundation. "Global Findings." http://www.globalslaveryindex.org/findings/.

What Is the Third Estate?

in the original French *Qu'est-ce que le Tiers-État?*
a political pamphlet written by Abbé Emmanuel Joseph Sieyès
published in Paris

1789

A quick glance at that place and date, and you know where we're headed: right into the teeth of the French Revolution. You might well know the story of the Estates-General and the Tennis Court Oath, though it's much less likely you know what, and who, led them there. In the months leading up to early 1789, the temperature was rising, at least politically, and while the writing wasn't quite yet on the wall, the pens were ready.

The Estates-General were the traditional advisory body to the French king, dating back to 1302, and drawn from the three components of French society: the clergy of the First Estate, the nobility of the Second Estate, and the Third Estate, meaning everybody else. Things had gotten bad enough that Louis XVI called them into session for the first time in over a century and a half and only then apparently started fishing around for ideas of what to do with them. A request to that effect by Jacques Necker, the king's minister, encouraged the pens that were already scratching, churning out pamphlets, generating first a trickle, then a flood, amounting to many thousands by the spring. The "pamphlet" form was of particular importance at the time, since newspapers were uncommon and little attended to.

Most pamphlets, however, were densely argued, contradictory, and frankly, confusing. It took a writer of clarity and the gift of a turn of phrase to coalesce those ideas into a simple—one might even say catechistical—refrain. He begins with:

What is the Third Estate? Everything.
What has it been until now in the political order? Nothing.
What does it ask? To become something.

Catchy, though one must also say, not terribly original. The author in question was Emmanuel Joseph Sieyès, the son of a lesser royal official who was educated at the Sorbonne, where he was introduced to the political philosophies of Locke, the Encyclopédistes, and others; drifted into the church; and, after some struggle, landed a position as an episcopal assistant. Rising through the ranks, he eventually made his way into the salon culture of the time and the emerging political discussions to be found there. His discontent was nurtured by a stint in the similarly politically imbalanced Estates of Brittany in the 1770s.

The pamphlet in question laid out ideas that were in common discussion, though presented in a clear, compelling, and understandable way, and importantly in the right place at the right time. His central argument was that sovereignty should come from those who produce, who generate services and goods for the benefit of society. The nobility, on the other hand, were fraudulent, parasitic, and unnecessary, and moreover, no particular group or class could or should be able to claim special privileges without the consent of the people. He said the Third Estate could sustain itself and has a right to complain: the nation can't be free if the Third Estate isn't. He even undertakes a thorough and detailed calculation of what proportion of the population comprises the Third Estate and comes up with 19 out of 20—95 percent.

The rallying cry of the day was "vote by heads, not by orders." The traditional structure of the Estates-General called for them to vote as orders, meaning transparently, that normal people would be continually outvoted two to one. Allow them to vote by person, and make sure the Third Estate's numbers were as large as the others combined, and all sorts of interesting things might happen, which wasn't necessarily what Louis or the rest of the power structure had in mind.

As for the document, "pamphlet" doesn't really convey the right image: this isn't the trifold brochure you pick up at an information booth. It came out in three increasingly compendious versions, starting at 86 pages and heading to 180, which apparently Sieyès self-published. The title page and verso of the third edition bear no printer's name or mark. It was, however, translated quickly into German and English and had a print run at least in the tens of thousands.

His work got Sieyès elected to the last available seat in the Third Estate. However, once his ideas caught fire and galvanized the political mood of the time, he no longer could control them. His positions were shot down numerous times in multiple venues, and he left behind a string of defeats and missed opportunities. He was, for example, on the wrong side of the question of confiscation of church lands (which he opposed), and apparently was a poor speaker, so his influence waxes and wanes over the next several decades. He didn't even prevail during the dramatic Tennis Court episode; it was he who moved that the Third Estate break away to the tennis court and invite the others to join them. That worked, and they swore to stay together until the other two saw the

A FAUT ESPERER Q'EU JEU LA FINIRA BEN TOT.

An engraving held at the Musée Carnavalet shows the nobility and the clergy riding on the back of a man representing the working class, or Third Estate. Alamy Stock.

light. But then he suggested they decamp from Versailles for Paris, where they might be safer, and they voted instead to stay put. Awkward.

After the fall of the Bastille, the abbé wafted in and out of a number of positions, including two separate constitutional committees, the Convention, the Committee on Public Safety, the Committee of Five Hundred, and the Senate, and also participated in an attempt to overthrow the Directory. He wrote quite a bit, though none of his other works had nearly such an effect. He's a bit of a slippery figure. Some histories depict him as a schemer and seasoned political operative, including arranging the coup of 18th Brumaire, which led to Napoleon's rise and eventual imperial dictatorship. Others portray a sputtering career that might have saved his life because his profile was low enough that he didn't attract enough attention during the Terror to be bothered with. In any event, when asked later what happened during those dark days, he said simply "*J'ai vécu.*" I survived. Which is more than many could say, though he was eventually made ambassador to Prussia, and even an Imperial count, before finally relocating to Brussels in 1815 in the aftermath of the Hundred Days.

It's hard, in hearing all of this, not to think of the Occupy movement and their rallying cry of the "99 percent," very nearly what Sieyès calculated for the Third Estate. And yet they effectively lacked what he provided, a central, unifying manifesto and program with goals. So much of the modern movement is driven by social media, which wins easily for speed and reach but maybe falls shorter on depth and texture of ideas. Other recent social and political movements, including Black Lives Matter, have also been quite successful in gaining and maintaining attention, though have not always been as successful at articulating a specific set of outcomes or results—which may or may not be the point. A hashtag, perhaps, can't do quite the same thing as an extended political argument.

Actually, I've struggled to find a recent political manifesto that has had substantial impact. The best I can manage is the Republican Party's Contract with America, which formed the basis of their stunning 1994 Congressional election victory. Right place, right time, right words . . . a combination that's hard to come up with, and when the lightning strikes, hard to beat.

SOURCES

Blanning, T. C. W. *The Pursuit of Glory: Europe, 1648–1815*. New York: Viking, 2007.

Encyclopedia Britannica. "Emmanuel-Joseph Sieyès." Last modified October 18, 2007. https://www.britannica.com/biography/Emmanuel-Joseph-Sieyes.

Scott, Samuel F., and Rothaus, Barry. *Historical Dictionary of the French Revolution 1789–1799.* Westport, CT: Greenwood Press, 1985.

Sewell, William H. *A Rhetoric of Bourgeois Revolution: The Abbé Sieyes and What Is the Third Estate?* Durham, NC: Duke University Press, 1994.

Sieyès, Emmanuel Joseph. *Qu'est-ce que le Tiers-État.* 1789. https://babel.hathitrust.org/cgi/pt?id=hvd.hxg153;view=1up;seq=13.

Van Deusen, Glyndon G. *Sieyes: His Life and His Nationalism.* New York: Columbia University Press, 1932.

11
"The Star-Spangled Banner"
a set of four verses, originally untitled
written by Francis Scott Key in Baltimore
original now housed in the Maryland Historical Society
1814

"The Star-Spangled Banner" asks a question. Am I the only one who didn't quite get that? It finally dawned on me when researching this story. It's precisely because we've all heard it so many times that it's become, for many, aural wallpaper, entirely familiar though rarely closely attended to. Almost every phrase has been repurposed; you can easily imagine book titles like "The Rockets' Red Glare," and "The Dawn's Early Light," and you'd be right; I found over 500 with that last one alone.

The backstory is well known, too, though as is so often the case, not in detail and not always correctly. In the midst of an otherwise overlooked war, best known for actually ending before the decisive battle and for Dolley Madison saving George Washington's portrait as the British burn the city bearing his name—in partial retaliation for the lesser-known abortive American invasion of Toronto—a day and a night of battle and uncertainty gave rise to one of the most recognizable songs in the world, which also tells us a story of quickly, and slowly, becoming.

It is September of 1814, Beethoven has premiered his Eighth Symphony, and Jane Austen has published *Mansfield Park*, anonymously. It's also a time of some geopolitical import; a continent away, the Congress of Vienna is gathering to reassemble Europe following the first wave of the Napoleonic Era. The once and future emperor himself has been in exile on Elba for four months, though he will linger there for only five months more before returning for the final hurrah and defeat of the Hundred Days. Indeed, it's in no small part because he's temporarily off the stage that the British are able to turn their fuller attention to a pesky conflict in North America.

At this point, coincidence smiles on Francis Scott Key, a lawyer, slaveholder, and occasional poet, who boards the British ship *Tonnant* on a mission to free an American physician wrongly arrested for treason. He and his party, however,

O say can you see through by the dawn's early light,
What so proudly we hail'd at the twilight's last gleaming,
Whose broad stripes & bright stars through the perilous fight
O'er the ramparts we watch'd, were so gallantly streaming?
And the rocket's red glare, the bomb bursting in air,
Gave proof through the night that our flag was still there,
O say does that star spangled banner yet wave
O'er the land of the free & the home of the brave?

On the shore dimly seen through the mists of the deep,
Where the foe's haughty host in dread silence reposes,
What is that which the breeze, o'er the towering steep,
As it fitfully blows, half conceals, half discloses?
Now it catches the gleam of the morning's first beam,
In full glory reflected now shines in the stream,
'Tis the star-spangled banner — O long may it wave
O'er the land of the free & the home of the brave!

And where is that band who so vauntingly swore,
That the havoc of war & the battle's confusion
A home & a Country should leave us no more?
Their blood has wash'd out their foul footstep's pollution.
No refuge could save the hireling & slave
From the terror of flight or the gloom of the grave,
And the star-spangled banner in triumph doth wave
O'er the land of the free & the home of the brave.

O thus be it ever when freemen shall stand
Between their lov'd home & the war's desolation;
Blest with vict'ry & peace may the heav'n rescued land
Praise the power that hath made & preserv'd us a nation!
Then conquer we must when our cause it is just,
And this be our motto — "In God is our trust,"
And the star-spangled banner in triumph shall wave
O'er the land of the free & the home of the brave. —

An original manuscript of "The Star-Spangled Banner," written by Francis Scott Key in 1814. Courtesy of the Maryland Historical Society, Item ID #54315.

get stuck there, as the attack on Baltimore is planned, so he has a front-row seat for the bombardment of Fort McHenry, which defends the harbor.

From the deck of the *Surprise*, where they've been moved, he witnesses the British use of the Congreve rockets, with roots back to 13th-century China, and the bombshells designed to detonate as they neared their targets. Through the rain and smoke of the long day and night of September 13, he has no way of knowing what happened until the following morning when he is able, finally, to see an enormous flag, raised to the tune of "Yankee Doodle," sewn by Mary Pickersgill and her family: 30 by 42 feet, three stories high, weighing 80 pounds, containing 350,000 hand-sewn stitches, and, as was the case then, bearing 15 stars and 15 stripes. A smaller and cheaper "storm flag" had flown during the battle itself; the large one, now in the Smithsonian Museum of American History, was reserved for calmer conditions.

An image of the original Star-Spangled Banner. Armed Forces History Division, National Museum of American History, Smithsonian Institution.

Inspired, Key makes notes, perhaps on the back of a letter in his pocket. After his release, he completes the four verses during his trip back to Baltimore, finishing at the Indian Queen Hotel. He's known to have written five copies in his own hand, each slightly different, of which only two survive, so we have no clear, definitive version. Many scholars are convinced that Key intended these to be lyrics, set to the tune of a song probably written around 1775 by John Stafford Smith, from the Anacreontic Society, a gentleman's musical club in London named for an ancient Greek poet. The tune is now usually mistakenly described as a "drinking song" because the club's meetings often took place in taverns. We do know that Key knew the song, having used it for an 1805 poem ending with "the brow of the brave."

The initial spread of the verses started almost immediately. It's probably Key's brother-in-law, Joseph Nicholson, a judge, former Congressman, and second-in-command at the fort, who took them to a print shop and got copies made in handbill form. These circulated quickly under the title, probably Nicholson's, of "Defence of Fort M'Henry." Given the circumstances, it's no surprise that it spread through the city within an hour, "like prairie fire" according to one account. It was performed first on the stage of the Holiday Street Theater and published as a poem now titled "Star-Spangled Banner" within the week. Within the month in it was published in 17 other cities up and down the East Coast. Carr's Music Store printed it with a musical score by November, bearing a 6/4 time signature and a tempo marking of *"con spirito,"* though with no mention of Key.

Things slow down a bit from there. "Yankee Doodle" and "Hail, Columbia" are the best-known and most popular patriotic songs at this time, and the "Banner" begins to take its place with them, often reinterpreted with altered lyrics for political expression supporting causes such as abolition or temperance, and appropriated by both sides during the Civil War. Slowly, it gathers momentum, perhaps being played at baseball games, though that practice is not well documented until 1918 and does not become regular until 1942. It becomes a military standard and is used by Puccini as the theme for the naval officer Pinkerton in *Madama Butterfly* in 1904. By 1917, it is designated to be played at official military ceremonies.

Somewhere in there, probably 1917, a standardized version was created. Five notable musicians were tasked with going through the song, measure by measure, and voting on how it ought to go. These included Oscar Sonneck, the first head of the music division at the Library of Congress, who had extensively researched it, as well as John Philip Sousa, no less. The two of them disagreed on the first two notes, which Sousa preferred syncopated. A manuscript from this process surfaced on the *Antiques Roadshow* in Eugene, Oregon, in 2011, and was valued between $10,000 and $15,000.

It now seems inevitable that the Star-Spangled Banner would become the national anthem, but it didn't happen quickly or without a fight. Congressional resolutions were introduced starting in 1912 with little success; a number of patriotic groups joined the cause, including the Veterans of Foreign Wars, who gathered five million petition signatures. One of the final acts passed by the 71st Congress made it the first and only official national anthem in 1931. It's in the same chapter of the U.S. Code that names the national motto of "In God we trust," the rose as the national floral emblem, the oak tree as the national tree, and "The Stars and Stripes Forever" as the national march. When played, people in uniform and members of the Armed Forces and veterans should salute, while others should face the flag and stand at attention with their right hand over the heart, as men remove their hats.

There was opposition throughout, somehow unimaginable today, because of the fact that the tune was of English origin, or that it was a wartime song rather than one dedicated to peace, or based on its supposed heritage as a drinking song during the Prohibition Era, or because, as we all know, it has a very wide range (an octave and a fifth) and thus, for many, is nigh impossible to sing, though we all do our best. Attempts to substitute the much easier "America, the Beautiful" have gone nowhere. It's made the Billboard chart twice, Jose Feliciano's controversial and very personal 1968 World Series version, and Whitney Houston's powerful rendition at the 1991 Super Bowl, which got to number 20 and then again to number 6 in the weeks following 9/11.

Those two versions, one performed with an acoustic guitar and one highly orchestrated, couldn't be more different, and they, along with all the others over the last two centuries, illustrate that this song still isn't finished, is still becoming. There is no "official" version, despite attempts to define it or lock it down, and for a nation as dynamic and experimental and occasionally fraught as the United States is, that somehow seems right.

Just for fun, let's put Francis Scott Key back on the deck of the *Surprise*, 200 years on. What does he do? Does he compose a four-stanza patriotic rhyme? It seems more likely he takes a picture and posts it to Instagram, maybe uploads a cell phone video to CNN, or heaven help us, tweets out a selfie. Whether by handbill, social media, or just word of mouth, ideas can travel fast, like a rocket. Some of the most powerful then germinate, deepen, and develop. The lines that became the song that became the anthem spread quickly, almost virally, at first, then at a more stately pace, adding layers of meaning and importance, still today.

SOURCES

Antiques Roadshow. Standardization Manuscript for "The Star-Spangled Banner." PBS video, 1:44. Posted 2011. http://www.pbs.org/wgbh/roadshow/archive/201101T20.html.

Billman, J. I. *The Star Spangled Banner: A Brief Story of the Song, Its Growth in Popularity and the Campaign Conducted by the Veterans of Foreign Wars of the United States Which Resulted in Its Adoption as Our National Anthem by Act of Congress*. Kansas City, MO: Veterans of Foreign Wars of the United States, 1932.

Cheatham, Katharine Smiley. *Words and Music of "The Star-Spangled Banner" Oppose the Spirit of Democracy Which the Declaration of Independence Embodies*. New York, 1918.

Gambino, Megan. "Document Deep Dive: The Musical History of 'The Star-Spangled Banner.'" *Smithsonian.com*. Accessed September 7, 2016. http://www.smithsonianmag.com/history/document-deep-dive-the-musical-history-of-the-star-spangled-banner-120158958/.

Glass, Andrew. "'Star-Spangled Banner' Becomes Official U.S. Anthem, March 3, 1931." *Politico*, March 3, 2010. Accessed September 7, 2016. http://www.politico.com/news/stories/0310/33775.html.

"H.R. 270 (104th): To Make 'America, the Beautiful' the National Anthem of the United States of America." *GovTrack.us*. Accessed September 7, 2016. https://www.govtrack.us/congress/bills/104/hr270.

Key, Francis Scott. "Defence of Fort M'Henry." September 17, 1814. Library of Congress. Accessed September 7, 2016. http://www.loc.gov/item/ihas.100010457.

Legal Information Institute. 36 USC § 301—National anthem.

Molotsky, Irvin. *The Flag, the Poet, and the Song: The Story of the Star-Spangled Banner*. New York: Dutton, 2001.

"Nicholson, Joseph Hopper." *Biographical Directory of the United States Congress*. Accessed September 7, 2016. http://bioguide.congress.gov/scripts/biodisplay.pl?index=N000100.

Taylor, Lonn, Kathleen M. Kendrick, and Jeffrey L. Brodie. *The Star-Spangled Banner: The Making of an American Icon*. New York: Smithsonian Books, 2008.

usmusicscholar. "Spangled Mythconceptions: Correcting the Anthem Story." *Star Spangled Music*, June 8, 2014. http://starspangledmusic.org/spangled-mythconceptions-a-flag-day-series/.

12
Webster's Dictionary
An American Dictionary of the English Language
published by Noah Webster
1828

As a kid, whenever I asked the question, "What does *that* mean?" the invariable response was "Look it up!" Which I did, and that explains a lot about the path my career took. Dictionaries do pretty much what you think they do, listing words and giving definitions, spellings, pronunciation and syllabication, history and origins, usages, parts of speech, and so on. There have been big, fat, impressive "unabridged" ones; smaller ones that you got when you graduated high school, called "collegiate"; others specific to a subject or geographic area or audience, such as children; or ones that translate between languages.

And then there are the even more exotic varieties, such as reverse dictionaries to help you find words given their definition (is there a word for being buried alive? Yep—"vivisepulture"), and even rhyming dictionaries based on the sounds in word endings. Not to mention other sources built around words: concordances, thesauri, style manuals, quotation sources, and one with the greatest name ever, the Internet Anagram Server, also known as I, Rearrangement Servant. Think about it.

Words define a language, and, in turn, languages help to define cultures and societies. And people define words, as Noah Webster, the last man who tried to define them all himself, knew. In the process, he was trying also to define and distinguish his developing nation.

Yes, I am one of those people who get those word-of-the-day e-mails—from two different dictionaries no less—so now you know what you're up against. Every so often you see stories about new words added to major dictionaries and the reactions they can provoke, ranging from "Why wasn't that already in there?" to "That's not a word" to "It's the end of civilization as we know it." "Bro hug" was added to the *Oxford English Dictionary* in 2016, with a first-noted usage in a Usenet newsgroup in 2001; "bro" in various guises goes back to 1530. The *OED* is the source of many great stories: the crazy man who contributed thousands of quotation references during its development, Tolkien's time there as a young man (he may have written the entry for "walrus" among others), the old definition for "abbreviator" as a Vatican official "for drawing up the pope's briefs." Hey, lexicographers need some fun too.

The earliest word lists may have been Sumerian about 5,000 years ago. Other ancestors include a dictionary-like thing in 2nd-century BCE Alexandria; examples in Rome; and the glosses in medieval Europe, where scholars helpfully defined the difficult Latin words in the margins of books as vernacular languages increasingly took hold. The first English dictionary was likely Cawdrey's *A Table Alphabeticall* in 1604; Samuel Johnson's 1755 work had some 40,000 words and 114,000 illustrative quotations, and that was largely that for three-quarters of a century.

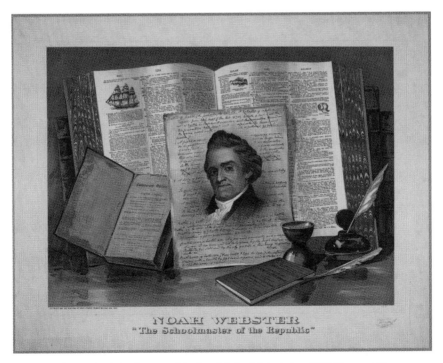

Noah Webster: "The Schoolmaster of the Republic," published circa 1886. Library of Congress.

Until along came Noah Webster—not to be confused with his distant cousin Daniel—a New Englander through and through. His father mortgaged the family farm to send him to Yale, from which he graduated in the height of the American Revolution in 1778. That education ill prepared him for most things, including farming, so after his graduation his father gave him $8 and sent him on his way; Noah never repaid the debt, and the farm was lost within a decade. He tried teaching, which he found unpleasant and poorly paying, and he passed the bar but never had a stable law practice. A biographer who calls him the "forgotten founding father" speaks of his "faith in himself, his work and his ability to promote both," and calls him "a young man on the make," whose "style apparently offended some"; I can't help envisioning an Early American Mark Zuckerberg or Jeff Bezos.

There are myriad aspects to Webster: stints in two state legislatures, editing, publishing, and participating in the founding of Amherst College. He was an early copyright advocate and an ardent revolutionary, Federalist, and friend of George Washington. But he later grew increasingly conservative, reactionary, and Calvinist, coming to see the masses as ignorant, dangerous, and not to be trusted in the wake of the French Revolution, Jefferson's election, and the War of 1812. He is best known, however, for two works: a speller published in 1783, which sold in the millions and made him famous, and of course his great dictionary, planned and worked on for almost 30 years. An 1806 attempt landed with a dull thud, but a second one finally came off the presses, all 70,000 words of it, in 1828, the same year as Dumas's *Three Musketeers*, the first Baedeker's travel guide, the opening of the London Zoo, and the first electric motor, invented in Budapest. Twenty-five hundred copies of that first edition were printed, a critical though not financial success at $20.

Its critical feature lies in the first of the 85 words in its title: *An American Dictionary*. In the first page of the preface, there it is: "Language is the expression of ideas; and if the people of one country cannot preserve an identity of ideas, they cannot retain an identity of language." In short, American English will deviate from British English because of our land, heritage, society, government, and people. He also sets out to, in his words, redeem the language from its corruptions, claiming that Americans spoke the purest version. The extensive introduction begins by laying out the biblical origins of all language, pausing to elucidate the "principal faults" in Johnson's work in areas such as orthography, pronunciation, grammar, syntax, and punctuation—and particularly origins. Word entries are considerably simpler than we're accustomed to, including accent, part of speech, definition, a few etymological and usage notes, a sample sentence here and there. He extensively cites American sources, including many of the Founders, such as Washington and Adams, as well as

Irving, though pointedly not Jefferson, Paine, or Cooper, and adds a great many new American words. There are also new senses of words like "marshal," "plantation," and "regent," each with different meanings outside the English context; Native American borrowings like "caribou," "hominy," and "podunk"; words from other languages such as "prairie," "chili," and "sleigh"; and brand new Americanisms, including "underbrush," "lumber," and "squatter."

Yes, I did what everybody does with a new dictionary—I looked up the dirty words. Yes to "damn" and "hell" and "piss" (with a strikingly extensive etymology), no to the F- and S-words. "Pimp" makes a surprising appearance, though, along with, shall we say, a curious selection of words beginning with S-E-X. And "abbreviator."

ADDITIONS.

ABANDON.
5. In *commerce*, to relinquish to insurers all claim to a ship or goods insured, as a preliminary towards recovering for a total loss.

ABANDONMENT.
2. In *commerce*, the relinquishing to underwriters all the property saved from loss by shipwreck, capture or other peril stated in the policy. This *abandonment* must be made before the insured can demand indemnification for a total loss.   *Park.*

ABLE. [Norm. *ablez, hable*; *habler*, to enable, from L. *habilis.*]

ABSCISSION.
2. In *rhetoric*, a figure of speech, when having begun to say a thing, a speaker stops abruptly, as supposing the matter sufficiently understood. Thus, "He is a man of so much honor and candor, and such generosity—but I need say no more."

AL'GATES, *adv.* [Sax. *algents*; *all* and *geat*, a gait, a way.] By all means; on any terms.   *Obs.*

ALIENISM, *n. al'yenizm.* The state of being an alien.
    The law was very gentle in the construction of the disability of *alienism.*   *Kent.*

Very grievous; violent; as *atrocious* distempers.   *Obs.*   *Cheyne.*

AUTOCH'THON, *n.* [Gr. αυτοχθων.] One who rises or grows out of the earth.

BAR'RATROUS, *a.* Tainted with barratry.

BAR'RATROUSLY, *adv.* In a barratrous manner.   *Kent.*

BARRELED.
2. In *composition*, having a barrel or tube; as a double-*barreled* gun.

BASIL'ICAL, *a. s* as z. In the manner of a public edifice or cathedral.   *Forsyth.*

BAWL'ER, *n.* One who bawls.

BA'REHEADEDNESS, *n.* State of being bareheaded.

BE'ASTISH, *a.* Like a beast; brutal.

BET'TERING-HOUSE, *n.* A house for the reformation of offenders.

BEWA'ILER, *n.* One who laments.

BLE'AKISH, *a.* Moderately bleak.

BO'NUS, *n.* [L.] A premium given for a charter or other privilege granted to a company.

BOOK'STORE, *n.* A shop where books are sold.

BLEB'BY, *a.* Full of blebs.   *Phillips.*

BREAKFAST, *v. t. brek'fast.* To furnish with the first meal in the morning.

CONDUCTION.
2. Transmission through or by means of a conductor.   *Henry's Chim.*

CRANIOG'NOMY, *n.* [Gr. κρανιον, L. *cranium*, the skull, and Gr. γνωμων, index.] The doctrine or science of determining the properties or characteristics of the mind by the conformation of the skull.   *Good.*

DAC'TYLAR, *a.* Pertaining to a dactyl; reducing from three to two syllables.   *Scott.*

DEN'ARCOTIZE, *v. t.* [*de* and *narcotic.*] To deprive of the narcotic principle or quality; as, to *denarcotize* opium.   *Journ. of Science.*

DEPOSITARY.
2. In *law*, one to whom goods are bailed to be kept for the bailor without a recompense.   *Kent.*

DIGESTIBIL'ITY, *n.* The quality of being digestible.

DIMIN'ISHABLE, *a.* Capable of being reduced in size or quantity.

DISHONOR, *v. t.*
4. To refuse or decline to accept or pay; as, to *dishonor* a bill of exchange.

DISOBLI'GEMENT, *n.* The act of disobliging.   *Milton.*

DISSOCIABLE.

An image showing additions, on page 143, to Noah Webster's *An American Dictionary of the English Language*, published in 1828. University of Washington Libraries.

The cruel joke here is that, despite his early and ardent support of copyright legislation, his name has entered the public domain. What is now the Merriam-Webster company is the direct heir, having bought the rights to Noah's work in 1843, but today anybody can publish a "Webster's" dictionary. Merriam-Webster is responsible for one of the most noteworthy 20th-century dictionaries, the 1961 *Third Unabridged* edition, which mostly undeservedly became the subject of denouncing editorials and condemnatory articles, partly because it included, apparently without sufficient disparagement, "ain't." Like people don't use it.

Today, lexicography has changed. While dictionaries are still being printed and bought, there won't be an *OED* third edition or a Webster's fourth, at least in print, though both continue in digital forms. New Internet sources such as WordSpy and the Urban Dictionary work much more quickly, and let's be honest, Microsoft Word's spell check and thesaurus prevail in many ways, not to mention the fun autocorrect games we all play on mobile devices.

Perhaps an apt metaphor for language is a river; as the ancient adage tells us, you can never step in the same one twice. Dictionaries and their cousins work to document words and languages and thus in a sense try to freeze that river, to make it be still so it can be understood. But they also help to thaw it, to facilitate change and renewal. And the words, as they are born, evolve, and sometimes die, continue to define us too.

Living languages are always in flux. Even Latin gets new words (*escariorum lavator* for dishwasher). And if you need any evidence that languages help to create community, go to a sci-fi convention and listen for Klingon or Na'vi or Dothraki. The Academie Française spends a great deal of effort barring the door, with minimal effect, from abominations such as "le weekend" or "le software." *Logiciel*, s'il vous plait. A 2016 proposal to reduce usage of the circumflex, the little hat thing, and to change the spellings of over 2,000 words including *oignon*, led to national protest and the #jesuiscircumflex hashtag. Which the Academie also frowns on, preferring *mot-dièse*. With an accent grave.

Webster's etymologies have been criticized as iffy, about a third of his definitions seem at least strongly influenced by Johnson's work, who also borrowed freely, as lexicographers are wont to do. Webster was also deeply committed to spelling reform, and had more luck there than most. We have him to thank for Americanized spellings of "favor" and "theater" and "defense" (not to mention "Americanize"), though he didn't get away with "tung," "wimmen," "ake," or dropping the final "e" from words like "doctrine." I do like "groop," though. His definitions reflect *his* view of a conservative, Christian society, and as one of the last dictionaries to be the work of a single person, that could hardly be surprising.

He's also been accused of "linguistic patriotism." In all of his works, here and throughout his long life, this complicated man wanted the best for the country that he loved deeply if not always unreservedly. It's safe to say this dictionary was a critical aspect of the emerging American identity, influencing and shaping how Americans write and speak and, by extension, think—then, and now.

SOURCES

Bilefsky, Dan. "French Spelling Changes, 26 Years in the Making, Cause a Fracas." *New York Times*, February 5, 2016. http://www.nytimes.com/2016/02/06/world/europe/french-spelling-changes-26-years-in-the-making-cause-a-fracas.html.

Friend, Joseph H. *The Development of American Lexicography 1798–1864.* The Hague: Mouton, 1967.

Horowitz, Jason. "How Do You Say 'Hot Dog' in Latin?" *New York Times,* June 1, 2003. http://www.nytimes.com/2003/06/01/weekinreview/how-do-you-say-hot-dog-in-latin.html.

Katz, William A. *Cuneiform to Computer: A History of Reference Sources.* Lanham, MD: Scarecrow Press, 1998.

Kendall, Joshua C. *The Forgotten Founding Father: Noah Webster's Obsession and the Creation of an American Culture.* New York: G.P. Putnam's Sons, 2010.

Latinitas Foundation. "Lexicon Recentis Latinitatis." Accessed December 6, 2016. http://www.vatican.va/roman_curia/institutions_connected/latinitas/documents/rc_latinitas_20040601_lexicon_it.html.

Micklethwait, David. *Noah Webster and the American Dictionary.* Jefferson, NC: McFarland, 2000.

Moss, Richard J. *Noah Webster.* Boston: Twayne Publishers, 1984.

Oxford Dictionaries. "Can the Académie Française Stop the Rise of Anglicisms in French?" March 20, 2014. http://blog.oxforddictionaries.com/2014/03/academie-francaise/.

Oxford English Dictionary Online. "abbreviator, n." Oxford University Press. Accessed December 6, 2016. http://www.oed.com.offcampus.lib.washington.edu/view/Entry/181.

———. "bro, n." Oxford University Press. Accessed December 6, 2016. http://www.oed.com/view/Entry/23492.

Samuel, Henry. "France's Académie Française Battles to Protect Language from English." *Telegraph.* October, 11 2011. http://www.telegraph.co.uk/news/worldnews/europe/france/8820304/Frances-Academie-francaise-battles-to-protect-language-from-English.html.

Singer, Natasha. "Scouring the Web to Make New Words 'Lookupable.'" *New York Times,* October 3, 2015. http://www.nytimes.com/2015/10/04/technology/scouring-the-web-to-make-new-words-lookupable.html.

Webster, Noah. *An American Dictionary of the English Language.* New York: S. Converse, 1828.

Wordsmith.org. "Internet Anagram Server / I, Rearrangement Servant." Accessed December 6, 2016. http://wordsmith.org/anagram/index.html.

The Book of Mormon

subtitled "Another Testament of Jesus Christ"
dictated and published by Joseph Smith Jr., in Palmyra, New York

1830

Growing up near the center of New York State, I can vividly remember commercials coming on every summer advertising something called the Hill Cumorah Pageant, and while I had no idea what it really was, I thought it looked pretty darned impressive—lots of lights and dramatic music, a cast of hundreds in historic-looking costumes—all acted out on a hillside maybe a couple of hours' drive away. I don't actually remember wanting to go see it, and I doubt my parents would have agreed, but I do remember thinking I might have been missing out on something. Little did the preadolescent me suspect that all the fuss was centered on a book with a mind-stretching backstory first published near that hill almost 150 years earlier, a book that begat a movement that started out and remains controversial and is still growing and spreading all over the planet.

Here's the deal. Joseph Smith Jr., aged 17, is visited by an angel in white, Moroni, who tells him there are golden plates buried not far away revealing a forgotten history of people who traveled to the Americas centuries before, their religious struggles and conflicts, and their visitation by Jesus just after his crucifixion and resurrection. Four years later, Joseph is allowed to take the plates along with devices that will allow him to translate them from their original characters he called "Reformed Egyptian." A series of hiding places, translation venues, helpers, and misfortunes ensue, including failed attempts from ancient-language experts to get help in understanding the characters, threats from local mobs, and the possible theft of the first 100 pages or so by an associate's wife—all done in secret. Later he is told, in a revelation now part of another central Mormon text, the *Doctrine and Covenants*, not to try to retranslate those, lest the originals reappear and any discrepancies undermine faith in the work.

He dictates translations from behind curtains or with the plates wrapped in linen, often wearing a set of eyeglass-like "interpreters" or with a "seer stone" in his hat to help out, sometimes without even looking at the plates. It's an

A portrait of Joseph Smith Jr. photographed by W. B. Carson, circa 1879. Library of Congress.

itinerant, on-again-off-again process, until he is joined in 1829 by a Vermont schoolteacher, Oliver Cowdery, who has heard of the plates. Then follows a burst of activity over three months, when at the rate of 3,500 words a day the work is largely completed, yielding a manuscript of about 600 printed pages. This doesn't include a series of plates that he's told must remain sealed until humanity is worthy. Joseph allows nobody to see the plates for years, not even his long-suffering wife, until he reveals them to a series of witnesses who later swear to their existence. Drawings of the plates resemble a very thick three-ring binder, holding together many hundreds of thin metallic sheets. When he's finished, Moroni then takes the plates back. "Mormon," Moroni's father, is one of the series of chroniclers who wrote the several books now collected and known as the *Book of Mormon*.

The first print edition, underwritten by a wealthy local farmer who mortgaged his farm, appears quickly, in 1830, and sells poorly, at $1.25 a copy, in no small part because of its length, complexity, and awkwardly simple wording (it uses only about 2,200 words); Mark Twain later refers to it as "chloroform in print." Slowly it gains traction, though; a second edition incorporating numerous revisions based on new revelations by Smith appears in 1837, followed by a British edition in 1841, and the first translation, into Danish, ten years later. By 1900, it's available in 10 languages, including Maori and Hawaiian, by 1950, 10 more, by 1980 a total of 40, and now well over 100 languages; it can be read by 90 percent of the world in their native language, and over 150 million copies have been printed.

The text is very precious to the Church of Jesus Christ of Latter-day Saints (LDS) that Joseph Smith chartered even before the book was published; any changes in wording must be approved by senior church leadership. The vast majority of copies are produced in one plant, on one press, to ensure quality and authenticity, the text is copyrighted and the name trademarked. It's been filmed a couple of times, in a 1915 silent version now lost, then an elaborate production in 2003 that flopped badly. The Hill Cumorah Pageant, with a mid-1980s script by science-fiction author Orson Scott Card, is by far the best and best known representation, not counting the musical, um, homage, that won nine Tony Awards in 2011. I was impressed, if not surprised, that the church bought several slick full-page ads in the program of the version I saw—betraying less a sense of humor about themselves, I think, than shrewd marketing: if you liked the musical, read the book that started it all!

Which is a bit of a slog. If the origin of the book is murky, so is the narrative. In a nutshell—or as much as something the size of a Russian novel can be summarized—it relays the centuries-long story of the descendants of Lehi, who make their way across the ocean to the Americas in about 600 BCE; their internecine religious battles; their evolution into what we now know as Native Americans; and the appearance of the resurrected Christ to set things right. Two centuries of peace, relayed in three pages, are followed by more fighting and the eventual destruction of the whole society in the fourth century.

The original manuscript had little punctuation and neither chapter nor verse markers, which have since been added, beginning with the original printing—as with the Old and New Testaments, those devices, like so many in printed books, are meant to make it easier to read and refer to. To make sure the book survived, a second manuscript copy was created by Cowdery as printing began; this is now known as the Printer's Manuscript, from which most, but not all, of the first edition was typeset. The original manuscript was sealed up in a cornerstone for 40 years, where it badly degraded. Only about a quarter of the pages are known to survive, many now held by the LDS church archives, while the Printer's Manuscript is owned by the Community of Christ, one of a number of rival denominations founded in the mid-19th century.

THE

BOOK OF MORMON:

C. S. albertson

AN ACCOUNT WRITTEN BY THE HAND OF MOR-
MON, UPON PLATES TAKEN FROM
THE PLATES OF NEPHI.

Wherefore it is an abridgment of the Record of the People of Nephi; and also of the Lamanites; written to the Lamanites, which are a remnant of the House of Israel; and also to Jew and Gentile; written by way of commandment, and also by the spirit of Prophesy and of Revelation. Written, and sealed up, and hid up unto the LORD, that they might not be destroyed; to come forth by the gift and power of GOD unto the interpretation thereof; sealed by the hand of Moroni, and hid up unto the LORD, to come forth in due time by the way of Gentile; the interpretation thereof by the gift of GOD; an abridgment taken from the Book of Ether.

Also, which is a Record of the People of Jared, which were scattered at the time the LORD confounded the language of the people when they were building a tower to get to Heaven; which is to shew unto the remnant of the House of Israel how great things the LORD hath done for their fathers; and that they may know the covenants of the LORD, that they are not cast off forever; and also to the convincing of the Jew and Gentile that JESUS is the CHRIST, the ETERNAL GOD, manifesting Himself unto all nations. And now if there be fault, it be the mistake of men; wherefore condemn not the things of GOD, that ye may be found spotless at the judgment seat of CHRIST.

BY JOSEPH SMITH, JUNIOR,

AUTHOR AND PROPRIETOR.

PALMYRA:

PRINTED BY E. B. GRANDIN, FOR THE AUTHOR.

1830.

Title page of an 1830 edition of *The Book of Mormon*. Library of Congress.

Its early appeal was partly due to the quite intriguing notion that heaven was open again, that God continues to speak, and that lost truths were being revealed in what was a time and place of great religious commotion. Moreover, Smith explained that Mormon and Moroni had crafted their text from a wide variety of sources, and in the book itself (2 Nephi 29:12), God says that he will "speak unto all the nations of the earth, and they shall write it," so this isn't the end of it, there will be more to come.

OK, OK, I can hear you saying—this is all fine and good, but is the thing legit? Is it on the level, or just the ravings of a religiously crazed dirt farmer from upstate New York? Let's say this—nobody likes the authenticity of their founding religious text called into question, let alone held up for public ridicule in, say, a big splashy hit Broadway musical including a number called "Making Things Up Again." There are reams of scholarship and speculation on both sides, including schools of thought about plagiarism, though in the absence of a strong candidate, this theory has faded. People have searched for places mentioned in the book and for evidence for the kinds of plants and animals and tools specified (like steel being used several centuries before it was developed) and found nothing of the sort. Instead, they find the whole origin story patently ridiculous—not to mention the original version's naming Jesus's birthplace as Jerusalem rather than Bethlehem. A computer analysis of the text in 2008 indicated "multiple 19th-century authors" were involved, but they couldn't incorporate any of Smith's other writings as examples—because there aren't any.

LDS scholars have developed ways around these objections, including the "limited-geography theory," which comes across like sticking your fingers in your ears and going la la la. They also raise the quite valid point that it seems highly unlikely that a lightly educated 24-year-old could make up something this complex and narratively unified on his own; even his own wife said at one point she didn't think he was capable of dictating a coherent letter, let alone this. And he apparently didn't dictate it in chronological order. If you're a believer, any evidence to the contrary hasn't swayed you; if you aren't, you've already made up your mind. Or if you haven't read it, go do so and decide for yourself.

With this, as with any religious text—or lots of other kinds of texts for that matter—the question is: Where did the words come from? Here we know, sort of. Joseph Smith dictated words that got written down, and it seems pretty certain what we have is what he said. So then the question is where he got them from. For every objection that the whole story is ludicrous on its face, and those are myriad, there's the counterpoint question of how he could have been able to pull this off? Whatever its actual genesis is, there's one thing that's certain: It comes from one source and one time, so its unity and intactness guarantee there's no partial credit. It either is what it purports to be, or it's not. Brigham Young's son once said, "If it is a humbug, it is the most successful humbug ever known."

And thus we get to faith. For which no amount of textual analysis, archaeology, or forensic psychiatry gives us answers. Words are so often the seeds of faith, and these words have taken root and flowered; the LDS church claims 15 million members worldwide, 6 million in the United States, about as many as Judaism and more than Presbyterianism. The signature number in the musical is a beautifully heartfelt—and scathingly funny—song called simply, "I Believe," and ultimately that's what this story is all about—belief, and the words that lead you there, no matter what anybody else thinks.

SOURCES

Gutjahr, Paul C. *The Book of Mormon: A Biography*. Princeton, NJ: Princeton University Press, 2012.

Hardy, Grant. *The Book of Mormon: A Reader's Edition*. Urbana: University of Illinois Press, 2003.

Larson, Stan. *Quest for the Gold Plates: Thomas Stuart Ferguson's Archaeological Search for the Book of Mormon*. Salt Lake City: Freethinker Press in Association with Smith Research Associates, 1996.

Morain, William D. *The Sword of Laban: Joseph Smith, Jr. and the Dissociated Mind*. Washington, DC: American Psychiatric Press, 1998.

14
First Woman's College Diploma
a diploma in the name of Catherine Elizabeth Brewer
issued by the Georgia Female College
now housed in the Wesleyan College Archives
1840

Diplomas—whether buried in a closet somewhere or beautifully framed to impress or intimidate, we all know what they are and what they represent: marking and recording the achievement of some accomplishment. Usually, these are considered academic in nature, though diplomas can also be given as awards or prizes; Nobel laureates receive diplomas, as do the top eight competitors in Olympic events.

The word comes to English from the Latin, derived from the Greek for "folding" or "doubling" and was first used to describe an official or state document in the 17th century. A few decades later, it began to be used to describe a document defined by the *Oxford English Dictionary* as "granted by a competent authority conferring some honor, privilege or license; that given by a university or college"; their first citation for that sense of the word comes from Cotton Mather in 1702. It's most often used today to represent the hard work of a student for at least four years of their life, either for high school, college, or some other academic degree. Clearly, these are objects we attach great importance to; otherwise there wouldn't be the pomp and ceremony (not to mention the ubiquitous "Pomp and Circumstance" marches) surrounding their presentation to a graduating class.

One might think the first diploma awarded to a woman would come from a place like Oxford or Cambridge, with centuries of tradition, or Oberlin, the oldest coeducational college in the United States. But the first woman we know of to get her diploma was Catherine Elizabeth Brewer Benson, who received hers on July 16, 1840, at the Georgia Female College, in Macon, now known as Wesleyan College, around the time of the Treaty of Waitangi in New

Adapted with permission from a podcast script originally researched and written by Kelsey Gibbons.

Graduates celebrating at the University of Washington Commencement exercises, 2016.
Dennis Wise/University of Washington.

Zealand and the Union Act, passed by the British Parliament uniting upper and lower Canada. (Oberlin's first four women were graduated the next year; women enrolled first at Cambridge in 1863 and weren't allowed to enroll at Oxford until 1920.)

The Georgia Female College was chartered in 1836 and received its first students in 1839, with Catherine Benson signing up on opening day. She became one of twenty girls in the junior class, since they had received schooling elsewhere for two years, and eleven of them graduated the next year.

So why was Catherine first? Pure happenstance; "Brewer" was the first in line alphabetically, and by virtue of that, she became the first woman ever to receive her baccalaureate diploma.

Catherine went on to marry and have eight children, and she also became part of the Wesleyan College Alumnae Association, formed in 1859, the first of its kind in the world. In 1888, she returned to speak to the graduating class, with words that have become known as the Benson Charge and are now spoken every time the graduating seniors are inducted into the Wesleyan College Alumnae Association. The Benson Charge goes like this: "Members of the graduating class, demands will be made upon you which were not made upon us. Your training, if you are true to it, will amply qualify you to meet those demands. No wiser blessing could I wish for you than that you may be true to every God-appointed work." Early artifacts such as diplomas and yearbooks are on display in the Benson Room in the Candler Alumnae Center, named after Catherine.

A photo of the Georgia Female College diploma awarded to Catherine Elizabeth Brewer on July 16, 1840. Wesleyan College.

The diploma looks only vaguely as you'd imagine. It is old and faded and quite fragile, and looks as though it was sewn together from multiple pieces of cloth, though it also has the words and the calligraphic writing that bespeaks a document that's official and meant to impress. That being said, it marked an important change in society—the dawn of a time when women were finally beginning to reach toward equality with men in terms of education. In fact, more women now go to college than men in the United States.

College diplomas are much more commonplace now, as well as an important part of society, especially in an economy where people who have a degree are more likely to get a job. As of 2011, fewer than one-third of adults in the United States held a bachelor's degree. According to a 2010 Education Pays report, having a college degree is linked to higher pay and healthier lifestyle choices. And a thirty-year study published in 2006 showed that having a college degree leads to lower blood pressure and lower stress. College diplomas also have personal meaning—they signify the fact that you made it through a higher education institution and represent the years of hard work you put into attaining the degree inscribed on the diploma. So, in important ways, they are more than just a pretty certificate on the wall—they symbolize dedication and self-improvement.

It is a document that is not going to disappear anytime soon if you ask most people, though there are those who think it might be time to upgrade them, imagining how the college diploma could be transformed into something more like a networked certification platform. Diplomas are sometimes called "sheepskins" because centuries ago they were just that, actually written on sheepskins. In many ways, it's a 12th-century document trying to do the work of a 21st-century world. The argument is that the college diploma should be enhanced and updatable, to be able to add new credentials and other experiences like internships, peer-to-peer learning, and online classes. It could show the whole picture of a person's skills, in real time, and not just that somebody failed to flunk out during four years through Stanford. And finally, it could be made machine-readable and discoverable. All this would make the college diploma less the traditional static piece of paper and more like a profile detailing all that a person has accomplished in furthering not only their education, but also their life.

These are all intriguing and certainly track the increasing technological impact on everyday life, but are they a good idea? The college diploma, while easily dismissed as just a piece of paper, shows the world what a person worked on for multiple years of their life to accomplish. It shows that a person was willing to be committed to a certain field for many years and more importantly that they valued their education and the promise it entails. If diplomas become digital, it will take away part of the magic that comes with receiving your diploma and being able to touch it and hang it up for everyone to see. And would commencements transform into simple ceremonial uploadings? Would it become just another file that is stored away on our computers, only glanced at when sent off to future employers?

Whatever happens to the diploma—whether it goes digital or stays as a tangible piece of paper—does not really change what it stands for and how important it is. College diplomas showcase people's successes and show their commitment and their drive in what they do. And no matter what their eventual form and no matter where you put it, a diploma is a mark of achievement for Catherine Benson and young women—and men—everywhere.

SOURCES

Atlanta Journal-Constitution. First Diploma Awarded at Wesleyan College, July 16, 1840, Presented to Catherine E. Brewer (Benson), Macon, Georgia. Atlanta: Special Collections and Archives, Georgia State University Library. Image. http://digitalcollections.library.gsu.edu/cdm/ref/collection/ajc/id/374.

Hardy, Marcelina. "7 Benefits of Earning a College Degree." *Yahoo Education.* Accessed February 10, 2014. http://education.yahoo.net/articles/benefits_of_higher_education.htm.

HistoryOrb.com. "Historical Events for July 1840." Accessed January 20, 2014. http://www.historyorb.com/events/date/1840/july.

Hoffman, Reid. "College Diplomas Are Meaningless. This Is How to Fix Them." *New Republic* (September 15, 2013). http://www.newrepublic.com/article/114692/college-diploma-time-upgrade.

O'Shaughnessy, Lynn. "20 Surprising Higher Education Facts." *U.S. News & World Report* (September 6, 2011). http://www.usnews.com/education/blogs/the-college-solution/2011/09/06/20-surprising-higher-education-facts.

Oxford English Dictionary Online. "diploma, n." Oxford University Press. Accessed December 07, 2016. http://www.oed.com.offcampus.lib.washington.edu/view/Entry/53198?rskey=4k48Vo&result=1&isAdvanced=false.

Wesleyan College. "Catherine Elizabeth Brewer Benson Class of 1840." Accessed December 10, 2013. http://www.wesleyancollege.edu/profiles/Catherine-Elizabeth-Brewer-Benson-Class-of-1840.cfm.

Wikipedia. "Catherine Brewer Benson." Accessed December 10, 2013. http://en.wikipedia.org/wiki/Catherine_Brewer_Benson.

15
John Snow's Cholera Map

a map, depicting the sites of deaths by cholera
compiled by John Snow and published in his monograph
On the Mode of Communication of Cholera
location of original unknown

1854

You've been sent on a simple errand. Your family needs water, and so you make your way to one of the neighborhood water pumps—the pump closest to your house. You fill a bucket with water and return home. You don't know it yet, but in choosing to use that particular pump, you've just determined whether your family will live or die.

On the one hand, this is a complicated story, inhabited by mysterious, microscopic organisms; a young and crowded metropolis strangled by dung heaps that stood as tall as houses; and factions of scientists and civic leaders at odds over how to eliminate an invisible killer.

On the other hand, it's a very simple story. It's a story about death. In Victorian London, lives hung in a delicate, unfair balance. Your life, and the lives of everyone you loved, depended on where you got your drinking water. You lived or died by the simple choices you made—choices we make fearlessly, unthinkingly, today. If you chose the water pump to your right, your family lived. If you chose the water pump to your left, your family is dead by dawn, their bodies suddenly, mercilessly emptied by cholera.

This is also a story about birth—the origins of the present-day metropolis, the emergence of modern epidemiology, and the ancestors of John Snow's cholera maps that foreshadowed information systems, like GIS, that allow us to analyze, visualize, and understand the patterns and trends that affect our lives. Just as we use social media tools to record where we've been and what we've experienced, Snow added layers of local and personal knowledge to available maps to tell the terrible story of an epidemic.

Adapted with permission from a podcast script originally researched and written by Andrew Brink.

Like all good maps, Snow's map inspired a journey. In illustrating the patterns created by a devastating epidemic, he opened the eyes and minds that would eventually subdue the killer named cholera. Snow's map gave Victorian England exactly what it was looking for—a way out.

Cholera is a terrible way to die. It arrives unseen, unannounced, and then kills with cruel and baffling speed. Snow's contemporary, the poet Elizabeth Barrett Browning, lamented cholera's ability to "catch" a person with "cramps" and "spasms" that turn gentlemen "dead-blue." A clinical description explains the cause of these deadly contractions: Cholera is a severe intestinal infection caused by ingesting food or water contaminated with the cholera bacteria. The bacteria cause the body to expel a profuse amount of watery diarrhea (euphemistically called "rice water") that leads to a sudden, lethal state of dehydration.

Just imagine: your child, husband, or wife complains of a stomachache. In the few minutes and hours it takes to fetch relief—the comfort of words, water, or a doctor—you witness your loved one vanish. Cholera can cause a person to lose up to 30 percent of their body weight in a matter of hours. Death is only the beginning for cholera. While cholera demands a lot from its victims, it requires little to multiply. The discharge caused by cholera is colorless, odorless, and contains a large amount of the cholera bacteria; all it needs to spread is an environment in which people frequently ingest other people's waste—and on and on it spreads.

In 1854, London was the world's most populous city, with two and a half million people. For all the marvels it contained—like the Crystal Palace—London lacked public health departments and sewage removal technology to effectively manage the waste generated by a city that would be considered dense even today. This resulted in overflowing cesspools that forced the River Thames to serve an ill-fated dual purpose—acting as both a main source of water and a sewer system. It made John Snow's London the perfect host city for an infectious disease.

So, what does a cholera map *look* like? This map documents the grim footprint left in London's Soho neighborhood during an outbreak that occurred there in 1854. As with most maps, you see street names and points of interest, like Golden Square and Piccadilly Circus. You also see hash marks rising, in varying heights, from the straight edges formed by streets. It's easy to imagine these lines representing some kind of score, and it's obvious that, regardless of who is winning or losing, all the action is emanating from a dot labeled "pump" sitting at the point where Broad and Cambridge Streets meet. Without knowing anything about cholera or London, you can see that something monumental happened at the corner of Broad and Cambridge.

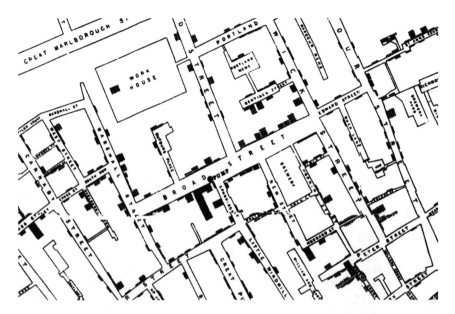

John Snow's map of the Golden Square outbreak, zoomed in on the vicinity of the Broad Street pump. It was published in 1854, with cholera cases highlighted in black. Wikimedia Commons (accessed at https://commons.wikimedia.org/wiki/File:Snow-cholera-map-1.jpg).

Which is true. The water pump sitting at this corner drew its water from a source contaminated with cholera. The towers of hash marks *do* represent a score—they tally the lives claimed by cholera. More than 500 people died within 250 yards of this water pump within a 10-day period.

At the time, Snow was a noted physician, celebrated for his pioneering work with anesthetics. Snow had mastered the use of chloroform, and this breakthrough brought much-needed relief to Londoners undergoing medical procedures. His work was so respected that he was called upon to comfort Queen Victoria, administering chloroform as she gave birth to her eighth child. His professional success allowed him to pursue a personal obsession: solving the riddle named cholera.

By the time he mapped cholera's impact on Soho, it had been killing Londoners for several decades. It wasn't uncommon for an entire family to be killed by cholera within a two-day period. People were dying, and there were many scientists trying to answer the anxious question: "why?" Some proposed that cholera was caused by foul air emanating from London's graveyards. Others suggested it was linked to atmospheric conditions. It even seemed possible that the disease was a poison leaking from the earth itself.

These were variations on the dominant worldview of the time known as the "miasma" theory. Miasmists believed that disease was caused by harmful mists and vapors that arose from filth. Given how filthy Victorian London was, it's not surprising that many of the most powerful people in London—members of Parliament, clergymen, and city commissioners—embraced the miasma theory.

Image, originally published as a lithograph, satirizing the London Board of Health during a cholera outbreak in 1832. The lettering reads: "A London Board of Health hunting after cases like cholera." Wellcome Library, London.

What is striking is something that can be hard for us to imagine today: in 1854, Londoners were suffering from information overload. Each theory about cholera had its own proponents, supported by streams of data recorded and disseminated in newspapers, dot maps, monographs, and lectures. Victorian England was home to an information revolution, with demographers recording births, marriages, weather, air quality, and, for the first time, tallying deaths by cause, location, age, and occupation. If you knew how to assemble the pieces, the patterns affecting British society—the ebb and flow of birth and death, cause and effect, illness and prevention—came into view.

Based on what he learned from studying a previous cholera outbreak in London, Snow developed a theory that cholera was transmitted by water. He arrived at this theory after examining the relationship between cholera deaths and sources of water in South London, where he found that far more people were killed by cholera in households that received water from a supply that mingled with sewage.

The Soho outbreak struck close to home—Snow lived and worked near the Broad Street water pump. In creating his famous cholera map, Snow wedded raw data—including the mortality rates recorded by the local registrar—with street-level knowledge of the patterns and habits of his neighbors acquired through observations, interviews, and being part of the neighborhood. Snow now knew which pumps individual families were known to drink from, and he knew the distance between the homes of those who died and the different water pumps they might have used.

He distilled all of this information into graphic representations of life, death, and water sources. The hash marks, street and building names, and dots noting the location of water pumps were placed on top of an existing map that had been produced by one C. F. Cheffins, a surveyor and mapmaker. The result is a map that paints a clear picture of how cholera travels through a community, a map that scientists, scholars, and writers still, to this day, consult for direction.

A historian notes that "part of what made Snow's map groundbreaking was the fact that it wedded state-of-the-art information design to a scientifically valid theory of cholera transmission." Geographers and statisticians both admire the pictorial aspect of the map, which resulted in placing data in the right context for considering cause and effect. In being so selective about what information was included—the street names, breweries, workhouses, and water pumps—the map revealed an obvious and overwhelming connection between the Broad Street pump and cholera transmission. In tallying cholera deaths while also showing the location of the area's other water pumps, the Broad Street pump was shown, starkly, standing at the epicenter of the epidemic.

This map was born out of Snow's previous attempts to condense and communicate his waterborne theory. He had previously created a map during his South London study that featured hand-inked dots, which were hard to read, and cloudy colors that tried, but failed, to show the connection between cholera deaths and water sources. Snow also published a table to tell the same story. But it wasn't quite right. It lacked key pieces of information gleaned later through interviews and observing the patterns of daily life in Soho. The 1855 map changed the minds of individuals who went on to change policies that transformed city living from a death sentence to a sustainable and life-affirming existence.

Given the effect this map has had on urban life, cartography, and science, you might wonder where the original map is today. If any original copies of the map exist, no one seems to know, or care. Which doesn't mean the map is hard to find. Authentic copies and versions of the map are found on university websites, in textbooks, and in popular science books. But the whereabouts of an original copy appear to be unknown. When it comes to determining the value of Snow's map, it seems that the information contained in the map is more important than the document itself.

The power contained in a map lies in its ability to provide sure footing in the midst of unknown territory. In providing direction, a map complements the imagination: it tells us where we are, where we are going, and where we've been. Snow's creation demonstrates that maps provide more than simple directions—they can also provide much-needed clarity.

The 1855 neighborhood is a place that can no longer be visited. Soho, as represented in this map, does not exist anymore, just as the world depicted in this map doesn't exist anymore. Today, Broad is now called Broadwick Street, and Cambridge is now Lexington Street. Today, cholera can be prevented and treated, though it still remains a scourge in parts of the world without access to clean, fresh water.

We may not be able to use this map to travel through present-day Soho, but we can use it for something even more meaningful. We can use it to return to the exact corner where the world changed.

SOURCES

Brody, H., M. Rip, P. Vinten-Johansen, N. Paneth, and S. Rachman. "Map-Making and Myth-Making in Broad Street: The London Cholera Epidemic, 1854." *Lancet* 355, no. 9223 (2000): 64–68.

Brody, H., P. Vinten-Johansen, N. Paneth, and M. Rip. "John Snow Revisited: Getting a Handle on the Broad Street Pump." *Pharos of Alpha Omega Alpha-Honor Medical Society* 62, no. 1 (1999): 2–8.

Frerichs, Ralph R. "History, Maps and the Internet: UCLA's John Snow Site." *Bulletin of the Society of Cartographers* 34, no. 2 (2000): 3–7.

———. *John Snow Site*. Accessed August 28, 2016. http://www.ph.ucla.edu/epi/snow.html/.

The John Snow Society. Accessed 2011. http://www.johnsnowsociety.org/.

Johnson, Steven. *The Ghost Map: The Story of London's Most Terrifying Epidemic—and How It Changed Science, Cities, and the Modern World*. New York: Riverhead Books, 2006.

Koch, Tom. *Cartographies of Disease: Maps, Mapping, and Medicine*. Redlands, CA: ESRI Press, 2005.

Tufte, Edward R. *Visual Explanations: Images and Quantities, Evidence and Narrative*. 5th print., with revisions. Cheshire, CT: Graphics Press, 2002.

Tulchinsky, Theodore H., and Elena Varavikova. *The New Public Health*. 2nd ed. Amsterdam: Elsevier/ Academic Press, 2009.

Vinten-Johansen, Peter. *Cholera, Chloroform, and the Science of Medicine: A Life of John Snow*. Oxford: Oxford University Press, 2003.

World Health Organization. "Cholera." Accessed 2012. http://www.who.int/topics/cholera/about/ en/index.html/.

16
Rules of Association Football (Soccer)

**a book of meeting minutes, containing what is
now referred to as the "Laws of the Game"**
written by Ebenezer Cobb Morley and approved by
the Football Association, in London
now held by the Football Association

1863

The game is starting to get exciting. Your team is driving, picking up yards in chunks, and a neat little run ends right about at the down marker. It looks like it might be a first down, but it's close. So close in fact that they have to measure, and in come the chains and the game comes to a screeching halt. OK, there does have to be a point at which it's a first down, and short of that point, it's not. But a system where one guy plops the ball down where he thinks it was when the running back's knee was down, and then another few guys come in to measure with chains based on where they thought it was before, to see if any tiny little part of the ball extends beyond the stick? Downright medieval. And people who have no idea how, say, the electoral college works or how a bill becomes law, can spout chapter and verse about what constitutes a touchdown or a legal reception. Remember: one knee equals two feet, any part of the ball breaking the imaginary plane counts, and the goal line goes around the world. Sheesh.

Rules are rules, though, and nobody knew that as well as the people who tried to bring some order and coherence to an ancient and sometimes dangerous game, now generally regarded as the most popular sport in the world. In the process, it tells us something about what makes creativity possible.

People have been kicking and throwing balls since there have been people and balls, or even things that act like balls. The Chinese game of *cuju* arose in the second century BCE and lasted until the Ming Dynasty; the 12th-century

91

Japanese game of *kemari* involved kicking a ball to keep it in the air as long as possible, and looking good doing it; the most desirable end was to catch it in the folds of one's kimono. The indigenous peoples of Australia and North America had games not unlike soccer. But it's in Mesoamerica where sports history is the strongest; at least 3,000 years ago there was a ball game so deeply ingrained in the culture that it's described in the Popol Vuh, and its rituals are bound up in their creation story and belief structure. These people also had the advantage of plants that could produce a form of rubber, so their balls could bounce, a source of amazement and even concern to the Europeans who, shall we say, largely put an end to the fun.

It fell, of course, to the English to codify and regulate all this, as they did with other sports—such as boxing as early as 1743, rowing, horse racing, and cricket. A game called "football" is the subject of a proclamation by Edward II in 1314 forbidding its play as a breach of the peace. It must have been a rough game without rules, causing property damage, riots, and even death at times, with an unlimited number of players, in the streets, using bushes and houses as goals. In *King Lear* "football player" is used as an insult. But slowly over the decades and centuries standards started to form.

The English public schools served as the incubators and crucible for football, each developing their own slightly different in-house version of the game, leading to inevitable confusion when they wanted to play each other. The first known set of written rules came from Rugby; compromise rules were compiled in Cambridge in 1846, though those didn't get wide acceptance. A collected set was published in 1861, revealing the depth of the differences, and this led to a series of meetings in 1863 to sort this out once and for all.

Those meetings were held in November in taverns across London, with people from a number of the important clubs in the area. Crafting a set of rules that everybody could agree on was not an easy task; they got stuck on whether the game should involve catching or not, and whether "hacking"—which we would call "kicking in the shins"—should be allowed. The gentleman from the Blackheath Club opined that eliminating hacking would "do away with the courage and pluck of the game, and I will be bound to bring over a lot of Frenchmen who would beat you with a week's practice." His motion to retain hacking was defeated 13–4, and Blackheath promptly withdrew from the whole business. His intellectual inheritors can be heard today in rueful debates about outlawing helmet-to-helmet tackling in the NFL and fighting in the NHL.

The rules under discussion covered aspects of the game we now think of as basic: the dimensions of the field and the goal, the introduction of the crossbar, lines, penalties, the nature of the ball, number of players, the officials, and even wardrobe. Originally there were only two officials; when this proved insufficient, a third was added, to whom differences of opinion would be referred; hence, the term "referee," a word already in use in boxing for a generation or more.

This was part of a larger movement, a period both of formalization and formation of sports: the Knickerbocker Rules for baseball were created in 1845, followed by Major League rules in 1877; the rules of American football were first codified in the 1870s, and tennis was largely standardized as a result of the first Wimbledon tournament in 1877. Basketball and volleyball were both created more or less from scratch in the 1890s.

The rules themselves were actually published in a sporting magazine, *Bell's Life in London*, a few days before the meeting and were then pasted into an otherwise handwritten book of minutes. The solicitor Ebenezer Cobb Morley took it upon himself to draft the rules at home and they were approved by the newly self-appointed Football Association ("soccer" is an abbreviated form of "Association") on December 8, 1863, only a matter of weeks after the Gettysburg Address was delivered; the FA itself was formed on the same day as

Photo of the original handwritten "laws of the game" for association football drafted for and on behalf of the Football Association by Ebenezer Cobb Morley in 1863, on display at the National Football Museum, Manchester. Adrian Roebuck/Wikimedia Commons (accessed at https://commons.wikimedia.org/wiki/File:Original_laws_of_the_game_1863.jpg).

the Red Cross. The book is now enshrined in the FA headquarters and handled with white gloves and the great reverence due to any founding document. Even though FIFA is now the international governing federation for soccer, it alone is not responsible for maintaining the Laws of the Game; instead that's entrusted to a board of eight, four appointed by FIFA and one each from the associations of Scotland, Wales, Ireland, and England in what must be a deeply uncomfortable arranged marriage, especially because it takes six of eight votes to make amendments to the rules.

That is also, though, an acknowledgment of the importance and centrality of rules to soccer and indeed to any sport. A sport or a game—or a society for that matter—without rules isn't worthy of the name. The rules are the game, and the game is the rules, no matter how ludicrous or over-specified they might be, and thus the rules define the distinctions between association football, rugby, rugby union, rugby sevens, American football, Australian Rules, Canadian, and so on and so on. All baseball fans, not to mention pitchers and batters, know that the strike zone varies from umpire to umpire, even pitch to pitch, but there has to be a strike zone. The debate over the charge vs. the block in basketball will never end, nor will disputes and frustration over judging in sports like gymnastics or figure skating.

Increasingly, these rules extend beyond the field of play. Consider the torturous NCAA compliance guidelines that require entire staffs to understand; salary caps; and, more recently, doping rules. Internationally there is now even a parallel legal structure in the form of the Court of Arbitration for Sport to sort out disputes.

All of which is part of a desire to get it right. That's why fencing uses automated systems to detect touches, and why tennis adopted the challenge system which (in theory) can see where a ball strikes the court within a 1 mm margin of error. It's also why instant replay is so seductive, no matter how long it takes or how counterintuitive the results are. And yet judgment—and necessarily error, or least subjectivity—is part of the quintessentially human nature of sport.

Sports rules, like any rules, provide structure. As one author has said, a sport without rules is just play. Rules create standards, limitations, boundaries, which is why most sports have lines of some sort. Mainly they provide constraints, and constraints promote creativity. Without those kinds of constraints would we have the desperate Hail Mary pass, the stunning alley-oop, the gracefully placed drop shot, or the beautiful bending shot of David Beckham? Doubtful, and it's the knowledge that any play, any moment, could produce an exquisite shot, a game-ending blunder, or yet another routine move that keeps us watching to see what happens next.

American Serena Williams returns a volley to Romanian Simona Halep during a quarterfinal match at the US Open tennis tournament, Wednesday, September 7, 2016, in New York. Associated Press/Charles Krupa.

SOURCES

FIFA. "Laws of the Game." Accessed February 5, 2013. http://www.fifa.com/aboutfifa/footballdevel opment/technicalsupport/refereeing/laws-of-the-game/index.html.

Goldblatt, David. *The Ball Is Round: A Global History of Soccer*. New York: Riverhead Books, 2008.

National Football Museum. "Football's Historic First Rule Book Arrives in Manchester." May 17, 2012. Accessed February 5, 2013. http://www.nationalfootballmuseum.com/about-us/latest -news/2012/05/soccers-historic-first-rule-book-arrives-in-manchester/.

Shearman, Montague. *Athletics and Football*. The Badminton Library of Sports and Pastimes. London: Longmans, Green and Co., 1899.

17
Alaska Purchase Check

a Treasury Warrant, #9759, payable to Eduard de Stoeckl,
in the amount of $7,200,000
for the purchase of the territory now known as Alaska
now housed in the National Archives

1868

Have you ever stood behind someone trying to pay for a purchase over $5 with just coins? Or using a $100 bill to purchase a candy bar? And it would seem unusual today to purchase a large-scale item like a computer with anything but a credit card, yes? It seems as though different circumstances require or at least lend themselves to different forms of payment. Throughout history, money could be anything from seashells to green slips of paper with the head of a United States president on the front.

It's still common to give high school graduates a little something to send them into the next stage of their lives. While the Alexander Hamiltons and the Andrew Jacksons are always great to see, in many cases the big bucks actually aren't in bills, but in the form of a check. Receiving cash meant you could just stuff it into your wallet and do whatever you wanted with it right away. However, with a check, there's at least another step involved. It's odd to think that a check can't purchase gas for your car but did purchase one of the biggest oil fields in the world. An area of the world that was originally dubbed "Seward's icebox" and "Jackson's polar bear garden" turned out to be more than America's last frontier, and also a region of the country that has surprisingly shaped our nation's history more than you might have expected.

It's widely believed the Russians were the first Europeans to reach Alaska, and by 1773 the land was known as Russian America. Colonies began sprouting as fur traders came to the area, dreaming of getting rich off the abundance of fur. They forced many Aleut people into slavery, ordering them to hunt sea otters to the brink of extinction. Along with the traders, Russian

---

Adapted with permission from a podcast script originally researched and written by Andrew Kyrios.

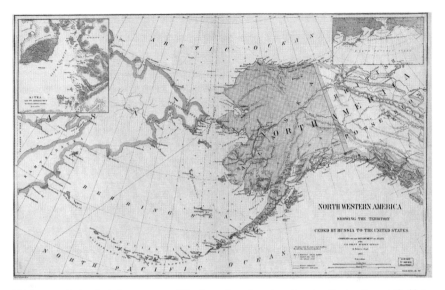

US Coast and Geodetic Survey map of Northwestern America, showing the territory ceded by Russia to the United States (Washington, D.C, 1867). Library of Congress.

missionaries also migrated to the area to convert the natives, specifically the Athabascan, Yup'ik, Koniag, Tlingit, and Aleuts, to the Russian Orthodox faith. They also taught them to read and write in Russian. As the colony progressed, New Archangel (current-day Sitka) was made the capital, and the fur tycoon Alexander Andreyevich Baranov was appointed to govern the settlement.

However, by the 1860s, the Russian government no longer valued their American colony. The fur-bearing animals were all but gone, and protecting and supplying the area became a burden. Even worse was the possibility of the British taking over the land for nothing. Financially troubled after the Crimean War, Alexander II, Emperor of all the Russias, offered to sell the land to either Britain or America, and hoped to start a bidding war. Britain, however, wasn't interested, and the United States was a bit distracted by the Civil War.

Negotiation resumed after the war. The Russians believed if America purchased Alaska, Britain's colony of British Columbia would be surrounded and thus greatly weakened. This was a time of considerable upheaval amid American westward expansion and the period of Manifest Destiny—the Transcontinental Railroad was completed just a year later—the impeachment of President Andrew Johnson, as well as Reconstruction. Nevertheless, on

March 30, 1867, Secretary of State William H. Seward negotiated the purchase of Russian America for a price of $7.2 million. America just increased in size by almost a quarter, nearly 600,000 square miles, for a mere two cents per acre.

Canceled check in the amount of $7.2 million for the purchase of Alaska, issued August 1, 1868; Records of the Accounting Officers of the Department of the Treasury. National Archives & Records Administration (NARA).

The Treasury Warrant, issued on August 1, 1868, at the Sub-Treasury Building at 26 Wall Street, was made out to Edouard de Stoeckl, a Russian diplomat (whose father happened to be an Austrian diplomat) who acted as Envoy Extraordinary and Minister Plenipotentiary of the Russians. The check was signed by Treasurer of the United States Francis E. Spinner, who, as signer of currency, liked to claim he had the most familiar autograph in the country. The Treasury check was cashed, with de Stoeckl's endorsement on the back, at Riggs Bank in Washington, D.C., and his handwritten receipt verifies he got the specified amount "in coin." Over $7 million must have been a lot of coin. The warrant itself looks like . . . a check, albeit a schmancy one, quite impressively featuring engraved figures, flowery 19th-century handwriting filling in the standard information, Spinner's distinctive signature, and a large blue stamp saying "PAID" with the date.

Some Americans were not pleased with the acquisition, which was famously known as "Seward's Folly." Although he faced criticism, when asked what his greatest achievement was as secretary of state, his response was "the purchase of Alaska—but it will take the people a generation to find it out." De Stoeckl didn't come out much better either. Accused of taking bribes, he decided to quit his job as a diplomat and move to Paris with his American wife, whom he had happened to meet while negotiating the deal in the States.

So was Alaska really worth the price? The name-calling ended in the 1880s when gold was first discovered, and the Klondike Gold Rush of 1896 attracted 100,000 people to the area, followed by the Nome Gold Rush. In the run-up to World War II, US General Billy Mitchell stated "I believe that in the future, whoever holds Alaska will hold the world. I think it is the most important strategic place in the world." The Aleutian Islands Campaign, often referred to as the forgotten battle of World War II, played a key part in the war between the Japanese and the Americans. The Lend-Lease program, which we're used to thinking of only concerning Great Britain, also involved flying airplanes to Alaska and then allowing the Soviets to use them in their fight against Germany. Alaska was admitted as the 49th state on January 3, 1959.

Check systems seem to have been common in the eastern Mediterranean and Muslim world by the 10th century and made their way to Europe, in fits and starts, by way of Crusaders and their experience with the monetary systems they encountered along the way. Because paper could be forged, early European banks made payments and transfers by oral order, meaning that everybody had to meet up in person and agree who was paying who how much. Forms such as "bills of exchange," which instructed someone in another city to make a payment after a certain period of time, gave rise to something closer to what we know today as a check by the 15th century or so, as their convenience, versatility, and acceptance increasingly outweighed the risk of fraud, abuse, and distrust of banks.

Modern usage of checks dates back to 17th-century England. At the time, they were known as "drawn notes" because they allowed the consumer to draw on the funds. A specific type of paper was also used to prevent fraud. A century later, this exclusive paper began to be personalized not only with the account holder's name, but also with a serial number that would be on each paper as a way for the banker to identify or "check" them; hence the name. The use of checks began to grow steadily in the mid-19th century into the 20th century and peaked during the early 1990s with a total of 50 billion checks written and collected per year.

Since then, the use of checks has sharply declined. Some say the death of the paper check was triggered by 9/11. Not only were many checks destroyed that day, the grounding of the air fleet for several days also held up the delivery of many more. Congress then passed the Check Clearing for the 21st Century Act, which permitted banks to use electronic copies of checks, and which also paved the way to take digital photos of checks for deposit using mobile devices. Banks were and still are fine with this because checks cost more to process so they're saving a pretty penny every year. The United States government is also doing away with checks. Starting in March 2012, federal benefits from Social

Security and Veteran's Affairs no longer were distributed in the form of a check, but through direct deposit or debit cards, which the government estimates saves millions a year.

With more payment options today, many people prefer to use credit or debit cards, along with electronic and online payments such as PayPal, not to mention bank and money-sharing apps and even digital currencies such as Bitcoin. However, some people are reluctant to see checks go. Some of us appreciate the actual object and believe it is safer or more reliable than purely electronic methods. In 2011, the United Kingdom banking industry actually planned to eliminate checks by 2018, but that idea went nowhere after complaints from senior citizens, small businesses, and charities.

Cutting money to save money seems to be the name of the game. Along with the decline of checks, critics have also demanded an end to the humble penny. It costs 2.4 cents to manufacture one penny, which honestly seems a little counterproductive. Canada phased out theirs in 2012.

The way money is spent is definitely evolving, and it will be interesting to see how the more traditional ways of spending will be complemented, or supplemented, by the digital world of electronic money. But for now, once a year, some of us can reliably expect a check from our grandmothers; and written in the memo, it says "Happy Birthday."

SOURCES

America's Library. "Purchase of Alaska." Accessed December 7, 2016. http://www.americaslibrary .gov/jb/recon/jb_recon_alaska_1.html.

Barat Primary Source Nexus. "Today in History: Alaska Purchase." March 30, 2012. http://primary sourcenexus.org/2012/03/today-in-history-alaska-purchase/.

Hemlock, Doreen. "Still Paying By Check? There Are Fewer of Us." *Sun Sentinel* (Fort Lauderdale, FL), February 19, 2012. http://articles.sun-sentinel.com/2012-02-19/news/fl-checks-in-decline -20120217_1_paper-checks-electronic-payments-direct-deposit.

National Archives and Records Administration (NARA). "Check for the Purchase of Alaska." Accessed December 7, 2016. https://www.archives.gov/historical-docs/alaska-purchase-check.

Office of the Historian, Bureau of Public Affairs. "Purchase of Alaska, 1867." United States Department of State. Accessed December 7, 2016. http://history.state.gov/milestones/1866-1898/alaska -purchase.

Our Documents. "Check for the Purchase of Alaska (1868)." Accessed December 7, 2016. http:// www.ourdocuments.gov/doc.php?flash=true&doc=41.

Quinn, Stephen, and William Roberds. "The Evolution of the Check as a Means of Payment: A Historical Survey." *Economic Review—Federal Reserve Bank of Atlanta* 93, no. 4 (2008). https:// www.frbatlanta.org/filelegacydocs/er08no4_QuinnRoberds.pdf.

Wikipedia. "Alaska." Last modified November 21, 2016. http://en.wikipedia.org/wiki/Alaska.

18
Robert's Rules of Order

The Pocket Manual of Rules of Order for Deliberative Assemblies
better known as Robert's Rules of Order
written by Henry Martyn Robert

1876

Who hasn't been in a meeting like this? It's not entirely clear who's in charge, or the person who is, is clueless. Nobody knows quite how to proceed, or more likely everybody thinks they do, and so the discussion can be unpleasant, difficult, counterproductive, even paralyzing. Then, at some particularly critical and contentious juncture, somebody, in a vain attempt to resolve the situation or just get the upper hand, will get really frustrated and fed up, and will blurt out the dreaded "Point of order!"

That, in my experience, is the beginning of the end. Then starts the scrambling for rules, often making them up as you go along, feelings get hurt, the volume rises, and everybody might just as well call it a day, 'cause now nothing's gonna get done. As our hero once said in a lecture, "Friction as to what constituted parliamentary law was indeed no uncommon thing." As true today as it ever was.

It's easy to mock "parliamentary procedure"; it's often portrayed as a technicality or tricky maneuver, as though using it is somehow underhanded or unfair, but of course it's precisely the opposite. Without these kinds of detailed and specific rules, stipulated and agreed to, what's the alternative? That's the question answered by an army engineer and general who, more than a century ago, laid down the law, or at least the rules by which the law can get made.

The idea of a body of people coming together to discuss or make decisions among themselves is ancient, recorded as far back as Thucydides 2,500 years ago. In the Anglo-Saxon tradition, this became the village "moot" and "witan," which eventually evolved into a "parliament," from the Latin for "meeting," by the 13th century. The rules for their debates took shape over time. They were first expressed in written form in the 1560s, and even at that early point they had many aspects that we find familiar today: discussing one topic at a time and staying on that point, alternating speeches between opposing points of view, the

TABLE OF RULES RELATING TO MOTIONS.

[*Containing Answers to Two Hundred Questions in Parliamentary Practice.*]

Section in Pocket Manual	Motion	Undebatable [§35]	Opens Main Question to Debate [§35]	Cannot be Amended [§23]	Cannot be Reconsidered [§27] — See Note 1	Requires a ⅔ Vote [§39]	Does not require to be Seconded [§3]	In order when another has the floor [§2]
	Explanation of the Table.—A Star shows that the rule heading the column in which it stands, applies to the motion opposite to which it is placed; a blank shows that the rule does not apply; a figure shows that the rule only partially applies, the figure referring to the note showing the limitations. Take, for example, "Lay on the Table;" the Table shows that §19 of the Pocket Manual treats of this motion; that it is "undebatable" and "cannot be amended;" and that an affirmative vote on it (as shown in note 5) "cannot be reconsidered;"—the four other columns containing blanks show that this motion does not "open the main question to debate," that it does not "require a ⅔ vote," that it does "require to be seconded," and that it is not "in order when another member has the floor." *[See page 11.]*							
11	Adjourn...	*		*	*			
10	Adjourn, Fix the Time to which to..........	2						
23	Amend [3]...							
23	Amend an Amendment.........................			*				
45	Amend the Rules.................................				*			
14	Appeal, relating to indecorum, etc. [4] ...	*		*				*
14	Appeal, all other cases........................	*		*				
14	Call to Order.....................................	*		*			*	*

NOTES.

(1) Every motion in this column has the effect of suspending some rule or established right of deliberative assemblies (see note to §39), and therefore requires a two-thirds vote, unless a special rule to the contrary is adopted.

(2) Undebatable if made when another question is before the assembly.

(3) An Amendment may be either (1) by "*adding*" or (2) by "*striking out*" words or paragraphs; or (3) by "*striking out certain words and inserting others;*" or (4) by "*substituting*" a different motion on the same subject; or (5) by "*dividing the question*" into two or more questions, as specified by the mover, so as to get a separate vote on any particular point or points.

(4) An Appeal is undebatable only when relating to indecorum, or to transgressions of the rules of speaking, or to the priority of business, or

Cropped image showing the top portion of "Table of Rules Relating to Motions" from 1895 copy of *Robert's Rules of Order*. Author's personal collection.

importance of decorum and not introducing personalities into the discussion, all of which were in place by the early 17th century.

These practices came to the American colonies and formed the structure for rules in colonial assemblies and the Continental Congress, not to mention the US Congress; Thomas Jefferson, presiding over the new Senate as vice president, wrote its first manual of procedure in 1801, based largely on that of the English Parliament. As the individual states formed their postcolonial governments and legislatures, they also developed sets of rules based on the English model, though naturally each in their own way.

Enter Henry Martyn Robert, a civic-minded minister's son who, after a bout of tropical fever, was reassigned by the army in 1863 to Massachusetts and promptly found himself presiding over a 14-hour meeting on the defense of New Bedford from Confederate attack. He was at a loss, and mortified, because he didn't know what to do. That embarrassment led to a resolution that he would never be in that situation again, and in typical 19th-century American fashion, he set out to do something about it.

He read all the books he could get his hands on for rules for meetings, including Jefferson's, and discovered there was great disparity—in no small part because of variations by state. He started to compile first a basic list, then what he thought would be a slim, 16-page guide that would be of general use so that people who belonged to multiple groups and societies didn't have to keep readjusting to new sets of rules. The army transferred him all over the country following the Civil War until he landed in Milwaukee one frigid winter, waiting for the ice to melt, and got to work.

For a book that's been around for over a century, now in an eleventh revised edition, and that has entered the popular vernacular, it's odd to think that, at first, he had difficulty getting it published. With no apparent interest, he paid for the printing of 4,000 copies, 1,000 of which he sent to educators, legislators, and parliamentarians nationwide in 1876, the year of Korean independence, the patenting of the telephone and combustion engine, the discovery of anthrax, and Brahms's first symphony. He sold out within months, and a second edition was out almost immediately. That first edition is now worth about $2,000, and much of its basic structure and even language remains in *Robert's* today.

Its intent was to free groups from confusion and dispute over rules so they could get on with conducting the business at hand. That's admirable, but now it's more than 700 pages of very precise—one might even say persnickety—language about often arcane, exotic, and rare situations, such as whether or not the motion to reconsider extending the limits of debate requires a second. I have to tell you, this stuff is not for the faint of heart; there are other, simpler sets of rules for smaller groups, though, of course, nothing so comprehensive, influential, or recognized. The truly committed professional can even receive certification from the National Association of Parliamentarians—and pause with me now for just a second to imagine what their meetings must be like.

Robert's personal legacy is in the book itself and the family business that keeps it going to this day. After his death, his only son, Henry Jr., took it on under a trusteeship, followed by Junior's widow, Sarah, and then her son, Henry III, who is still credited, along with a number of others, on the eleventh edition. For Henry Sr., I could find only a couple of minor biographies and a master's thesis about his life; even his tombstone in Arlington National Cemetery makes no mention of his parliamentary work and contributions. His military engineering career was also quite distinguished, and he worked on major projects from the Puget Sound to Long Island to the Mississippi River, rising eventually to brigadier general and US Army Chief of Engineers, a position he held, apparently, for exactly three days, before retiring in 1901.

It's easy to get lost among the parliamentary trees and miss the forest; Robert was striving to promote order, not only at your local Rotary Club meeting but in the wider society as well. One of Robert's better-known quotes goes like this: "The great lesson for democracies to learn is for the majority to give to the minority a full, free opportunity to present their side of the case, and then for the minority, having failed to win . . . gracefully to submit and to recognize the action as that of the entire organization, and cheerfully to assist in carrying it out, until they can secure its repeal." An appealing, if quaint, notion in an increasingly partisan, polarized world.

Voting stations in the Washington State House of Representatives chamber, Olympia. Washington State Office of Legislative Support Services (LSS).

SOURCES

Donadio, Rachel. "Point of Order." *New York Times*, May 20, 2007. http://www.nytimes.com/2007/05/20/books/review/Donadio-t.html.

Find a Grave. "Henry Martyn Robert." January 1, 2001. http://www.findagrave.com/cgi-bin/fg.cgi?page=dfl&GRid=2119.

National Association of Parliamentarians. "Accreditation." Last modified 2016. http://www.parliamentarians.org/services/accreditation/.

Robert, Henry M. *Robert's Rules of Order Newly Revised.* 11th ed. Edited by Sarah Corbin Robert. Philadelphia, PA: Da Capo Press, 2011.

19
Alfred Nobel's Will

a will, written by Alfred Nobel in his own hand
signed and witnessed in Paris
now housed in the Nobel Foundation vault in Stockholm

1895

Do you ever wonder what you'll leave behind? For most of us, it'll be our friends and loved ones' memories, and for many, our families will be our legacy. Some of us will be remembered for our important achievements, and a very few of us will live on for generations and centuries based on the works and ideas that survive us, for good or for ill.

Each of us, though, no matter how grand or humble, has the opportunity to leave one thing behind, one last word, that in most cases has to be heard, and obeyed: a will. Much as people don't like to talk about or even contemplate it, making a will gives us all a chance to make our wishes known about our worldly goods and how they should be dispensed, and perhaps also a chance to get in one final dig or demonstration of affection.

One will, penned in firm black ink, doing just about everything wrong and constructed so poorly that it should likely never have been honored, nevertheless changed the fortunes of nearly a thousand beneficiaries its author could never have imagined, and of their benefactor as well.

You've seen it a dozen times; Great Aunt Hildegarde has finally croaked, so now the greedy, ne'er-do-well family gathers to find out who got what from the old girl at the reading of her last will and testament. In early England, those two things were actually different: the "testament" was for personal property, the "will" for real property, and originally referred to the declaration itself, only over time coming to mean the document. So a last will is precisely that, your "last will" about how to dispose of your stuff.

In reality, those readings are rare and largely the purview of lazily written scripts, though there remains here a hint of ancient history: the earliest Roman wills were made in public, by male heads of households, in an oral ceremony before the *comitia calata*, a body of witnesses convened twice a year for just such a purpose; upon death, the seals were broken and the document read aloud. Later provisions were made for wills to be executed by men who were going into battle (*in procinctu*) or in imminent danger of death. By and large, the only women who could make wills were those who were unmarried after the death of their father, or widows not in the power of their father, and even then they were under the authority of a guardian called a *tutor*.

The functions of a Roman will feel very familiar. Then, as now, the law dictated what happened when a person died without a will, or intestate. So a will is a means to deviate from that pattern, to more specifically designate who gets what, to favor some, disappoint or even disinherit others, to name guardians for minor children, and so on. It's a final mechanism for control of one's property, no matter how seemingly bizarre or capricious, and it's also a one-way street, with no opportunity for rebuttal or negotiation other than legal challenge of its provisions. According to one estimate, such challenges accounted for 60–70 percent of all Roman civil litigation.

Requirements for making a will today vary by jurisdiction. In general, though, the person making one has to be of a certain minimum age, free from duress or influence, and capable of reasoning and making decisions. The will must then be witnessed by people who aren't named in it. Signatures or marks are often, but not always, required and, in some cases, handwritten or even oral ("nuncupative") wills can be acceptable as well. It's not hard to find fascinating tidbits in the history of will making; in the late 19th century it was common for state laws to explicitly address inheritance rights of illegitimate children and whether or not married women could even make wills. Louisiana today has a provision for forced heirship; you can't disinherit your child without a reason, like if he ever hit you, accused you of murder, or got married as a minor without your permission.

There are limits, but laws generally give the maker of a will quite a bit of leeway. Good news for Alfred Nobel, in his own words, "a misanthrope and yet utterly benevolent [with] more than one screw loose yet . . . a super-idealist." An inventor from an early age, he patented dynamite at the age of 35, shortly after a brother was killed in an explosion in their experimental shed. When another brother died in 1888, an obituary mistakenly named him as Alfred and was titled "The merchant of death is dead." That would get to anybody. The story is told that in Alfred's case it seems to have contributed to a morbid fear of "apparent death" and a desire to have his veins opened after he died, followed by cremation in a bath of hot sulfuric acid. Perhaps this was also linked to his claustrophobia; he joined the Société pour la Propagation de la Crémation for 100 francs in 1881. The mistaken obit is a great story, repeated many times in many places, including published biographies, though some recent investigative reporting couldn't verify it or the supposed newspaper that ran the obituary, *Ideotie Quotidienne*, so perhaps it's just a little too good to be true.

Image of Alfred Nobel's will, dated November 27, 1895. Wikimedia Commons (accessed at https://commons.wikimedia.org/wiki/File:Alfred_Nobels_will-November_25th,_1895.jpg).

Something, anyway, prompted his writing of a new will, his third, in 1895, about a year before his death. This one was quite the impromptu affair; he seems to have grabbed four men in the Swedish Norwegian Club in Paris and asked them to witness the will he had just dashed off. Frankly, it's a mess, running some four pages (and is now locked in a vault at the Nobel Foundation in Stockholm), with writing up the sides in the margins. It leaves small bequests to nephews and nieces, servants, and to the former Sofie Hess, an Austrian flower salesgirl with whom, though he never married, he had the longest relationship of his life. Then, in a sharp turn, he specifies that the bulk of his estate, amounting to something like $200,000,000 in current dollars, was to be invested in a fund, "the interest on which shall be annually distributed in the form of prizes to those who, during the preceding year, shall have conferred the greatest benefit to mankind."

Which is a lovely thought, except for a few minor difficulties. The executors he specified had no idea they'd been named until after his death; the will was contested by several family members who felt shortchanged; the press criticized it for being unpatriotic, since the prize money wasn't reserved for Swedes; the institutions he named to choose the prize winners had not been consulted; and, most seriously, there was no foundation, no institution, no place for the money to go. He had only established what would become the Nobel Foundation by the terms of the will itself.

Thus began the saga of making all his dreams into reality, which, as we all know, did eventually happen, though not without the spectacle of the executor gathering up Nobel's securities and assets in secret in the Swedish embassy, driving away with them in a horse-drawn cab through the streets of Paris to the Gare du Nord, revolver at the ready to protect himself from thieves, and perhaps the relatives, and spiriting the loot out of France and into Britain and Sweden, where the will would eventually be probated.

In any event, the deeds were done, and the prizes started to flow in 1901, including to Wilhelm Röntgen for Physics for his discovery of X-rays, which was made just weeks before Nobel wrote his will. The bitching started almost immediately as well, with criticism of the first Literature award going to the poet Sully Prudhomme rather than Tolstoy. For all the worthiness of Marie Curie and Martin Luther King and Mother Teresa and Malala Yousafzai, there have also been some notable clunkers: a 1927 Physiology or Medicine award for "discovering" that injections of malaria parasites might help in treating syphilis, and another in 1949 for development of the prefrontal lobotomy. Not to mention the omissions: Gandhi, Eleanor Roosevelt, Chekhov, Joyce, Proust, Rosalind Franklin. These things happen. Winners, forever after known as "laureates" because that sounds very grand, receive a gold medal, a diploma, and prize money based on the current size of the endowment, lately something over $1 million each; people who share prizes also have to share the cash, and not always equally at that, which must make for some stilted conversation at the banquet table.

There's one other curious omission that has drawn some speculation over the years. With awards given in several scientific disciplines such as Physics, Chemistry, and Medicine, why is there no prize in Mathematics? The most popular story is based on Nobel's supposed bitterness because his wife either

Detailed image of Nobel Prize Medal in Chemistry. Adam Baker (flickr user: atbaker).

had an affair or ran away with a mathematician. Salaciously delicious, yes, though sadly false, because, as we know, Nobel never married. So what's the deal? Apart from the outside chance that Nobel's occasional paramour Sophie was carrying on with one Gösta Mittag-Leffler, it seems more likely that he just gave money to things that interested him or he thought worthwhile or practical, or because King Oscar II of Sweden had already endowed a mathematics prize. You can rest assured that there is a major prize for them now, the Fields Medal, given every four years. It's a nice medal, but unfortunately, no cash.

Since Nobel kept his last will secret, we don't know for certain what his motivations were. His prior will, from two years earlier, also had provisions for prizes and a donation to the Austrian peace association, though no prize in literature. It's easy to say that the inventor of dynamite regretted its misuse and thus wanted to atone somehow, though dynamite was used mainly at the time for construction purposes, and he's said to have thought his inventions might end war since the consequences of using such powerful weapons would be too horrible to contemplate.

We can only speculate how Alfred Nobel would be remembered today, if at all, had he not written that third will and had it not been made to work. But succeed the will did, perhaps beyond his imaginings. Consider the Fields Medal, established in 1936. Or the Turing Award in computer science in 1966, the Pritzker Prize for architecture, the Pulitzer Prizes, the Oscars, even the Darwin Awards or the Ig Nobel Prizes for seemingly trivial achievements.

Apart from the prizes themselves, they also likely helped to give rise to the notion of acknowledging and rewarding intellectual or professional achievement in general. While we might not know what he really intended, we know what he got; in a word, not what he wanted. So often, hopes and dreams and wishes are bound up in what's in a will—who gets the car, the house, the silver, the love. For a man who shunned publicity and wanted peace, he got the reverse; the world stumbles on in its familiar chaotic and bloody way, and Nobel's name lives on, year after year, a symbol for over a century for the fact that you can't always get, or leave behind, what you want.

SOURCES

Altman, Lawrence K. "Alfred Nobel and the Prize That Almost Didn't Happen." *New York Times,* September 26, 2006. http://www.nytimes.com/2006/09/26/health/26docs.html.

Champlin, Edward. "*Creditur vulgo testamenta hominum speculum esse morum*: Why the Romans Made Wills." *Classical Philology* 84, no. 3 (July 1, 1989): 198–215.

———. *Final Judgments: Duty and Emotion in Roman Wills, 200 B.C.–A.D. 250.* Berkeley: University of California Press, 1991. eBook Collection (EBSCOhost) (accessed March 17, 2015).

Long, George. "Testamentum." In *A Dictionary of Greek and Roman Antiquities,* edited by William Smith, 1113–18. London: John Murray, 1875. Accessed March 8, 2015. http://penelope.uchicago .edu/Thayer/E/Roman/Texts/secondary/SMIGRA*/Testamentum.html.

Mikkelson, David. "The Prize's Rite." *Snopes.com,* October 4, 2013. Accessed March 8, 2015. http:// www.snopes.com/science/nobel.asp.

National Paralegal College. "Statutory Requirements for a Valid Written Will." Accessed March 8, 2015. http://nationalparalegal.edu/willsTrustsEstates_Public/ExecutionValidityComponents OfWills/StatutoryRequirementsForWill.asp.

Nobelprize.org. "The Will." Last modified 2014. Accessed March 8, 2015. http://www.nobelprize.org/ alfred_nobel/will/.

———. "Full Text of Alfred Nobel's Will." Last modified 2014. Accessed March 8, 2015. http://www .nobelprize.org/alfred_nobel/will/will-full.html.

Redsteer, Andrine. "Laws Governing Estate Inheritance for Children in Louisiana." *LegalZoom.com.* Accessed March 8, 2015. http://info.legalzoom.com/laws-governing-estate-inheritance-chil dren-louisiana-21808.html.

Schultz, Colin. "Blame Sloppy Journalism for the Nobel Prizes." *Smithsonian.com,* October 9, 2013. http:// www.smithsonianmag.com/smart-news/blame-sloppy-journalism-for-the-nobel-prizes -1172688/.

Shammas, Carole, Marylynn Salmon, and Michel Dahlin. *Inheritance in America: From Colonial Times to the Present.* New Brunswick, NJ: Rutgers University Press, 1987.

Wikipedia. "Nobel Prize." Last modified March 7, 2015. http://en.wikipedia.org/w/index.php? title=Nobel_Prize&oldid=650269550.

20
The First X-ray

An X-ray image of the hand of Anna Bertha Ludwig
taken by Professor Wilhelm Röntgen in Munich

1895

At the airport, when you're going through one of those giant whirling back-scatter X-ray machines, how do you feel about it? Are they an inconvenience? A necessary security measure? An invasion of privacy? We're told that the images being captured and read are unidentified, not kept, and that they can't really see you practically naked, but who really knows? And, in any event, it's nothing that hasn't been seen before, right?

That wasn't always the case. More than a hundred and twenty years ago, at the turn of the 19th century, the human body was still inscrutable. The late 1890s were the height of inhibited Victorian sensibilities, and most bodies were kept under tight wraps—sometimes literally, in the case of the hourglass corsets fashionable at the time.

In today's age of oversharing, when we post ultrasounds of our babies on Instagram before they're even born, we're used to seeing and being seen, inside and out. So, it's hard for us to imagine how shocking, thrilling, and even titillating it was in early 1896 when newspapers began to broadcast the news that a German scientist had found a way to see through solid objects—had, in fact, discovered some new kind of invisible light that could pass right through clothing and even skin to reveal what lay underneath. Accompanying this news as it raced around the world was an even more astonishing image, which showed the dim skeletal outline of the bones in a woman's hand, punctuated by a substantial ring that seemed to float around the boney finger. This wasn't a picture of a skeleton from a medical school, but a glimpse inside a living, breathing person.

Adapted with permission from a podcast script originally researched and written by Eli Gandour-Rood.

Portrait of Wilhelm Röntgen. National Library of Medicine (NLM).

It was November 8, 1895. A Friday night. A 50-year-old German physicist, little known outside his own university, was diligently replicating a fairly routine experiment when he stumbled across a phenomenon that would change the modern world forever. Wilhelm Röntgen had been preparing to conduct an observation of cathode rays, which he knew he could create by passing an electric current through a partial vacuum within a glass tube. He also knew that he could observe them because they would make a particular kind of screen glow if it was held quite close to the tube. Before he could even get started, he noticed an unexpected faint light coming from the screen, even though it was all the way across the room and not in the right position to be hit by the cathode rays.

Röntgen realized that there must be a new kind of electromagnetic radiation coming from the tube and striking the screen, causing the mysterious glow. He spent the next six weeks feverishly investigating this strange new phenomenon, barely leaving his lab, while his wife Anna left his meals outside the door. This radiation was unlike anything that had ever been seen before, and he was single-minded in his investigation. For convenience, he used the letter "X" in his notes to describe this new phenomenon, a designation we still use today.

X-rays seemed to be a new kind of light, invisible to the naked eye, that could shine right through what had previously been considered impenetrably solid objects, like wood, or paper . . . or skin. A few days before Christmas, Röntgen invited his patient wife into the lab and asked her to lay a hand on the table, on top of a photographic plate. The mysterious new rays streamed through her skin, and fifteen minutes later, they had the image soon to be seen round the world, slightly blurred but definitely real, showing each of the delicate bones in Frau Röntgen's left hand.

Professor Röntgen wasted no time in sharing his findings. He wrote up the results in a short scientific paper called "On a new kind of rays"; two weeks later, the front page of the major newspaper in Vienna carried the story of the discovery, along with the striking image of Frau Röntgen's skeletal hand. The day after that, the news spread by telegram to London and then to New York and, soon, newspapers all over the world were breathlessly describing Professor Röntgen's discovery. "Hidden solids revealed" trumpeted the *New York Times* headline.

These "ghost pictures," as the press called them, inspired scientific curiosity and unease in roughly equal measure. Editorials and cartoons from popular magazines and newspapers of the time were quick to speculate about whether

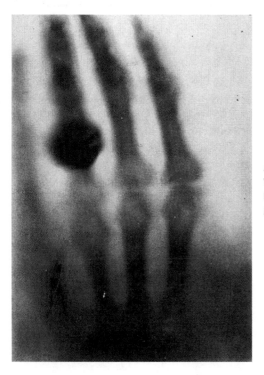

An image of the first X-ray, taken by Wilhelm Röntgen of his wife Anna's hand in 1895. National Library of Medicine (NLM).

this ability to take pictures through solid walls was the end of decency, morality, and respectful privacy. Some suggested a new market for lead-lined underpants to keep out the prying eyes of scientists and photographers.

The market for lead underpants never really took off, undoubtedly because uneasiness didn't last in the face of the immediate positive applications of this new technology. Not two months after X-rays made their world debut, they were being used to create evidence in a legal trial, when a Canadian man who'd been shot in a bar fight was able to submit for the judge's consideration an X-ray image showing the bullet lodged in his leg.

Even faster came the first instance of a doctor using an X-ray as a diagnostic tool when, less than a week after Röntgen's findings were widely published, an English physician used an X-ray image to locate a needle embedded in a patient's hand.

After all, once they knew what to look for, it wasn't all that difficult for other scientists to reproduce the astonishing new X-rays. Within months, even weeks, X-rays had spread all over the world. Machines were hastily constructed everywhere from London, where visitors to Hyde Park could pay two pence to see inside their bodies, to Chicago, where "slot-machine–style" apparatuses allowed curious individuals to put in a coin and see the bones in their hands. In New York, even Bloomingdale's got into the act, luring in customers with demonstrations of the new rays.

Now, anyone who has been smooshed under a bulky lead vest while getting X-rays done at the dentist might be astonished at such casual lengthy radiation exposures. But you've got to remember that at the time, the dangerous effects of X-rays were completely unknown. Unfortunately, it wasn't until much later that the first dangers of radiation began to be recognized, as the most avid experimenters began to experience unpleasant and painful effects, like burns and mysterious cancers. It was many years before the dangers were fully understood and addressed.

In fact, the immediate concerns about X-rays weren't physical, they were psychological, or even spiritual. "I have seen my death!" Anna supposedly exclaimed when she saw that first ghostly image of her own bones. And no wonder; before X-rays, the only opportunity to see the inside of the human body was after death, or in moments of terrible trauma, such as accidents or amputations. Now curiosity seekers could gawk at their own mortality for two pence a pop.

In fact, many of these demonstrations took place alongside another new technology that was causing a sensation. During the same month that Röntgen was squirreled away in his lab investigating a glowing screen, another visual revolution had happened, this time in France, where the Lumière brothers were putting on the world's first projection of film before a paying audience. They thrilled audiences with their new moving pictures, but strangely it took time before movies caught on in the fashion of X-rays, which garnered far more attention over that first year. After all, while these moving pictures were a wondrous thing, they still showed mostly what could already be seen with one's own eyes: scenes of everyday life, trains moving, people and horses in the streets. In a way, they were a natural, even expected progression in the field of photography.

X-rays, on the other hand, came out of nowhere to reveal hidden mysteries of the human body, and they brought about an unprecedented, almost magical expansion of the visible world, a public spectacle that also brought about immediate practical improvements in science and medicine. Röntgen refused to take out patents on his discovery, and even donated the money when he was awarded the very first Nobel Prize in Physics in 1901, claiming that this discovery was far too useful for one man alone to profit from it. The instant and overwhelming public response proved that to be very true indeed.

Now, more than a century later, blasé as we are about our overexposed, over-shared bodies, it's still hard not to be impressed by the image of that shadowy, skeletal hand when Professor Röntgen's new rays allowed us to take our first good look inside ourselves.

SOURCES

Glasser, Otto, Jessie C. Tucker, and Margret Boveri. *Wilhelm Conrad Röntgen and the Early History of the Roentgen Rays*. Springfield, IL: C.C. Thomas, 1934.

Hessenbruch, Arne. "A Brief History of X-rays." *Endeavour* 26, no. 4 (December 2002): 137–41.

Kevles, Bettyann. *Naked to the Bone: Medical Imaging in the Twentieth Century*. Reading, MA: Addison-Wesley, 1998.

Natale, Simone. "The Invisible Made Visible." *Media History* 17, no. 4 (November 2011): 345–58.

New-York Times. "Hidden Solids Revealed." January 16, 1896.

Fannie Farmer Cookbook

The Boston Cooking-School Cook Book
written by Fannie Merritt Farmer, later known as the "Fannie Farmer Cookbook"

1896

There are few more soul-shriveling questions than this: What do you want for dinner tonight? We all have to eat, and much as we often like to think about food, that doesn't mean we have time or ability to *really think* about it, so we fall back on the old standbys. In my house, that's red lentil soup, meatloaf, salmon . . . when things are really dire, pasta, and then there's always take-out, delivery, or, heaven forbid, something frozen. Now and then, I'll get inspired and crack open a book or go online and try to find a new recipe that doesn't sound impossible or require three things I've never heard of and wouldn't know where to get.

Today, we largely think of recipes as simple or at least straightforward: ingredients, procedure, time, temperature, and so on; follow the path and you'll be OK. Which sometimes leads to frustration when for some reason—never your fault—it doesn't work. Yet for a long time it wasn't often like that, until a remarkable woman from Massachusetts helped to codify much of what we take for granted in recipes and cooking and helped to change how, and perhaps why, we think about food.

For this story I don't have to go any further for inspiration than my dining room bookshelf to find my grandmother's Fannie Farmer; it's a 1915 printing of a revised second edition from 1906, inscribed to her as a Christmas present from her father when she was 17. I also have my mom's somewhat spiffier copy, from the 1950s. This is so often the way of these things; cookbooks are used, shared, passed down, smudged, spilled on, stained, written on, occasionally destroyed, and eventually the best ones become part of the family. Apparently somebody in my grandmother's household very much liked the "Thanksgiving Pudding II" recipe, since her copy opens right to page 402 and bears more than a few battle scars. I might try that, though where I'm going to get a third of a cup of suet I don't know. Witness also the Betty Crocker, where I found my favorite molasses oatmeal cookie recipe, which my friend Bryan and I tried out

A GROUP OF KITCHEN UTENSILS. — *Page 14.*

Page 14 of *The Boston Cooking-School Cook Book* by Fannie Farmer, showing "A Group of Kitchen Utensils" from a 1915 printing of a revised 2nd edition. Author's personal collection.

in high school and in the process trashed the kitchen, a tale my mother never tired of telling at my expense.

Cookbooks are ancient, as are recipes (from the Latin word that also gives us "receipt"; "recipe" entered English first as a formula for compiling medicine, a century before its culinary sense). Old ones, though, are almost always in rudimentary form: take six figs and a cow, boil until done, that sort of thing. The first known printed cookbook is *De Honesta Voluptate et Valetudine*, "On honorable pleasure and health," published in 1474 by one Bartolomeo Platina, jailed by one pope (for something, it's not entirely clear what) and made Vatican librarian by the next. The first American cookbook appears to be, appropriately, *American Cookery* from 1796 by Amelia Simmons. In its second edition, she apologies for what she thinks might have been intentional errors in the first, added by her ghostwriter to sabotage her, but it sold anyway, and like so many other cookbooks then and now, it borrowed from other sources without bothering with a lot of attribution. If you think about it, many of the earliest American stories are around food, including the near-starvation of the early settlements at Jamestown and Plymouth, and of course the Thanksgiving story made possible by the help provided by indigenous peoples to the newcomers in adapting their familiar European recipes to native ingredients. And everybody lived happily ever after, right?

Over time, cookbooks grew more sophisticated, mirroring improvements in publishing. Straight narrative gave way to graphics, then black-and-white photographs, then color. Recipes have also been doled out in booklets, promotional forms, binders, not to mention the ubiquitous 3x5 cards, eventually CDs, and now a myriad of online forms. They also reflect their times and places and can be valuable sources for social history, telling us about what foods were available, equipment, measurements, fuels, even methods of cleaning and the rituals of serving and eating. Mostly, cooking has been passed down by example or imitation. As one author puts it, they're "the scarce, flawed, irreplaceable records" of the voices of untold numbers of cooks, mostly "illiterate or bound by trade secrets . . . convey[ing] craft skills and cultural traditions."

Around the turn of the 20th century in America, we see the rise of what became the "domestic science" movement, which emerged from increased attention to food and nutrition, an acknowledgment that eating well was key to good health and perhaps the solution to other social ills in a rapidly industrializing and urbanizing country. It was also an earnest attempt to provide greater opportunity to young women to undertake professional careers as cooks as well as to prepare them to cook for their own families. One example is the Boston Cooking School, founded in 1879 by the Women's Educational Association, and headed by Mary Johnson Lincoln. It not only catered to women of means to help them supervise their staffs, but also offered affordable courses—$1.50 for six lessons—and even free classes in the largely immigrant North End. Ellen Richards, the first woman to earn a degree from MIT, lectured on food chemistry.

Eight years later, 30-year-old Fannie Merritt Farmer, prevented from attending college after what was likely an attack of polio as a child, which left her with difficulty in walking for the rest of her life, at the encouragement of her employer, entered the school aspiring to eventually become a teacher of cooking. And did she ever. Upon graduating in 1889, she was asked to stay on as assistant principal. She took over the school five years later until 1902, when she left to found her own. She is universally described as an engaging and infectious teacher and presenter, including lecturing at Harvard Medical School on the importance of nutrition on convalescence, a topic she returned to repeatedly in her teaching and writing, perhaps because of her own ongoing mobility impairments. One author remarks on the "intimacy and sympathy" with which she writes about this: "Men and women are certainly but children of an older growth, which fact is especially emphasized during times of sickness and suffering."

In 1896, the year of *La Boheme*, the first modern Olympic Games, and the discovery of helium and radioactivity, Fannie published her first cookbook, running to some 1,800 recipes. Her publisher, Little, Brown, wasn't confident in its success, so she had to pony up for the printing costs for the first run of 3,000 copies. Cannily, she retained the copyright, which yielded a tidy profit as it took off, eventually selling in the millions. OK, yes, Fannie's book is in fact a reworking of an 1884 book by Mrs. Lincoln, which apparently was dull as dishwater; she was rightly criticized for that, but as we all know, history is written (or in this case eaten) by the winners. Fannie wrote in the first person and an informal voice, and as one biographer says, she seems to be one of the few cookbook authors of the day who really enjoyed eating.

Her first sentence tells you a lot: "Food is necessary for growth, repair, and energy," which is followed almost immediately by a chemical breakdown of the human body, thus indicating what kinds and amounts of food were most necessary. She goes on in similarly simple but effective ways, highlighted by a systematic, thorough, thoughtful tone. On page 17, we learn how to build a fire, and on page 25, we get what many consider among her major contributions: a painstaking and specific set of instructions about measurements of ingredients—dry, liquid, and otherwise—continually stressing the importance of being methodical and purposeful, using standardized spoons and cups and level measurement techniques. And yet she makes it all seem engaging and easy to prepare.

Pages 250–251 of *The Boston Cooking-School Cook Book* by Fannie Farmer, from a 1915 printing of a revised 2nd edition. Author's personal collection.

The first actual "recipe" is how to make tea. The book's structure and form are very familiar to any cookbook user today: breads, biscuits, cereals (including "macaroni"), eggs, soups, fish, beef, lamb, and so on, including several chapters on desserts. It ends with sample menus with pictures and chapter 37 on "Helpful Hints for the Young Homemaker." There we learn, among other things, that fruit stains can be removed by "pouring boiling water over [the] stained surface, having it fall from a distance of three feet" (for ink stains you should wash in a solution of hydrochloric acid and rinse in ammonia water) and that one part beeswax to two parts turpentine, heated and dissolved in a saucepan, yields a polish for hardwood floors.

So, apart from being the "mother of level measurements," what did Fannie Farmer give us? In her preface, she says she's not only trying to provide a set of yummy recipes, but also hoping "that it may awaken an interest through its condensed scientific knowledge which will lead to deeper thought and broader study of what to eat." Her aim, she later says, "is to elevate cookery to its proper place as a science and an art."

She helped to promote and change not just thinking about food but *thinking* about food. Today, with cable cooking channels and blogs, reality programs, umpteen magazines, celebrity chefs, Instagrams of meals, the whole foodie culture, I think she succeeded beyond her wildest imaginings. The structure and form of what we think of today as a recipe owes a great deal to her influence, though as technology continues to evolve, this might change as well. Videos and apps on a laptop or smartphone can depict and demonstrate processes and techniques in ways that words on paper can't always get across, so the means by which the practice of cooking might be codified and thought about are changing yet again, which I think would make Fannie very happy— and hungry—indeed.

SOURCES

Biblio. "Collecting *The Boston Cooking-School Cook Book* by Farmer, Fannie Merritt—First Edition Identification Guide." Accessed July 15, 2015. http://www.biblio.com/the-boston-cooking -school-by-farmer-fannie-merritt/work/42133#first.

Farmer, Fannie M. *The Boston Cooking-School Cook Book*. Boston: Little, Brown & Co., 1915.

Feeding America: The Historic American Cookbook Project. "The Boston Cooking-School Cookbook." Accessed July 15, 2015. http://digital.lib.msu.edu/projects/cookbooks/html/books/book_48 .cfm.

Fisher, Carol. *The American Cookbook: A History*. Jefferson, NC: McFarland, 2006.

Freedman, Paul, Joyce E. Chaplin, and Ken Albala. *Food in Time and Place: The American Historical Association Companion to Food History*. Berkeley: University of California Press, 2014. http:// public.eblib.com/choice/publicfullrecord.aspx?p=1711036.

Gilbert, Sandra M. *The Culinary Imagination: From Myth to Modernity*. New York: W. W. Norton & Company, 2014.

Levenstein, Harvey. "Farmer, Fannie Merritt." *American National Biography Online*. Last modified February 2000. http://www.anb.org/articles/20/20-00334.html.

The Library of Congress—Science Reference Services. "Selected Works on Gastronomy in the Rare Books and Special Collections Division, Library of Congress." Accessed July 15, 2015. http://www.loc.gov/rr/scitech/SciRefGuides/gastronomylist.html.

Pilcher, Jeffrey M. *The Oxford Handbook of Food History*. Oxford: Oxford University Press, 2012.

Oxford English Dictionary Online. "recipe, n." Oxford University Press. Last modified June 2009. http://www.oed.com/view/Entry/159522.

Wikipedia. "Boston Cooking School." Last modified January 30, 2013. https://en.wikipedia.org/w/index.php?title=Boston_Cooking_School&oldid=535764409.

———. "Boston Cooking-School Cook Book." Last modified September 14, 2014. https://en.wikipedia.org/w/index.php?title=Boston_Cooking-School_Cook_Book&oldid=625473635.

22
The Protocols of the Elders of Zion

a fraudulent book

of uncertain authorship, perhaps at the instigation of the Russian Secret Police
first known to be published in serialized form in St. Petersburg

c. 1900

Aren't these lovely images? "The sun on the meadow is summery warm / The stag in the forest runs free" and "The branch on the linden is leafy and green / The Rhine gives its gold to the sea." Those picturesque and bucolic words are lyrics from a pleasant Teutonic-sounding folk song, one of the lesser-known numbers from the score of *Cabaret*. You can envision happy German people swaying together and singing this, beer steins firmly in hand. The words seem completely innocuous, if evocative. And then they turn, just slightly: "But somewhere a glory awaits unseen / Tomorrow belongs to me."

In the film, this is sung in a beer garden where a tow-headed youth sings the opening stanza as the camera slowly pulls back to reveal his light brown shirt and, eventually, the accessorizing swastika armband. His voice becomes louder and more strident, and others in the garden join in, at first seated, then rising, more and more, louder and harsher, ending practically in a shout with an iconic stiff-arm salute. It's a catchy, memorable tune, and this scene is way more disturbing than anything in any *Friday the 13th* movie, I can tell you that.

Slowly, more and more is revealed about this song, until we realize it's not exactly what it first appears to be. Its power and impact aren't diminished as a result—far from it, they're enhanced. It can often be the case that no matter how much of the "truth" is known, people go right on believing as they like, sometimes with terrible consequences.

It's hard to know anything for certain about *The Protocols of the Elders of Zion*, other than that over the last century it has swept the world and left hatred and bigotry and pain in its wake. Its form is quite clever—it purports to be the transcripts of 24 lectures, or "protocols," delivered in secret meetings of the Elders of Zion, a Jewish cabal bent on global domination, by their chief. In most editions, these are surrounded by material explaining and describing the text, all of which

Cover of an edition of *Le Peril Juif: Les Protocoles des Sages de Sion* (*The Jewish Danger: The Protocols of the Learned Elders of Zion*), c. 1940 (color lithograph). Bridgeman Images.

lends an air of credibility. The book lays out a plan to subvert morals, control the press and economic systems, wipe out all governments, and replace them with a single world order ruled by an absolute monarch. These include easy-to-understand steps such as "Methods of Conquest," "Materialism Replaces Religion," "Take-Over Technique," "Provisional Government," "Ruthless Suppression," "Brainwashing," and "Instilling Obedience." In this plan, the Jews will use as their unwitting dupes—in a conspiracy theory twofer if ever there was one—the Freemasons, who will eventually get wiped out for their troubles after the dust settles.

Pretty much everything is murky here. Since the text itself says it's presenting what amount to meeting minutes of a conspiracy, in reading about it, it's hard to know at times whether people are referring to the conspiracy in the text or the conspiracy to spread the text as warning of a conspiracy. Still with me? At least one author asserts that its vagueness and lack of detail regarding time and place was important to its success. Books and articles about the Protocols tend to toss around references to the League of Nations, Czar Nicholas I, and Napoleon III, among others, in a dizzying array of boldface historical names.

Multiple origin stories have been offered: that scribal spies copied the *Protocols* in the dark of night as an emissary carrying them slept unaware in an inn, or that they were stolen from a Zionist archive or lifted from an iron chest by the lover of a Masonic leader. It appears that the original version, whatever it was, was constructed in Paris just before the turn of the 20th century, perhaps at the initiation of one Pyotr Ivanovich Rachkovsky, a name to conjure with, the head of the local office of the Russian Secret Police. The first known printing was in abbreviated and serialized form in the St. Petersburg newspaper *Znamya* in 1903, and the first full edition followed some two years later appended to another anti-Semitic book with the catchy title *The Great within the Small: The Coming of the Anti-Christ and the Rule of Satan on Earth*. It spread first through Russia before exploding around the world about 1920, likely due to the dispersal of White Russians following the Russian Revolution, appearing in German, English, French, Polish, and Arabic versions in rapid succession. A particular American fan was Henry Ford, who sponsored a printing of half a million copies and serialized it himself in his *Dearborn Independent* newspaper. He apologized in the face of a libel suit a few years later, though without evidence that he ever fundamentally changed his ideas.

What it really is is a fraud, and a plagiarized fraud at that, meant to deceive. The text is taken largely from the little-known 1868 German novel *Biarritz* and from the colorfully named political satire *Dialogue in Hell between Machiavelli and Montesquieu*, written by a Jewish French author. It was exposed as a forgery in 1921 by the *Times* of London and ruled a forgery by a Swiss court in 1935, which naturally has had no effect whatsoever on its acceptance as legitimate. Like any good conspiracy theory, the more it's denied, even with, or perhaps especially with, evidence to the contrary, the stronger it becomes. It continues to be published around the world and is, of course, easily available on the Internet. A version, complete with 30 pages earnestly debunking the debunking, can be found online from an Australian apocalyptic website that also helpfully links to recent earthquake reports.

It's impossible to say how great an influence the *Protocols* had, for example, in the atrocities of the Holocaust, though the Nazi party did obtain the rights to the German translation in 1929. It isn't clear if Hitler actually read them, but he was an enthusiastic fan, encouraging its reading and distribution, including to the Hitler Youth. One scholar suggests its most pronounced effect might have been in encouraging inaction in people who had been exposed to it and thus made less willing to question or stop what was happening, a chilling notion.

One online version, accompanied by an extensive commentary about its history, says on the bottom of each page: "WARNING: This document is a provem [*sic*] anti-Semitic forgery and hoax. Abuse is strictly forbidden." Well, OK, but this raises a couple of questions: Forbidden by whom? What exactly constitutes "abuse," and who gets to say so? It's certainly understandable why someone trying to expose this for what it is wouldn't want their own version used to further hate, which explains the prominent red "Antisemitic Forgery and Hoax" on the front page. Although . . . once you start down that road, labeling words or ideas or people for that matter, unforeseen and unwelcome consequences can sometimes follow. A more positive and hopeful approach was taken in a four-page public statement in 1920 by the American Jewish Committee; the last paragraph begins: "We have an abiding confidence in the spirit of justice and fairness that permeates the true American, and we are satisfied that our fellow-citizens will not permit the campaign of slander and libel that has been launched against us to go unreproved."

Finally, just in case you're still having difficulty believing that people can believe what they want to believe, no matter what the "truth" is, there's this. Remember "Tomorrow Belongs to Me"? It was written by John Kander and Fred Ebb in 1966 for *Cabaret*, which won the Tony Awards for Best Musical and Best Original Score. The song is meant to disturb, to warn, to shock us into an acknowledgment of the ease with which evil can seduce. Much more perniciously, the song has since been appropriated by white-power rock groups such as Skrewdriver, who have recorded and played it at concerts and rallies, to audiences who are certain it is an authentic Nazi anthem. It's not hard to find white-power Internet forums praising the song as the only redeeming

Released for publication Wednesday, December 1, 1920 (Archives AJC)

The American Jewish Committee
31 Union Square West, New York City

A national organization instituted in 1906 and incorporated by an act of the New York State Legislature in 1911, "to prevent the infraction of the civil and religious rights of Jews in all parts of the world; to render all lawful assistance and to take appropriate remedial action in the event of threatened or actual invasion or restriction of such rights, or of unfavorable discrimination with respect thereto; to secure for Jews equality of economic, social and educational opportunity; to alleviate the consequences of persecution and to afford relief from calamities affecting Jews wherever they may occur."

President, LOUIS MARSHALL; Vice-Presidents, CYRUS ADLER AND JULIUS ROSENWALD; Treasurer, ISAAC W. BERNHEIM; EXECUTIVE COMMITTEE: CYRUS ADLER, Philadelphia, Chairman, ISAAC W. BERNHEIM, Louisville, SAMUEL DORF, New York City, ABRAM I. ELKUS, New York City, ALBERT D. LASKER, Chicago, IRVING LEHMAN, New York City, LOUIS MARSHALL, New York City, A. C. RATSHESKY, Boston, JULIUS ROSENWALD, Chicago, HORACE STERN, Philadelphia, OSCAR S. STRAUS, New York City, CYRUS L. SULZBERGER, New York City, MAYER SULZBERGER, Philadelphia, ISAAC M. ULLMAN, New Haven, A. LEO WEIL, Pittsburg.

PUBLIC STATEMENT

New York, November 30, 1920—A conference to discuss the widespread campaign of secret anti-Jewish propaganda in the United States was called by the American Jewish Committee. This conference was participated in by the foremost national Jewish organizations and authorized the issuance of a public statement in which the so-called "Protocols of the Learned Elders of Zion" now being circulated in large numbers by secret agencies are condemned as a forgery, and the charge that Bolshevism is part of a conspiracy of Jews and Freemasons to secure world domination is denounced as a malicious invention inspired by foreign reactionary forces for the purpose of breeding suspicion and hatred of the Jews and Freemasons in the United States in order to discredit "free government in the eyes of the European masses and thus facilitate the restoration of absolutism in government."

The signatories of the declaration which is addressed "To Our Fellow Citizens," include the following representative Jewish organizations: The American Jewish Committee, the Zionist Organization of America, the Union of American Hebrew Congregations, the Union of Orthodox Jewish Congregations, the United Synagogue of America, the Provisional Committee for an American Jewish Congress, The Independent Order of B'nai B'rith, the Central Conference of American Rabbis, the Rabbinical Assembly of the Jewish Theological Seminary, and the United Orthodox Jewish Rabbis of America. The complete address follows:

TO OUR FELLOW CITIZENS:

During the war, by secret agencies, a document variously called "The Protocols of the Elders of Zion," "The Protocols of the Meetings of the Zionist Men of Wisdom," and "The Protocols of the Wise Men of Zion," was clandestinely circulated, in typewritten form, among public officials and carefully selected civilians, for the purpose of giving rise to the belief that the Jews, in conjunction with Freemasons, had been for centuries engaged in a conspiracy to produce revolution and anarchy, by means of which they hoped to attain the control of the world by the establishment of some sort of despotic rule. Some months ago this document was published in England. More recently it has appeared in print in the United States and thousands of copies have been circulated with an air of mystery among legislators, journalists, clergymen and teachers, members of clubs, and indiscriminately to the general public. The London *Morning Post* has given out a series of articles as a commentary upon The Protocols, in which the charge of an unholy conspiracy between Jews and Freemasons is elaborated, and Bolshevism is characterized as a movement of, for and by the Jews and is declared to be a fulfilment of The Protocols. These articles, whose authorship is not disclosed, have now appeared in book form under the title "The Cause of World Unrest." During the past six months there have been sent forth weekly in Henry Ford's organ, *The Dearborn Independent*, attacks of extraordinary virulence upon the Jews. These assaults upon the honor of the Jewish people are all founded on The Protocols and on the discredited literature of Russian and German anti-Semitism, inspired by the minions of autocracy. Parrot-like they repeat the abominable charges that can only appeal to the credulity of a stunted intelligence—charges long since conceded to be unfounded by all fair-minded men. Ford is employing his great wealth in scattering broadcast his fulminations, regardless of consequences.

When the Jews of the United States first learned of these malevolent prints, they deemed it beneath their dignity to take notice of them, because they regarded them as a mere recrudescence of mediaeval bigotry and stupidity showing upon their face their utter worthlessness. These publications have, however, been put in circulation to such an extent that it is believed that the time has come, humiliating though it be to them, for the Jews to make answer to these libels and to the unworthy insinuations and innuendoes that have been whispered against them.

Speaking as representatives of the Jewish people, familiar with the history of Judaism in its various phases and with the movements, past and present, in Jewish life, we say with all solemnity:

(1) The Protocols are a base forgery. There has never been an organization of Jews known as The Elders of Zion, or The Zionist Men of Wisdom, or The Wise Men of Zion, or bearing any other similar name. There has never existed a secret or other Jewish body organized for any purpose such as that implied in The Protocols. The Jewish people have never dreamed of a Jewish dictatorship, of a destruction of religion, of an interference with industrial prosperity, or of an overthrow of civilization. The Jews have

The first page of "AJC Statement on the Protocols of the Learned Elders of Zion," published in 1920 by the American Jewish Committee. Reprinted with permission. © 1920, American Jewish Committee, www.AJC.org. All rights reserved.

aspect of an otherwise distasteful or "demoralizing" film, and seeking the original German lyrics or other information about its origins. All of which demonstrates, as if that were necessary, that words have potential for all kinds of meanings, that people believe what they're ready to believe, and that the future belongs to those who shape our view of the present and the past.

SOURCES

The American Jewish Committee. "Public Statement." *American Jewish Committee Archives.* December 1, 1920. http://ajcarchives.org/AJC_DATA/Files/F-45.PDF.

Bible Believers. "The Protocols of the Learned Elders of Zion." Accessed October 16, 2016. http://www.biblebelievers.org.au/przion1.htm.

Bronner, Stephen Eric. *A Rumor about the Jews: Reflections on Antisemitism and the Protocols of the Learned Elders of Zion.* New York: St. Martin's Press, 2000.

IMDb.com. "Cabaret (1972): Trivia." Accessed October 16, 2016. http://www.imdb.com/title/tt0068327/trivia.

Marsden, Victor E., trans. *The Protocols of the Learned Elders of Zion. Tikkun Olam: David Dickerson's Web Site.* Accessed October 16, 2016. http://ddickerson.igc.org/The_Protocols_of_the_Learned_Elders_of_Zion.pdf.

Pipes, Daniel, and Mazal Holocaust Collection. *Conspiracy: How the Paranoid Style Flourishes and Where It Comes from.* New York: Free Press, 1997.

Segel, Benjamin W. *A Lie and a Libel: The History of the Protocols of the Elders of Zion.* Translated and edited by Richard S. Levy. Lincoln: University of Nebraska Press, 1995.

Stormfront.org. "Tomorrow Belongs to Me." Forum thread last modified April 3, 2015. Accessed October 16, 2016. http://www.stormfront.org/forum/t6509/.

23
IQ Test

**The Binet-Simon Scale, later revised and translated
as the Stanford-Binet Intelligence Scales**
an intelligence test developed and first employed in Paris
1905

What's your number? I don't mean your phone number, or for that matter your zip code, or Social Security number—useful though they all are. No, I mean those numbers that everybody secretly wants to compare, and that can truly affect the course of your life: your SAT scores. Or your ACT scores, your GRE scores, your LSAT scores, TOEFL, GMAT, MCAT, ASVAB, and on and on.

Those scores count in so many ways; whether or not you advance in school or graduate, what college or graduate school you get into, what scholarships you win, your licensing as a professional, entry into the military. One can even save your life, in a more macabre way: in 2002 the Supreme Court, in *Atkins v. Virginia*, declared it was unconstitutional to execute the "mentally retarded," usually defined by an IQ score of less than 70 or so.

But where did that score, and the idea for that score, come from? Even though systematic testing goes back at least as far as the seventh-century imperial examinations for the Chinese civil service, standardized testing as we know it today began much more modestly, with a reserved French psychologist who was determined to find a simple way to quantify the emerging concept of intelligence, and in the process moved us down the road to an increasingly measured and numbered society.

Let's try a few questions from one of those early tests. Think hard. Remember, the rest of your life may be affected by your answers. In what ways are these things alike: a star, the sun, and the moon? If you said they all shine, are in the sky, or are bright, you get credit. How about a cloud, steam, and ice? All water, all vapor, both acceptable answers. A stone, a nail, and a cannon? All are hard. However, if you said that the first three are round, you get no credit, or that the next three are all white, or that the last three are heavy or can hurt somebody, you're out of luck—even though most of these latter answers seem more evocative and frankly interesting to me.

Maybe these will be easier, under the heading "Problematic Situations." What's the thing to do "when you are lost and cannot find the way home?" You'll get credit for asking somebody or using a compass, but not waiting for somebody to find you. How about "if your lessons at school are too hard for you"? Talking to the teacher is acceptable; studying hard isn't. How about "if you have nothing to eat and nobody will give you food or money"? Full marks for going to work or earning money, no credit for "Borrow. Ask someone. Die." And if these weren't problematic enough, even for a 1922 test, try Test 8 (Æsthetic Discrimination, reproduced here): "Which is prettier?"

Palms started to sweat yet? The very idea of taking one of these tests—facing those little bubbles, no. 2 pencil grimly in hand, or, more recently, clicking on a computer screen—is enough to make anybody shudder. While it may feel as though that's an ancient, lizard-brain terror, it's only in the last 150 years or so that people have thought seriously about trying to quantify intellectual ability. The concept of "intelligence" as something other than innate, God-given, and universal only begins to arise in the mid-19th century, fueled by a number of factors, including the coalescing of psychology as a discipline and the development of more sophisticated techniques for statistical analysis of data.

Enter Alfred Binet, born into a family of doctors, but who went into law after his first unfortunate encounter with a cadaver. He then drifted into the new psychology and became fascinated by what we would now call child

[*Page 23*]

An illustration from the *Herring Revision of the Binet-Simon Tests, Examination Manual: Form A*. In this test, "Aesthetic Discrimination," the person taking the test is asked to indicate which figure in each pair is prettier. University of California Libraries, Internet archive.

development, anticipating the work of Jean Piaget and others, which seems to have begun with years of intense investigation and testing of his own two daughters, Madeline and Alice. He began to form a notion of the sorts of abilities one might expect of a child as they grow, which he later came to call "mental age." With a pupil-turned-colleague, Théodore Simon, he broadened his investigations to hundreds of children in schools and in mental institutions.

Then in 1905, after several frustrating years with little progress, including numerous papers on cephalometry, the measurement of heads, the Paris school authorities were seeking a way to identify children who either needed extra assistance in being educated by virtue of their diminished ability, or who were completely unable to be helped by the schools. Binet and Simon took on the challenge and within months hit on a method using a series of questions, gauged to what would be "normally" expected at certain ages. These 30 questions, ranging from following a moving object with one eye, all the way up to defining abstract concepts such as the differences between "boredom" and "weariness," became the Binet-Simon Scale. Later revisions compared "mental age" to "chronological age" and others later added the idea of dividing these to form a ratio: a child of 10 with a mental age of 15 would then get a score of $15/10$, converted to 150 . . . their "intelligence quotient": IQ. Somewhere along the line, we also got formal definitions for terms once clinical and today used only crudely and interchangeably: "moron" (originally an IQ from 50–69), "imbecile" (20–49), and "idiot" (less than 20).

The scale itself was first published in a journal that Binet founded and edited, *L'année psychologique*, in June of 1905, only a few weeks after Mata Hari debuted in Paris and in the midst of Albert Einstein's annus mirabilis—that same month he published his major work on special relativity. It didn't take long for word to spread and the scale to be widely used. It was revised once before Binet's untimely death in 1911 and then came to the United States in 1916 in a translated and edited version by Lewis Terman called the Stanford-Binet Scale, named for the university where he taught. The Stanford-Binet is still used, along with a number of other intelligence tests, one of dozens of standardized tests, part of the multibillion-dollar testing and test-coaching industry.

Binet worked very hard to be rigorous and make his tests and processes as fair as possible, with extensive directions on how to conduct the tests and score responses. He was deeply engaged with the clinical and educational practice of the day, and aware of his method's limitations, though seemingly also oblivious to the profound influences of background, preparation, and environment. Three-year-olds are expected to point to body parts, identify objects, repeat syllables, say their family name; 13-year-olds must "correctly" identify differences between a president and a king, and "superior adults" must be able to draw an image of what a folded and cut piece of paper would look like, which I feel quite certain I wouldn't be able to accomplish.

Entire shelves have been written about these tests and the testing industry, both pointing out perceived unfairness and bias and defending the core assumptions and results. Once you start down this road, though, it's hard to turn back. If we can measure and quantify something, it must be real, right? Even though we can't always satisfactorily define or explain what the test is testing, now that there's a number for it, that number's usefulness, importance, and validity seem beyond question. And if the lower classes or lesser races get lower scores, ignoring lots of reasons why that might be the case, well, what can you expect? So now the numbers rule: IQs, SATs; state achievement tests; and, by extension, credit scores, actuarial tables, and on and on.

More recently, broader notions of "intelligence" have been proposed, including the idea of multiple intelligences—linguistic, musical, spatial, interpersonal, and so on—which has a certain appeal. Indeed, the 2003 version of the Stanford-Binet explicitly calls out eight different kinds of abilities, including quantitative reasoning, visual-spatial processing, and nonverbal IQ. And yet the tests continue, perhaps because of inertia or perhaps because they serve useful purposes.

Or perhaps, these tests have ongoing appeal because they just make things so much easier. Think about it. Now we can characterize people by using a number or two that seems to say all that needs saying. If that's your SAT score, you *can* get into these colleges and you *can't* get into those. That bubble you fill in so carefully becomes a pigeonhole. It makes sorting people easier, into the high and the low, the worthy and the not, the ones who can and the ones who can't. It's so much simpler than all that messy detail and background and complexity, reducing us all to an easily located point on the curve, determining your future, no matter your past.

SOURCES

Becker, Kirk A. *History of the Stanford-Binet Intelligence Scales: Content and Psychometrics*. (Stanford-Binet Intelligence Scales, Fifth Edition Assessment Service Bulletin No. 1). Itasca, IL: Riverside Publishing, 2003. Accessed August 15, 2016. http://www.hmhco.com/~/media/sites/home/hmh-assessments/clinical/stanford-binet/pdf/sb5_asb_1.pdf?la=en.

Castles, Elaine E. *Inventing Intelligence: How America Came to Worship IQ*. Santa Barbara, CA: Praeger, 2012.

Harris, Phillip, Bruce M. Smith, and Joan Harris. *The Myths of Standardized Tests: Why They Don't Tell You What You Think They Do*. Lanham, MD: Rowman and Littlefield, 2011.

Herring, John P. *Herring Revision of the Binet-Simon Tests, Examination Manual: Form A*. Yonkers-on-Hudson, NY: World Book, 1922. http://catalog.hathitrust.org/Record/001280856.

Kohn, Alfie. *The Case against Standardized Testing: Raising the Scores, Ruining the Schools*. Portsmouth, NH: Heinemann, 2000.

Phelps, Richard P., ed. *Defending Standardized Testing*. Mahwah, NJ: L. Erlbaum Associates, 2005.

Sternberg, Robert J., ed. *Encyclopedia of Human Intelligence*. 2 vols. New York: Simon and Schuster Macmillan, 1995.

Terman, Lewis M. *The Measurement of Intelligence: An Explanation of and a Complete Guide for the Use of the Stanford Revision and Extension of the Binet-Simon Intelligence Scale*. Riverside Textbooks in Education. Boston: Houghton Mifflin, 1916.

Terman, Lewis M., and Maud A. Merrill. *Measuring Intelligence: A Guide to the Administration of the New Revised Stanford-Binet Tests of Intelligence*. Riverside Textbooks in Education. Boston: Houghton Mifflin, 1937.

Wolf, Theta Holmes. *Alfred Binet*. Chicago: University of Chicago Press, 1973.

24
The Zimmermann Telegram
a coded telegram
sent from German Foreign Minister Arthur Zimmermann
to the German Ambassador in Mexico City
now housed in the National Archives
1917

In a world of seemingly endless revelations of surveillance by governments, corporations, and heaven only knows who else, it seems very few of us can keep a secret, whether we want to or not. Not to mention hacks and unauthorized downloads of materials from banks, e-mail services, retail stores, websites, hospitals, and on and on.

Today, it seems, you can't be too careful. Nor could governments, a century ago, in a world engaged in the war to end all wars, or so they thought, which after two-and-a-half gruesome years was going nowhere slowly. Long before text messages, e-mails, and cell phones, the telegraph was the mode of choice for the embassy set, and one telegram in particular, designed to tip the balance of the war, backfired completely and spectacularly, and eventually became an example not only of terribly misjudged diplomacy, but of a secret about a secret about a secret.

———

As 1917 dawned, things were just plain ugly throughout much of Europe as alliances and empires were at each other's throats. The United States had so far remained studiously neutral, profitably trading with both sides. And Woodrow Wilson fancied himself a peacemaker-in-waiting to a world that nonetheless seemed little interested in his services, though he eventually won the 1919 Nobel Peace Prize for his troubles, and little else. The delicate game of

———

Adapted with permission from a podcast script originally researched and produced by Jill Fenno.

maintaining that neutrality for as long as possible in order to reap the maximum financial rewards survived U-boat attacks, the 1915 sinking of the *Lusitania*, and a presidential election the following year.

As the war dragged on, Germany was subsisting on potatoes and sending fifteen-year-olds onto the battlefield, so something dramatic was required. Arthur Zimmermann, the newly appointed German Foreign Minister, had just the thing: What if Mexico could be persuaded to attack the United States from the south, occupying their attention and distracting them from the unrestricted submarine warfare Germany was about to unleash, and thus keeping them out of the war in Europe? And if Mexico obliged, they might get Germany's gratitude, some financial support, and, oh, I don't know, how about Texas, New Mexico, and Arizona, which they had lost over the previous 80 years. Great idea, huh? So, Zimmermann sends this brainstorm in a message to Heinrich von Eckardt, his ambassador to Mexico.

Naturally, you can't send something like this just any old way. Plan A is to use a merchant submarine, but its journey is canceled, so instead, off it goes by telegram. Telegraphy had been around for several decades, from the earliest experimentation at sending messages by wires in the 1830s to the first stable transatlantic cable in place by 1866, running from Ireland to the poetically named Heart's Content in Newfoundland. It quickly became a popular, if expensive, means for sending messages much faster and much farther than ever before possible, the first time in human history that people at distance could be connected effectively in real time. The new Pony Express could move the mail from coast to coast in 10 days, but couldn't compete with the speed of telegrams and ceased operations within days of the completion of the transcontinental telegraph, after a run of a mere 18 months.

Telegrams were fast and could go far, but they could also be expensive, so codes—not unfamiliar to us in an LOL OMG kind of world—were developed to save space and money, from a simple "73" for "goodbye" to "ewvgl" for "Natives have plundered everything from the wreck," which apparently happened often enough to merit its own code. At least 1,000 codebooks were published during the telegraphy era, for both general and specialized uses.

Needless to say, the Germans were employing a rather more sophisticated set of codes for their messages, necessary because their telegraph cable had been cut by the British early in the war, and so the obligingly still neutral Americans were allowing them to use theirs, for ostensibly diplomatic purposes. The Zimmermann telegram thus went from the American embassy in Berlin, via Copenhagen and London to Washington on its way to Mexico City, across a diplomatic cable meant in part to carry President Wilson's peace overtures. It was sent on January 16, 1917, the same day the United States bought the

Mark Transatlantic Cablegrams for United States, Canada, Cuba, West Indies, Mexico and beyond   241
"Via Western Union," "Via Anglo," or "Via Direct."

38906	Enxavega.....	Inform us if you hear anything further concerning.
38907	Enxelharia ...	Inform us of any change.
38908	Enxequetar ..	In order to inform.
38909	Enxetar	Is it advisable to inform?
38910	Enxiar	Must inform.
38911	Enxilhar	Must not inform.
38912	Enxoada	Not advisable to inform.
38913	Enxofrar	Not to inform.
38914	Enxombrar ...	Regret to inform you.
38915	Enxosinha....	Should inform.
38916	Enxotador ...	Should not inform.
38917	Enxotadura...	To inform.
38918	Enxoval......	Until they inform.
38919	Enxovalhar...	Until we inform.
38920	Enxovalho....	Until you inform.
38921	Enxovedo ...	What did they inform?
38922	Enxovia......	What did you inform?
38923	Enxundia.	What shall we inform?
38924	Enyalius	When did they inform?
38925	Enyesar......	When did you inform?
38926	Enyesarian...	When shall we inform?
38927	Enyus.......	When will they inform?
38928	Enzainaban..	When will you inform?
38929	Enzainais.....	Whom did they inform?
38930	Enzaino.......	Whom did you inform?
38931	Enzarzaban ..	Whom shall we inform?
38932	Enzarzados...	Why did they inform?
38933	Enzarzais	Why did they not inform?
38934	Enziba.......	Why did you inform?
38935	Enzinha......	Why did you not inform?
38936	Enzinheira...	Will inform.
38937	Enzoned.....	Will inform you as soon as possible.
38938	Enzootique...	Will inform you when there is any chance.
38939	Eogeno......	Will not inform.
38940	Eolidias	**Information.**
38941	Eolina.......	According to best information at hand.
38942	Eolipyla......	All the information we can get is.
38991	Epaulais......	Have no definite information.
38992	Epaule........	Have obtained the following information concerning.
38993	Epaulement ..	Have secured information to the effect that.
38994	Epaullets ...	Have secured the information you want.
38995	Epaxial.......	Have secured the necessary information.
38996	Epebolus.....	Have sent all the information in our possession.
38997	Epelant......	Have sent full information by letter.
38998	Epelasses....	How soon can you secure information?
38999	Epeliez.......	How was the information sent?
39000	Epelons	If——applies to you for information.
39001	Ependymite...	If entitled to the information.
39002	Ependyte	If information is not refused.
39003	Epentosi......	If information is refused.
39004	Epenthese....	If not entitled to the information.
39005	Epenthesis...	If the information is confirmed.
39006	Epenthetic....	If the information is definite.
39007	Epépiner......	If the information is not confirmed.
39008	Eperlan......	If the information is not definite.
39009	Eperonner....	If the information is not reliable.
39010	Epeuleuse ...	If the information is reliable.
39011	Epeum.......	If the information is satisfactory.
39012	Epeumakten...	If the information is unsatisfactory.
39013	Epexegesis...	Information came direct from.
39014	Ephah.......	Information has been received here.
39015	Epheboe.....	Information is satisfactory.
39016	Epheboum....	Information is unsatisfactory.
39017	Ephébies.....	Information sent by.
39018	Ephébique....	Information sent by letter.
39019	Ephedrarum..	Information sent by telegram.
39020	Ephédrisme...	In order to confirm the information.
39021	Ephelide	Is the information reliable?
39022	Ephémere ...	Is there any information concerning?
39023	Ephemerist...	It is reported, and we believe the information to be correct.
39024	Ephéphi......	It is reported, but we do not believe the information to be correct.
39025	Ephesiorum...	Make use of the information.

Sample page from Western Union telegraphic code (published 1900 by International Cable Directory Company). University of Washington Libraries.

Danish Virgin Islands, and six days before Wilson called for "peace without victory" in Germany.

The message got through just fine, though not without other, unknown and unintended, eyes on it, in this case in the prosaic-sounding Room 40 of the British Admiralty office, which by this point employed 800 telegraphers and 80 cryptographers busily intercepting and decoding communications in the way one does during wartime. The message they started with was numbers, lots of numbers. About 175 four- and five-digit numbers, obviously in code. Mostly they stood for words: 98092 was "U-boat," 36477 was "Texas," 67893 was "Mexico"; the Germans hadn't had time enough yet to create a code for the newly admitted Arizona, so it was encoded phonetically. The code breakers also used knowledge of German syntax, for example, that verbs often occur directly before periods.

By this point, the British have gotten very good at decoding German messages and thus this one was cracked within days, so now the British knew what the Germans were up to in enticing the Mexicans to attack the Americans. It was then just a simple matter of telling the Americans. Except, you don't necessarily want everybody to know just how good you are at this, so as not to spoil the surprise and give up your hard-won advantage. So the coded message about the secret operation is decoded in secret and kept a secret.

Coded Zimmermann Telegram, dated January 19, 1917, as received by the German Minister to Mexico. National Archives and Records Administration (NARA).

Zimmermann Telegram contents decoded, on the second page of a telegram from Ambassador Walter Page to Secretary of State Robert Lansing, sent February 24, 1917. National Archives and Records Administration (NARA).

With typical British can-do spirit, they devised a means of letting the cat out of the bag without letting the whole cat out of the whole bag, so to speak. The head of Room 40, one Reginald "Blinker" Hall—no kidding—passed the text to the Foreign Office, which contrived multiple stories to cover their tracks. They knew the text would be sent by regular means from Washington to Mexico, so they got the coded text from the Mexican telegraph office, perhaps by the bribery efforts of one "Mr. H." And it just so happened that that version used a different code from the original, but one that had previously been captured, thus the British could give away that code, and still conceal their other superior cryptography capabilities.

The decoded message finally made its way to Wilson in late February, and by the end of the month, he released it to the press. And then the proverbial matter hit the proverbial fan. There isn't any "Pearl Harbor" moment at which the Americans entered World War I, but this is about as close as it gets. Zimmermann actually confessed, in an interview and then a speech, that it was genuine, in the apparent calculation that Americans wouldn't be all that angry, so long as they understood Germany would only bankroll Mexico's attack if the United States entered the war. A stratagem that failed. Within days, Wilson's hand is forced. Within weeks, the resolution is introduced in Congress (though this is still not universally accepted; six senators and 50 representatives vote against it), and the Americans take up arms in April 1917 for the final 17 months of the war. For the record, Mexico never seriously entertained this offer, dismissed it out of hand, and never entered World War I. Zimmermann lost his job just after the fall of the German government that summer, never to regain it, though before he left office, he cemented his reputation by taking time to facilitate Lenin's return to Russia through German territory, thus helping to nudge along the approaching Russian Revolution.

One contemporary method used for this sort of thing is the diplomatic pouch, often mentioned in spy thrillers, which strangely enough does actually exist. A 26-page State Department manual lays out its uses and restrictions; it's authorized by Article 27(3) of the 1961 Vienna Convention on Diplomatic Relations, permitting documents and articles for official use to be sent without being "opened or detained" or for that matter inspected. Classified materials go in tangerine-colored canvas or nylon bags (white bags for unclassified stuff), and there are some restrictions, in particular hazardous materials or personal items, including, specifically, hair-dressing products and cookies.

Now, of course, the telegram has all but vanished. Western Union, with roots back to the dawn of telegraphy in the 1850s, ceased its service in 2006, by which time it was delivering only 20,000 or so messages a year. It is now a global money order and transfer service. In a retro-charming historical twist, the Telegram app bills itself as a "a cloud-based mobile and desktop messaging app with a focus on security and speed," including encryption and timed destruction of messages. Physical telegrams can still be sent, via services such as iTelegram, though in a world of texting and Twitter, that's a bit of a secret too. One wonders, in fact, if the NSA is even bothering to monitor telegrams; perhaps it's worth a second look as a secure medium once again.

SOURCES

Cobb, Stephen. "New Harris Poll Shows NSA Revelations Impact Online Shopping, Banking, and More." *We Live Security*. Last modified April 2, 2014. http://www.welivesecurity.com/2014/04 /02/harris-poll-nsa-revelations-impact-online-shopping-banking/.

History.com. "U.S. Enters World War I." Accessed May 8, 2014. http://www.history.com/this-day-in -history/us-enters-world-war-i.

Kennedy, Paul M. *The War Plans of the Great Powers, 1880–1914*. London: Allen & Unwin, 1979.

Kutler, Stanley I. *Encyclopedia of the United States in the Twentieth Century*. New York: Charles Scribner's Sons; Simon & Schuster and Prentice Hall International, 1996.

National Archives and Records Administration (NARA). "The Zimmermann Telegram." Accessed May 8, 2014. http://www.archives.gov/education/lessons/zimmermann/.

Nickles, David Paull. *Under the Wire: How the Telegraph Changed Diplomacy.* Cambridge, MA: Harvard University Press, 2003.

Reeds, Jim. *Commercial Telegraphic Code Books.* Accessed May 7, 2014. http://www.dtc.umn.edu/~reedsj/codebooks.html.

Rogers, John. "150 Years Ago, a Primitive Internet United the USA." Associated Press. October 23, 2011. Accessed December 5, 2016. http://www.boston.com/news/nation/articles/2011/10/23/150_years_ago_a_primitive_internet_united_the_usa/.

Telegram.org. "Telegram—a New Era of Messaging." Accessed October 14, 2016. https://telegram.org/.

Tuchman, Barbara W. *The Zimmerman Telegram.* London: Constable, 1959.

US Department of State. "14 FAM 720 Diplomatic Pouch." In *Foreign Affairs Manual and Handbook.* March 30, 2015. Accessed October 14, 2016. https://fam.state.gov/fam/14fam/14fam0720.html.

Western Union. "About Us." Accessed October 14, 2016. https://corporate.westernunion.com/index.html.

The 19th Amendment

to the United States Constitution
of uncertain authorship, perhaps written by Susan B. Anthony and others,
passed by Congress and ratified and adopted by the States
*now housed in the National Archives, General Records of
the United States Government; Record Group 11*

1920

Where is the Constitution?

That's not as ridiculous a question as it sounds. I've asked a lot of people this, and gotten a wide variety of answers, and the vast majority are wrong, or at least partially wrong. Think about this for a moment, and all will be revealed shortly.

In the meantime, consider this: are there any words in the United States Constitution that were written by women? Since all the members of the Constitutional Convention were men, there's little likelihood there, though I wouldn't put it past Dolley Madison or Abigail Adams to have had a go if the opportunity had presented itself. So if there are, they would probably have to be in an amendment. Article V lays out the process of amending, and it's not at all easy. It requires two-thirds of both houses of Congress, plus ratification by three-quarters of the states, now usually with a deadline attached, which probably explains why there have only been 27 successful attempts so far.

None of which has stopped people from trying; amendments have been proposed to abolish the death penalty and the Electoral College, to prevent both interracial and same-sex marriage, flag desecration, and abortion; to require a balanced budget, and to deny citizenship to native-born children unless their parents are already citizens. None of these got anywhere near the states. Curious, isn't it, in a document all about liberty, how many of these are meant to stop people from doing something?

One amendment maybe, just maybe, was of female authorship. It came in the course of a remarkable two-decade period when fundamental constitutional changes seemed almost commonplace. Six amendments, the 16th through the 21st, were adopted from 1913 to 1933, instituting such things as a federal income tax, direct election of senators, and Prohibition, as well as its subsequent repeal. Along with Prohibition, the 19th is one of the first amendments to come as a result of popular demand for change rather than from within the government apparatus itself. It's only 39 words, but powerful words they are, opening the door to full participation in civic life for half a nation.

Photograph with the caption "Bastille Day spells prison for sixteen suffragettes who picketed the White House," taken July 19, 1917. National Archives and Records Administration (NARA).

It isn't entirely clear that Susan B. Anthony wrote it. Some sources say yes; others say it was cowritten with Elizabeth Cady Stanton; a few say somebody else or that nobody knows. If we're not certain of who wrote it, we definitely know how and when. This amendment was first introduced in 1878 with no success. A number of states, largely in the West, passed referenda in the early 20th century granting suffrage to women, which reenergized the push for it to become a national constitutional guarantee. It was reintroduced several times beginning in 1914, failed by one vote in the Senate in February 1919, and then finally was passed that June and sent to the states. Ratification began within the week in Wisconsin, Illinois, and Michigan; a steady stream followed until

March 1920, with one state short of the 36 needed. That 36th vote, somewhat surprisingly at the time, came from Tennessee, after several days of parliamentary chicanery and nail-biting drama. But by one vote it succeeded, and the deed was done.

That leaves the question of *where*, as in where did it go? Up until 1818 there was no actual process for the states to let anybody know they'd ratified an amendment. The Constitution doesn't say, and it's a sobering thought that the adoption of the Bill of Rights was a haphazard, make-do kind of affair, not entirely well documented. (Don't tell anybody.) From 1818 to 1951, the secretary of state was designated to receive these notices, so Governor Roberts of Tennessee signed a certification of the legislature's action, dated August 24, 1920 (he wrote in the time, 10:17 a.m.), and off it went.

Now, the process is housed in the National Archives. When Congress passes an amendment, it's the Archivist of the United States who sends copies to the states and receives notification of their actions, examines those and then when the necessary number (now 38) are received, verifies that the amendment is valid and therefore officially part of the Constitution, rather prosaically printing that official notification in the *Federal Register*. Finally, the records are added to the Archives' collection for safekeeping. That includes the amendment itself, in the form of a joint resolution of Congress, in this case a single page signed by the Speaker of the House and vice president as president of the Senate. Even though the US president has nothing at all to do with constitutional amending, that didn't stop LBJ and Richard Nixon from horning in on certification ceremonies as superfluous "witnesses."

In the case of the 19th Amendment, after Tennessee put it over the top, ratifications continued, though at a more leisurely pace, concluding with Mississippi, which finally got around to it in 1984. It also survived a challenge under a loopy states' rights argument in a unanimous Supreme Court decision in *Leser v. Garnett* in 1922.

So, back where we started: Where is *the* Constitution?

There are specific documents at the National Archives that record and memorialize the stages of constitutional development, including the manuscript versions of the original and of the Bill of Rights, kept in large glass cases in the rotunda, as well as these amendment resolutions and certifications, all kept safe from harm and protected from physical degradation. This is what an archive does, what it's for. Specifically, it keeps and maintains the records of an organization, corporation, or government.

Yes, fine, I hear you say, so where do they keep the real thing? That's the secret that really isn't a secret—there isn't one. You could, theoretically, construct "the Constitution" from all those individual pieces, connecting up

H. J. Res. 1.

Sixty-sixth Congress of the United States of America;

At the First Session,

Begun and held at the City of Washington on Monday, the nineteenth day of May,
one thousand nine hundred and nineteen.

JOINT RESOLUTION

Proposing an amendment to the Constitution extending the right of suffrage
to women.

Resolved by the Senate and House of Representatives of the United States
of America in Congress assembled (two-thirds of each House concurring therein),
That the following article is proposed as an amendment to the Constitution,
which shall be valid to all intents and purposes as part of the Constitution when
ratified by the legislatures of three-fourths of the several States.

"Article —————.

"The right of citizens of the United States to vote shall not be denied or
abridged by the United States or by any State on account of sex.

"Congress shall have power to enforce this article by appropriate
legislation."

F. H. Gillett

Speaker of the House of Representatives.

Thos. R. Marshall

Vice President of the United States and
President of the Senate.

Joint Resolution of Congress proposing a constitutional amendment extending the
right of suffrage to women, approved June 4, 1919. National Archives and Records
Administration (NARA).

how it all happened and demonstrating the validity of the process, if anybody thought it was necessary. However, there is no unique, tangible, singular, definitive "Constitution." The one you find in a textbook or website somewhere, assuming it's correct, is just as valid, just as useful, just as "authentic" as one sitting on the desk of the president or the chief justice. So from a purely documentary perspective, the Constitution just *is*. The text that underlies and undergirds the entire American system of law and society doesn't really exist.

Well, that's not quite right; it's more that it exists everywhere. There doesn't have to be a single authoritative version for it to work. The public and overt nature of the processes renders that unnecessary. We all have access to the process and results; there's nothing secret or hidden involved. Even though very few of us have ever seen these critical documents that together make up the Constitution, we know they're there or that they can be produced, and that suffices. Lots of eyes keep it honest.

In an era when there's so little agreement, so little apparent common ground, the idea of new amendments requiring such a broad national consensus seems almost fanciful today; the most recent amendment, limiting Congressional pay raises, pales in comparison and grandeur, not to mention it took over 200 years to ratify. And even if we do, often passionately, disagree about what the words in the Constitution mean, we all agree on what they are, a testament to the power of documents, even when you can't see them.

SOURCES

Clift, Eleanor. *Founding Sisters and the Nineteenth Amendment*. Hoboken, NJ: John Wiley & Sons, 2003.

DocsTeach. "Nineteenth Amendment to the United States Constitution." Accessed October 12, 2016. https://www.docsteach.org/documents/document/nineteenth-amendment-to-the-united -states-constitution.

General Assembly of the State of Tennessee. "Certificate of Ratification of the Nineteenth Amendment to the Constitution, Accompanied by Resolution and Transcript of the Journals of the Two Houses of the General Assembly of the State of Tennessee." National Archives and Records Administration (NARA). Accessed August 24, 2010. https://www.wdl.org/en/ item/2720/.

Kyvig, David E. *Explicit and Authentic Acts: Amending the U.S. Constitution, 1776–1995*. Lawrence: University Press of Kansas, 1996.

National Archives and Records Administration (NARA). "America's Historical Documents." Accessed October 12, 2016. http://www.archives.gov/historical-docs/document.html?doc=13.

———. "Constitutional Amendment Process." Last modified August 15, 2016. http://www.archives .gov/federal-register/constitution/.

Smentkowski, Brian P., and Michael Levy. "Nineteenth Amendment." *Encyclopedia Britannica*. August 20, 2010.

26
Statistical Significance
the book *Statistical Methods for Research Workers*
written by Sir Ronald Aylmer Fisher, published by Oliver & Boyd
1925

Nobody likes to admit they're wrong, particularly on any matter of real importance. Sometimes there comes a point when it's just obvious: realizing you've
made a wrong turn and have to double back, or that that shirt doesn't go with
that jacket after all. But what about those times when right and wrong aren't
so evident—when, even though you're almost certain you're correct, the tiniest
of doubts lurks in the background? That's no big deal when the decision is a
minor one, but when a lot is riding on the outcome, the question becomes:
how much niggling doubt is too much?

For the really major stuff, like whether or not to accept the result of a
scientific research project, you'd think there would be a structured and rigorous
process for making decisions. And you'd be right, though the origin of one of
the critical components of that process is a bit on the murky side, emerging
decades ago in a surprisingly offhand manner. It was likely crystallized, unintentionally, by one of the founders of modern research methods. You've probably
never heard of Ronald Fisher, but his work and ideas have affected nearly every
statistical study and the way we understand the way we understand the world,
for nearly a century.

Fisher was nearly blind from a young age, married in secret because his
16-year-old wife's family disapproved, and taught in public schools for a while,
though as one source puts it, "neither he nor his pupils enjoyed the experience."
He was, by all accounts, a man of great personal charm and a loyal friend. He
was also quick to anger, especially when he perceived error or misrepresen-
tation in an argument, and his temper led to famous feuds with other early
statisticians, including Karl Pearson, who developed the best-known quantifi-
cation of correlation. Fisher was often right, but his disposition and sometimes
abbreviated writings frequently alienated colleagues. His early work, typical for
the emerging world of experimental design, was in agriculture, which led him
to interest in genetics and, eventually, eugenics, cofounding the Cambridge

A portrait photo of Sir Ronald
Aylmer Fisher, taken by Elliott & Fry.
© National Portrait Gallery, London.

University Eugenics Society in 1911. But the question of certainty was where
Fisher made his mark.

Here's the basic idea. Let's say you wanted to find out whether people have
better memory of things they read on paper or on a tablet. You recruit a bunch
of people, and have half of them read a chapter of a physical book, and the
other half read the same text on an iPad. You then test their memories for facts
in the chapter. Whichever group has the higher score gives you your answer.
Simple, yes?

Well, maybe. The higher score *might* indicate that, in general, people
remembered better in one mode or the other. Or it might be that the people
in one group happened to be better readers, or have better memories, or had
a natural preference (or hatred) of the format you gave them, or were just
having a crummy day. How could you separate any real difference resulting
from format from these other factors? One way would be to randomly assign
people to the two groups to mix all those things up. Fine, so now you get
to this question: How much higher does one group need to score for you
to be sure that the difference was really because of the format and not just
random chance?

That question was very much on the minds of Fisher and his colleagues as the field we refer to as "quantitative research" was coalescing. The underlying concepts of statistics are embedded in probability theory, which was first explored seriously in the 16th and 17th centuries to better understand games of chance; the earliest notions date back to ancient dice games using animal bones. In the early 20th century, the focus turned to science, with early statisticians using a variety of techniques and guidelines to try to identify the appropriate level of certainty that a scientific result wasn't just random error.

In the midst of this, along comes Fisher. His book on the subject, *Statistical Significance*, was published in 1925, the same year as the debut of the *New Yorker*, publication of *The Great Gatsby* and *Mein Kampf*, the Scopes Trial, Mount Rushmore, and an August march of 40,000 KKK members down Pennsylvania Avenue in Washington. *Statistical Significance* wasn't intended to be a textbook, at least not in a classroom setting. Rather, it was meant to collect, popularize, and spread the considerable number of threads of work in statistics that had been developing in earnest for a few decades.

Ultimately, the question of appropriate certainty was framed as how much likelihood, what probability, of a result being wrong we should be willing to live with. In his book, Fisher seemingly tosses this off on page 79: "In practice we . . . want to know . . . whether or not the observed value is open to suspicion. . . . We shall not often be astray if we draw a conventional line at .05." A year later, in another paper, he reinforces this: "Personally, the writer prefers to set a low standard of significance at the 5 per cent point, and ignore entirely all results which fail to reach this level." Modern researchers would refer to this as a *p* level of 0.05, no more than a 5 percent probability that a research result comes from some random source rather than indicating a real effect.

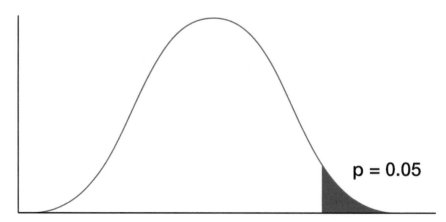

A depiction of a normal distribution curve, or bell curve, showing 5 percent shaded on the right tail and marked with p = 0.05. Created by Tim Blankemeyer.

If you think that sounds a bit casual to be the lodestone of the means by which we decide which studies to believe and which to reject, you're not alone. There's no evidence that Fisher intended this dictum to be universal or definitive or exclusive, but it stuck. If you look more deeply, though, a bit more context emerges. The 1926 paper continues: "A scientific fact should be regarded as experimentally established only if a properly designed experiment *rarely fails* to give this level of significance." Yet here we are: In the vast majority of settings, if you want a quantitatively based science or social science research study published, and you don't hit that 5 percent mark, it's an uphill battle. Moreover, many researchers won't even submit such results for publication, because who wants to be seen as a failure? In acknowledgment of Fisher's achievements, one of the most often used statistical tests, the analysis of variance, is denoted as *F*.

Important consequences emerge from this process. First of all, if you have a hard-and-fast rule, it's hard-and-fast, so a study result that *just* makes it across the line, winding up with a *p* value of .0499, gets to be called "statistically significant," and one that falls *just* short, with .0501, doesn't. It's quite likely that, without Fisher's writings, some similar threshold would have been developed, but it's safe to say that this standard has profoundly impacted the development of quantitative research. And who can say how many potentially interesting and valuable findings never saw the light of day because they just missed the mark?

Also, consider this. If each statistically significant result has a 5 percent chance of being spurious, then it follows that 5 percent of all the "statistically significant" results that have been published are actually due to random chance. I hasten to point out that studies in the medical and pharmaceutical fields often have considerably more stringent thresholds—1 percent or even .01 percent— since health and safety are involved. Still, this means that some small fraction of findings . . . aren't findings at all.

Think of that 5 percent as the likelihood of a false positive on a test, or, as one often hears in beginning stats classes, the likelihood of convicting an inno- cent person ("beyond a reasonable doubt"). Researchers know these happen, and they want to minimize those chances, and yet they don't want to require so much certainty that they wind up missing something potentially inter- esting. The balance between screening false positives and false negatives is very important to researchers, and the focus on *p* values reveals how they feel about it. There's a firm line on false positives, and yet in many cases there's no calcula- tion or even consideration of the probability of a false *negative*, of failing to see a real effect. By this means, the scholarly community wants to be assured that results in the literature are credible, sometimes to the exclusion of meaningful results that might otherwise be shared. This preference is reinforced by the very way they refer to false positives and false negatives as Type I and Type II errors, respectively. Note which comes first.

It could, however, go the other way around. Today, some researchers are increasingly of the opinion that this significance-level business is less important than how big, how important, how meaningful an observed effect is. If people remember things twice as well when reading from a printed book than an e-book, that might merit our attention more than a smaller effect we're surer about. That would give us a different kind of scholarly record and would require a different way of reading and thinking about and navigating the literature, perhaps with a greater desire and necessity for replication and the accompanying effort and money and time that would require.

Neither approach is inherently better; they're just different. You could even imagine combining the two somehow, factoring in the size of effects and certainty in some hybrid way. Is that possible? Could it happen? Getting to agreement on something like that would likely take more than just a line or two in a book, so it would appear that here, as in so many cases, the only thing we can truly be certain of is . . . maybe.

SOURCES

Cowles, Michael, and Caroline Davis. "On the Origins of the .05 Level of Statistical Significance." *American Psychologist* 37, no. 5 (1982): 553–58.

Encyclopedia Britannica. "Sir Ronald Aylmer Fisher." Last modified January 18, 2011. http://www.britannica.com/biography/Ronald-Aylmer-Fisher.

Fisher, Ronald Aylmer. *Statistical Methods for Research Workers.* Biological Monographs and Manuals. Edinburgh: Oliver and Boyd, 1925.

———. "The Arrangement of Field Experiments." *Journal of the Ministry of Agriculture of Great Britain* 33 (1926): 503–13.

Huberty, Carl J. "On Statistical Testing." *Educational Researcher* 16, no. 8 (November 1987): 4–9.

O'Connor, J. J., and E. F. Robertson, "Sir Ronald Aylmer Fisher." *MacTutor History of Mathematics Archive.* Accessed July 14, 2015. http://www-history.mcs.st-andrews.ac.uk/history/Biographies/Fisher.html.

Salsburg, David. *The Lady Tasting Tea: How Statistics Revolutionized Science in the Twentieth Century.* New York: W.H. Freeman, 2001.

Siegfried, Tom. "P Value Ban: Small Step for a Journal, Giant Leap for Science." *Context* (blog). *Science News* (March 17, 2015). https://www.sciencenews.org/blog/context/p-value-ban-small-step-journal-giant-leap-science.

Spencer, Hamish G. "Fisher, Sir Ronald Aylmer." *Oxford Dictionary of National Biography.* Oxford: Oxford University Press, 2015.

University of Minnesota Morris. "Sir Ronald Aylmer Fisher." Accessed July 14, 2015. http://mnstats.morris.umn.edu/introstat/history/w98/RAFisher.html.

Wikipedia. "1925." Accessed April 23, 2015. http://en.wikipedia.org/w/index.php?title=1925&oldid=658834075.

———. "Ronald Fisher." Accessed July 10, 2015. https://en.wikipedia.org/w/index.php?title=Ronald_Fisher&oldid=670783312.

27
Stock Market Ticker Tape
recording transactions on the New York Stock Exchange in late October
1929

In our 24/7 world, it's possible to follow events great and small almost anywhere, effectively in real time, while also keeping up with what your friends are wearing and eating and what your favorite celebrities are up to via their Instagram accounts. We take that ability so much for granted that it can be frustrating to wait even for up-to-the-microsecond details or updates reloading and refreshing on a screen, so it's difficult to imagine what it would be like not to be completely connected all the time.

Here we have a story of fortunes lost, lives ruined, a world plunged into a decade of depression, the end of an era. It's also a story of infrastructure, which is, almost by definition, pretty dull. Don't lose heart, though, it's suitably gory—and there's even a parade at the end.

Stock market tickers were nothing more than specialty telegraph printers for stock transactions, introduced in 1867, most popularly by E. A. Calahan of the American Telegraph Company. Numerous innovations ensued, including one of Thomas Edison's earliest successes, the Universal Stock Ticker in 1871. They are part of the long tradition of devices and means of getting information about financial matters, including via boats, stagecoaches, horses, carrier pigeons (no kidding), and even the development of a private semaphore signaling system between New York and Philadelphia in the 1830s. Securities trading was among the first uses of the telegraph in 1844, and, by 1887, 87 percent of Western Union's revenue came from stock traders and racetrack gamblers. All those innovations were meant to squeeze out that little bit of extra time to get the jump on rival investors.

The telegraph, and then the stock ticker, provided a number of important advantages, chiefly up-to-date, continuous access to information, without having to be physically present on a trading floor, thus lowering costs and cutting out middlemen.

Financial information was now in the hands of the many; more information was flowing to more people in more places more quickly, while simultaneously reinforcing the central positions of the exchanges in New York and Chicago. More subtly, access to that much information had an allure to the point of addiction; a cartoon from 1903 shows a businessman on vacation out in a field, fully decked out in bowler hat and spats, newspaper in hand, secretary and messenger boys at the ready under a lovely tree, right next to his stock ticker. And how long has it been since you checked your phone?

Scanned image of an illustration by Charles Dana Gibson, published in 1906 in a collection called *The Gibson Book*. The caption reads "Mr. A. Merger Hogg is taking a few days' much-needed rest at his country home." University of Washington Libraries.

So how did it actually work? Let's put ourselves back on September 3, 1929, and you want to buy 100 shares of U.S. Steel. You call your broker, who in turn calls the floor of the exchange, reaching a trader in that stock, who will find the best possible price; it closed that day at $262/share. You say yes, the purchase is made, and the sale is recorded at the exchange, first on a slip of paper, then handed to a keyboard operator who types it in using the stock symbol (in this case X), the number of shares, and price. This entry joins a queue from other operators and eventually gets inserted—and this is all manual work throughout—into an integrated stream sent out by telegraph to print on many thousands of tickers, on a three-quarter-inch tape, in codes still used, chattering away all over the world. Another copy, printed on celluloid and known by its trade name as the Trans-Lux, was displayed on lighted screens in many brokerage offices, for all to see. The ticker was named for its characteristic sound when printing; to this day, any movement of a stock's price is called a "tick."

By the late 1920s, it was widely known that there was a problem. Numerous articles from the period point out the shortcomings of then-current technology that was unable to keep up, at 300 characters a second, with dramatically increasing trading volumes. As one article said in 1928, "Anything less than right now is slow," discussing efficiencies like better queueing, the availability of a backup system, and even using fewer characters to represent stock names all in "a battle to gain . . . thousandths of a second." Newer, faster systems were in the works and being deployed, but out of fairness they couldn't be used until they could be universally available, likely in late 1930.

Too late. But I can hear you asking: Surely the ticker tape merely *recorded* the awful events; where's the "changing the world" part? Good question. The causes of the market crash have been dissected for decades: widespread speculation based on buying stock on increasingly overextended margins, soft business fundamentals, and so on; we won't rehash all that here. Instead, let's focus on the days themselves. In 1921, the *New York Times* index of major company share prices stood at 65, and it rose steadily throughout the decade; by September 1929, it stood at 449, meaning investments had increased by about a factor of seven. Trading volumes in the 1920s begin at about one to two million shares per day, routinely going over three million or four million and even higher by 1928 and 1929, which causes occasional minor delays as the ticker tries to keep up. But in a rising market, who cares? You're making money all the time.

On October 21, things start to turn. It's a big day, volume over six million shares, the third-largest day ever, and now prices fall. The ticker falls behind early and consistently, and it doesn't finish printing out trades until 4:40 p.m., an hour and 40 minutes after the market closes. Even more worrying, a second service, meant to quote bond prices, was giving real-time updates on major stocks every ten minutes, and that showed values even lower than the delayed stock ticker, merely confirming that things were going south but leaving people without precise information as to how bad.

More bad days followed. On the 23rd, another six-million-share day, another hour and 45 minutes late by the end, and the *Times* index drops 31 to 384, as the market sheds about $4 billion in value. Then Thursday the 24th, a day characterized as "blind, relentless fear," and "a wild scramble," so bad the stock exchange visitors' gallery is closed. A total of 12.4 million shares trade, and the ticker finishes after 7 p.m., *four hours late.* Newspapers later report on extraordinary scenes of special weekend bus runs and sightseers touring the usually vacant financial district, and even picking up scraps of ticker tape off the street (compared, in one article, to "visitors seiz[ing] upon spent bullets on a battlefield as souvenirs") as staff worked for the first time ever on a Sunday to help clear backlogs—they estimated they would need another week to get caught up.

It was a week they didn't have. Monday the 28th: 9.2 million shares, ticker 167½ minutes late, down 49 points, "mob psychology" rules. Tuesday the 29th, the day usually referred to as the Great Crash: 16.4 million shares, or more—some trades were likely never recorded—152 minutes late, along with other information problems: rumors, mistakes, fatigue. Words like "vertical," "perpendicular," and "sickening" are used. The *Times* index loses 43 points that day; by November 13 it stands at 224, half of what it was at the peak, and it would bottom out in July 1932 at just 58. Volume dropped dramatically as well, all the way down to 83,000 shares in mid-1940; the trading record of 16.4 million wouldn't be broken until April 1, 1968, the day after Lyndon Johnson announced he would not run for reelection. Oh, and that U.S. Steel stock you bought at 262? It closed at 174 on October 29, and by July 1932, it will be a bargain at 22.

Ticker tape from October 29, 1929, showing the first trades of the historic day. Collection of the Museum of American Finance, New York.

It was likely only a matter of time; the bubble had to pop. When it started to fall, and the ticker fell behind, and then when it became clear that things were getting worse fast, it was the not knowing, and moreover not knowing what you didn't know, that helped to feed the panic. So this is an unusual example of a document that is likely simultaneously record, and cause, of events.

And, a story of infrastructure. It's easy to conceive of the ticker device that way, like a faucet or an electrical outlet. Behind the scenes there's a process, a system, wires, people, tubes, whatever, and that's all part of it too, and like any infrastructure, nobody pays any attention until it goes wrong.

It's also, yes, a business story, a technology story, even a psychology story. To me, though, the critical aspect here is the information itself, the numbers and symbols tumbling out on the little strip of tape spelling doom for a way of life for so many. How it's created, how people get it, what they do with it, and then what happens when it's wrong, or gone. The entire securities enterprise was built on that information and its availability, timeliness, and accuracy to support individual and corporate decisions wise and less wise. When that was interrupted, the foundations of those decisions and that enterprise was challenged, which may well have been what pushed over the second domino.

Finally, the parade. If people think at all about ticker tape today, it's about a parade in what's called the Canyon of Heroes in lower Manhattan, a tradition going back to 1886. Over 200 such parades have been held, originally with actual ticker tape thrown from windows lining the route; today the tradition goes on, but copier paper is used. But you could go really old-school and buy a working replica ticker machine to print your own tape—for only $30,000— another example of an information system that moves with the times. More or less.

SOURCES

Flynn, John T. "The Ticker's in a Jam." *Collier's* (December 15, 1928): 18, 56–57.

Galbraith, John Kenneth. (1972). *The Great Crash, 1929.* 3rd ed. Boston: Houghton Mifflin, 1972.

Hochfelder, David. "Where the Common People Could Speculate: The Ticker, Bucket Shops, and the Origins of Popular Participation in Financial Markets, 1880–1920." *Journal of American History* 93, no. 2 (2006): 335–58.

New York Times. October 21–31, 1929.

NYSE.com. "NYSE: Transactions, Statistics and Data Library." Accessed November 18, 2015. https:// www.nyse.com/data/transactions-statistics-data-library.

Olson, James Stuart. *Historical Dictionary of the Great Depression, 1929–1940*. Westport, CT: Greenwood Press, 2001.

Pisani, Bob. "Plundered by Harpies: An Early History of High-Speed Trading." *Financial History*, no. 111 (2014): 20–24.

Scientific American. "High-Speed Tickers to Serve Brokers." (March 1930), 199.

The Stock Ticker Company. "Stock Ticker History." Accessed November 18, 2015. http://stockticker company.com/stc/history/.

Willson, Dixie. "Johnny, Bring the Ticker Tape!" *American Magazine* (January 1930), 70, 115.

28
The Richter Scale

"An Instrumental Earthquake Magnitude Scale"
published in *Bulletin of the Seismological Society of America* by Charles F. Richter
1935

When the earth moves, the first question is usually, "Did you feel that?" followed almost immediately by, "How big do you think that was?" It seems we're hardwired to try to quantify natural phenomena; consider the Saffir–Simpson scale for hurricanes, the Modified Fujita scale for tornadoes, decibels for sound, and so on.

Having lived through exactly one meaningful earthquake, the Nisqually quake of 2001, the 6.8 magnitude was less important to me at that moment than trying to decide whether or not I should turn off the clothes dryer. (I didn't, and we both survived.) The Nisqually still gets referenced when people in the Puget Sound region talk about seismic preparations, but, honestly, way more recent attention had been paid to the so-called "Beast Quake," the Marshawn Lynch touchdown run that cemented the Seahawks' improbable comeback win in an NFC Wild Card game in 2011, because the noise and vibration generated in the stadium after that play set off a local seismograph.

That 6.8 qualifies as a "strong" quake; in an understatement for the ages, anything over about an 8 is called "great," although described using words like "destroyed," "collapsed," and "permanent changes." The genesis of all this, the source of those numbers and the way we derive, react to, and think about them, was a paper written by a unique man, an inadvertent seismologist with many idiosyncrasies who might have been perfectly positioned to feel his way toward creating a way of thinking about the Earth that nobody had before.

If this story doesn't want to make you go buy a month's worth of survival supplies, I'm losing my touch. Each year, about 50,000 earthquakes big enough to be detected occur, about 100 of which are big enough to cause damage if near population centers. The first known device to measure them, the precursor of today's seismographs, was invented by Chang Heng in China in 132 CE. It was a cylinder festooned with eight dragon heads holding balls; an earthquake would dislodge one of the balls, causing it to fall into a sculpted frog's mouth.

Replica of a Chinese seismograph, photo taken at the Museu de Macau. Wikimedia Commons (accessed at https://commons.wikimedia.org/wiki/File:Seismograph_IMG_5401.JPG), credit to Wikimedia user: Deror avi.

Clang. Scales to rate quakes based on their intensity date back to Europe in the 18th and 19th centuries, leading to what's now known as the Modified Mercalli scale, ranging from Roman numeral I, "not felt," through VII, "difficult to stand"; IX, "general panic"; and XII, "damage nearly total."

Those scales, though, were based on perception and effects, what could be felt or seen. As the study of the movement of the Earth became more systematic, attention began to focus on ways of measuring the actual size of an earthquake. This is where Charles Richter comes in; his original interest was theoretical physics, but he drifted into seismology by accepting a research assistantship while in his doctoral program at Caltech. He began by making precise measurements from many quakes to help in determining their location. This work, tedious and exacting, by hand with a slide rule, led him to the insight that the amount of shaking diminished as you got farther from the site of an earthquake and that this relationship could be represented on a single curve.

That led to his development of a simple scale to quantify the amount of energy released by a quake, which he was first to refer to as "magnitude," perhaps borrowing the word used to describe the brightness of stars, an echo of his childhood interest in astronomy. The scale is logarithmic, meaning that an increase in magnitude from 5 to 6, say, represents 10 times more energy released—a suggestion from a colleague, Beno Gutenberg, that somehow never quite got fully recognized in the press or certainly in the naming of the scale, which became a point of contention for many. If you'd rather be more precise, here's the definition from the paper itself: "The magnitude of any shock is taken as the logarithm of the maximum trace amplitude, expressed in microns, with which the standard short-period torsion seismometer . . . would register that shock at an epicentral distance of 100 kilometers." Richter never named the scale for himself; that appears to have started with a press interview by another colleague, Perry Byerly, who actually suggested a usage like "a Richter of 5," though that didn't catch on.

The scale itself has no maximum or minimum and in fact can take on negative values. A -0.2 is equivalent to the energy released by lighting 30 matches; +0.2 to a large hand grenade. The Oklahoma City bombing was roughly a 3, the Chernobyl explosion not quite a 4, the bombing of Hiroshima a 6, and the largest earthquake yet measured, the Valdivia quake in Chile in 1960, a 9.5. It's estimated that the meteor impact that wiped out the dinosaurs was about a 13, and the release of energy from an ultra-compact stellar corpse detected in 2004, 50,000 light-years from Earth, was rated at a 32, something called a "starquake," which for all the world sounds to me like a bad 1980s science fiction movie.

Richter was using the scale by 1932, though the paper wasn't published until 1935, the same year as Social Security, *Porgy and Bess*, radar, and nylon came on the scene, and while the Hoover Dam and the Golden Gate Bridge were being built, Mao was on the Long March, and Germany was building the Luftwaffe and imposing the Nuremberg Laws. The data presented in that paper also lays out the frequencies of quakes of various sizes, leading eventually to the understanding that not only are large quakes less frequent, but also that the smaller ones don't release that much energy and thus don't mitigate the strain that is always building up. This would take decades to prove, but Richter just seemed to know it from the numbers and tossed it off in the last paragraph of the paper. Years later, in an unpublished note, he also seems to have recognized long before anybody else that one quake can trigger another remotely at much greater distances than the familiar aftershocks.

So we all know the Richter scale, sort of: 6 is big, 3 is small, and 8 is really bad, and all these interpretations are due to him. But if you listen very carefully to seismologists today, you won't hear its name any more. Because they don't use it. Richter himself was clear that he was developing a scale specific to Southern California and, for that matter, to a particular kind of instrumentation. It got widely adopted and used, yes, but by the 1970s it had largely been superseded. The US Geological Survey implemented a policy in 2002 officially preferring the more general if prosaically named moment magnitude scale (MMS), while quickly acknowledging that all subsequent work would be designed to be consistent with Richter's original scale. So it goes.

American seismologist Charles Francis Richter, who developed the first widely used seismic magnitude scale, studies earthquake tremors in his laboratory in Pasadena, California, in 1963. Associated Press.

Charles Richter was one of the handful of people responsible for coalescing seismology into the scientific discipline it is today, and later in his life, he was a leading voice in awareness of earthquake preparedness and improving building codes. He was also a nudist. And a poet. And kept a seismograph in his living room. And appears to have had multiple affairs. And, if his biographer is to be believed, probably had Asperger's syndrome. He had a difficult childhood, only met his father once and was the product of his parents' second marriage to each other, each time ending after the birth of a child. As a young adult, he spent time in a sanitarium after a nervous breakdown. He was intensely personal, with a small circle of friends, few students, and no children, and was certainly awkward and socially uncomfortable—to the point of preparing long remarks that he never finished and never read for the retirement party that he deeply didn't want to have. His grave went unmarked for ten years.

It's easy to cast him as a kook or a weirdo who had a great idea, but I think that does him an injustice. I think there was something about him, in the way his mind worked, that was perfectly suited for this work: the laborious calculation, the observation and digestion of large amounts of data, long before sophisticated tools for analysis, visualization, or display existed. After spending some time with him, I get the sense that he was sensitive to all of this, a sensitive soul who was perhaps far better attuned to the rumblings of the Earth and the nuances of the numbers than to the norms and strictures of a world he never fully understood.

I got all this way without talking about the Big One. Yes, those of us who live in seismically active zones know that it's coming, that it's only a matter of time. Arguably, Richter's paper could also be called the Big One, not just because of the scale and the technical prowess that led to it, but also because it marks a clear before and after. It moved thinking about quakes from impact to energy, from perception to reality. Richter gave us the numbers and the feel for what the numbers mean. And even though his name is no longer there, that sensation continues.

SOURCES

Encyclopedia Britannica. "Charles F. Richter: American Physicist." Accessed August 8, 2015. http://www.britannica.com/biography/Charles-F-Richter.

———. "Seismograph." Last modified June 10, 2016. https://www.britannica.com/science/seismograph.

Hough, Susan Elizabeth. *Richter's Scale: Measure of an Earthquake, Measure of a Man.* Princeton, NJ: Princeton University Press, 2007.

Israel, Brett. "How Are Earthquakes Measured?" *Live Science,* August 20, 2010. Accessed August 8, 2015. http://www.livescience.com/32779-measuring-earthquake-magnitude-richter-scale.html.

Jones, Richard. "Group Wants to Keep Richter Name Alive." *Journal-News* (Hamilton, Ohio), April 22, 2013. Accessed August 8, 2015. http://www.journal-news.com/news/news/group-wants-to-keep-richter-name-alive/nXRcp/.

Oskin, Becky. "What Ever Happened to the Richter Scale?" *Live Science*, April 24, 2013. Accessed August 8, 2015. http://www.livescience.com/29005-why-richter-scale-no-longer-used.html.

Pacific Northwest Seismic Network. "Seahawks FAQ." Accessed August 11, 2015. http://pnsn.org/seahawks/faq.

Richter, Charles F. "An Instrumental Earthquake-Magnitude Scale." *Bulletin of the Seismological Society of America* 25, no. 1 (1935): 1–32.

Spence, William, Stuart A. Sipkin, and George L. Choy. "Measuring the Size of an Earthquake." *Earthquakes & Volcanoes (USGS)* 21, no. 1 (1989): 58–63. Accessed August 8, 2015. http://earthquake.usgs.gov/learn/topics/measure.php.

UPSeis. "How Are Earthquakes Studied?" Michigan Tech. Last modified April 16, 2007. Accessed August 8, 2015. http://www.geo.mtu.edu/UPSeis/studying.html.

US Geological Survey. "Earthquake Glossary—Magnitude." Accessed August 8, 2015. http://earthquake.usgs.gov/learn/glossary/?term=magnitude.

———. "Earthquake Glossary—Richter Scale." Accessed August 8, 2015. http://earthquake.usgs.gov/learn/glossary/?term=Richter%20scale.

———. "USGS Earthquake Magnitude Policy (implemented on January 18, 2002)." Accessed August 8, 2015. http://earthquake.usgs.gov/aboutus/docs/020204mag_policy.php.

Valone, David A. "Richter, Charles Francis." *American National Biography Online*. Last modified February 2000. http://www.anb.org/articles/13/13-02219.html.

Wikipedia. "Charles Francis Richter." Last modified June 26, 2015. https://en.wikipedia.org/w/index.php?title=Charles_Francis_Richter&oldid=668817200.

———. "Richter Magnitude Scale." Accessed August 6, 2015. https://en.wikipedia.org/w/index.php?title=Richter_magnitude_scale&oldid=674765677.

Einstein's Letter to Roosevelt

a letter signed by Albert Einstein, written in collaboration with Leó Szilárd

addressed and delivered to President Franklin Roosevelt

now housed in the FDR Presidential Library and Museum

1939

What was the last real letter you wrote, or received, for that matter? We all get lots of things in the mail that one could politely call "junk"—flyers, credit card offers, and those annoying big political postcards around election time—along with the bills and, once in a great while, an actual letter. Overall, as the doggedly earnest US Postal Service commercials betray, the mail ain't what it used to be. Statistics go back a couple of centuries; the annual number of items handled peaked in 2000 at 207 billion, and by 2015 it had fallen to 154 billion, only 62 billion of which were first-class mail, roughly the same number as 1982. If you add it all up, somewhere between nine and ten trillion pieces of mail have been sent in the United States since 1789.

Of that staggering mass of letters that have been written, sent, read, ignored, lost, treasured, one—which didn't even get mailed—went from one of the greatest minds of the 20th century to one of its greatest political leaders, politely and reservedly calling his attention to a situation of some concern that wound up putting us all under a cloud we may never emerge from.

It all started with the Queen Mother of Belgium. Sort of. In the summer of 1939, the Hungarian physicist Leó Szilárd is growing progressively concerned about the possibility of the use of newly discovered atomic fission to make bombs, particularly by increasingly belligerent Germany. He's also worried because Germany has stopped exporting uranium ore from newly occupied Czechoslovakia. He tries to figure out how to get somebody to raise the alarm—and who better than Albert Einstein, who was inconveniently enjoying a sailing vacation. The story is repeatedly told of Szilárd and another colleague driving around Long Island without knowing quite where Einstein was living, about to give up, until they asked a kid on the street, who led them right to the world famous Nobel laureate, father of relativity, in a T-shirt and grubby pants.

Photograph showing Albert Einstein receiving his certificate of American citizenship from Judge Phillip Forman. Photo taken by *New York World-Telegram & Sun* staff photographer Al Aumuller and gifted to the Library of Congress. Library of Congress.

As they talked, the question got around to whom to contact. Another major source of uranium was in the Congo, then a colony of Belgium, which was itself in jeopardy of further invasion by the Nazis, so perhaps their foreign minister or ambassador would do. Or the queen mother, whom Einstein knew and had a correspondence with. A moment's reflection led them away from writing to foreign governments on the eve of war, so they turned their minds toward Roosevelt. Szilárd composed a four-page draft, which Einstein thought too long; he dictated a shorter alternative in German and around they went through several drafts until finally agreeing on a two-page version, dated August 2. That's about a month after the last Jewish businesses were closed in Germany and only a few days after another extraordinary and even less-well-known letter, from Gandhi to Hitler, dated July 23, which reads in part, "It is quite clear that you are today the one person in the world who can prevent a war which may reduce humanity to a savage state. Must you pay that price for an object however worthy it may appear to you to be?" It's tragic, though not surprising, that this letter had less eventual impact than Einstein's.

Einstein's letter itself is unremarkable. Typed and double-spaced, it starts out more like a scientific paper, and the tone is detached, unemotional, even understated in parts. The word "bombs" doesn't appear until the third paragraph, and only on the second page do we get "You may think it desirable to have some permanent contact [with] . . . physicists working on chain reactions in America." Today, one might expect something more like "OMG Hitler's gonna nuke us." The typist hired by Szilárd to take his dictation recalled later

Albert Einstein
Old Grove Rd.
Nassau Point
Peconic, Long Island

August 2nd, 1939

F.D. Roosevelt,
President of the United States,
White House
Washington, D.C.

Sir:

Some recent work by E.Fermi and L. Szilard, which has been communicated to me in manuscript, leads me to expect that the element uranium may be turned into a new and important source of energy in the immediate future. Certain aspects of the situation which has arisen seem to call for watchfulness and, if necessary, quick action on the part of the Administration. I believe therefore that it is my duty to bring to your attention the following facts and recommendations:

In the course of the last four months it has been made probable - through the work of Joliot in France as well as Fermi and Szilard in America - that it may become possible to set up a nuclear chain reaction in a large mass of uranium,by which vast amounts of power and large quantities of new radium-like elements would be generated. Now it appears almost certain that this could be achieved in the immediate future.

This new phenomenon would also lead to the construction of bombs, and it is conceivable - though much less certain - that extremely powerful bombs of a new type may thus be constructed. A single bomb of this type, carried by boat and exploded in a port, might very well destroy the whole port together with some of the surrounding territory. However, such bombs might very well prove to be too heavy for transportation by air.

August 2, 1939, letter personally delivered to FDR on October 11, 1939 (the outbreak of the war intervened) by Alexander Sachs, a longtime economic adviser to FDR. After learning the letter's contents, President Roosevelt told his military adviser, General Edwin M. Watson, "This requires action." FDR Presidential Library & Museum.

that she was convinced she was working for a nut. Roosevelt replied with a brief note of his own, just a few bland if not quite curt paragraphs: "I found this data of such import that I have convened a Board . . . to thoroughly investigate the possibilities of your suggestion regarding the element of uranium." You'd think they were discussing the weather or the price of fish, not the very real potential of unleashing annihilation on an unthinkable scale.

But how does one get a letter to the president? Charles Lindbergh was briefly considered as a conduit and was actually contacted, though in retrospect it's just as well he never responded, since he was likely a crypto-Fascist anyway. Alexander Sachs, an economist at Lehman Brothers and unofficial Roosevelt adviser, offered to hand-deliver it. That was all very fine and wonderful, except he couldn't get in; his reputation as a talker led FDR's staff to keep him at arm's length to save the president's time, frustrating everybody. Finally, on October 11, over a month after the invasion of Poland, Sachs gets an appointment and reads the letter out loud, to which Roosevelt drolly replies, "Alex, what you are after is to see that the Nazis don't blow us up." He forms that committee, things move slowly, Einstein writes a second letter to prod things along, J. Edgar Hoover gets involved to blackball Einstein from participating in what would become the Manhattan Project in 1941 because he's a pacifist, and it's all just too dreary. Einstein wrote four letters in all, the last of which in 1945 urged FDR to meet with scientists to discuss the implications of the atomic bomb and its potential internationalization—it was found on Roosevelt's desk, unread, when he died that April.

Letters are likely one of the earliest forms of writing; many scholars believe that administrative and business records came first but that letters both personal and diplomatic were commonplace about 4,000 years ago, as were relay and messenger systems for delivery. The Romans even had postal inspectors. One of the most specific functions allocated to the Congress in the Constitution is to "establish Post Offices and post Roads." For a long time, the sending of mail was largely a catch-as-catch-can enterprise. Letters would be sent by special messenger (if you were rich), and private services started to arise following the development of printing in the 15th century. National systems followed and eventually monopolies and the development of international agreements in the 1870s, leading to the Universal Postal Union in 1878, which has been an agency of the United Nations since 1948. I've always marveled that the only really efficient, well-managed, and profitable aspect of the Confederate government was their post office.

Back in the day, official written texts were often read aloud; after all, writing can be forged, and perhaps the receiver couldn't read. It's possible that some conventions of letters—the opening greetings, the sincerely-yours close—emerge from that oral tradition. Letters also formed the foundations of other written forms such as newspaper and scholarly journal articles, passports, and bank notes. And of course some novels and a number of books of the Bible are epistolary.

Letters are generally private, or at least one-to-one; perhaps that's why there's no suggestion Einstein and his colleagues considered any other method of communication like a memo or technical report. That's just one of many forms or genres of letters—a 1945 handbook describes letters of condolence, introduction, recommendation, invitation, and apology, among others, and it further suggests that effective letters should be brief, neat, attractive, well-worded, and opportunely timed. There are also open letters, intended to be public, chain letters, hate mail, form letters, and love letters. In all cases, these are forms deeply embedded in social practice and also affect how letters are written and sent. Think of the different kinds of paper, tone, and vocabulary used for different genres, for example, especially the distinctions between expectations for personal as opposed to business or official correspondence. Particularly important or meaningful examples can be cherished (or loathed) and kept for generations as reminders of a person's handwriting, a momentous event, even a scent.

No doubt digital message sending will continue to specialize as time and experience go on as well, though it's difficult to imagine this kind of rich variety and complexity evolving for texts or e-mails or emojis. The number of e-mails sent is much more difficult to quantify with any accuracy; a report from 2016 indicates there will be nearly 250 billion sent per day by 2019. At that rate, it would take only forty days to equal the ten trillion pieces of physical mail sent over two centuries.

You know how the story ends—the bomb got built; the bomb got dropped. *Time* magazine's cover of July 1, 1946, shows Einstein beside a mushroom cloud, and the improbably simple $E = mc^2$ formula; he told *Newsweek* a year later that if he'd known Germany wouldn't develop one of their own, "I never would have lifted a finger." In one of those heartbreaking quirks of history, because of that single letter, Einstein, the avowed lifelong pacifist, has gotten the credit, or taken the blame, for kick-starting the atomic age.

SOURCES

Atomic Archive. "President Roosevelt's Response to Dr. Einstein." Accessed June 10, 2013. http://www.atomicarchive.com/Docs/Begin/Roosevelt.shtml.

Barton, David, and Nigel Hall. *Letter Writing as a Social Practice.* Philadelphia, PA: John Benjamins, 2000.

Brix, Andrew C. "Postal System." *Encyclopedia Britannica*. https://www.britannica.com/topic/postal-system.

Butterfield, William Henry. *Effective Personal Letters, for Business and Social Occasions*. New York: Prentice-Hall, 1945.

Dannen, Gene. "Einstein to Roosevelt, August 2, 1939." *Leo Szilard Online*. Last modified July 26, 1998. Accessed June 10, 2013. http://www.dannen.com/ae-fdr.html.

Franklin D. Roosevelt Presidential Library & Museum. "Letter, Albert Einstein to FDR, August 2, 1939." www.fdrlibrary.marist.edu/archives/pdfs/docsworldwar.pdf.

———. "Sachs, Alexander Index." Accessed June 10, 2013. http://docs.fdrlibrary.marist.edu/psf/box5/folo64.html.

Isaacson, Walter. *Einstein: His Life and Universe*. New York: Simon & Schuster, 2007.

Kelly, Cynthia C. *The Manhattan Project: The Birth of the Atomic Bomb in the Words of Its Creators, Eyewitnesses, and Historians*. New York: Black Dog & Leventhal Publishers: Distributed by Workman Pub., 2007.

Mauro, James. *Twilight at the World of Tomorrow: Genius, Madness, Murder, and the 1939 World's Fair on the Brink of War*. New York: Ballantine Books, 2010.

The Radicati Group, Inc. "Email Statistics Report, 2015–2019." March 2015. http://www.radicati.com/wp/wp-content/uploads/2015/02/Email-Statistics-Report-2015-2019-Executive-Summary.pdf.

Rowe, David E., and Robert J. Schulmann. *Einstein on Politics: His Private Thoughts and Public Stands on Nationalism, Zionism, War, Peace, and the Bomb*. Princeton, NJ: Princeton University Press, 2007.

United States Postal Service. "Postage Rates and Historical Statistics." Accessed June 26, 2013. http://about.usps.com/who-we-are/postal-history/rates-historical-statistics.htm.

30
FDR and Thanksgiving

A presidential proclamation, #2373, titled "Thanksgiving Day"
issued by President Franklin Roosevelt in Washington
now housed in the FDR Presidential Library

1939

What date is Thanksgiving this year? All holidays move around, because 365 doesn't divide evenly by 7, so days like New Year's and your birthday creep their way through the week as the years go by. And holidays that are pegged to particular days of the week, such as Labor Day on Monday, fall on different days of the month. Some religious holidays also float because they're tied to the complication of the lunar cycle; that's why Easter and Jewish holidays move around within a several-week period, and why Islamic holidays, determined by an entirely lunar calendar, march through the months.

But Thanksgiving is, reliably, on the fourth Thursday of November. Except that it wasn't always. It wasn't always in November, it wasn't always on a Thursday, and it wasn't even on the same Thursday for a couple of years. It's now largely forgotten, but before our brief national nightmare was put to rest, it divided a nation, broke up families, and threatened to shake the very foundations of one of our most cherished institutions.

Thanksgiving for many people is the quintessential American holiday, honoring the English Pilgrims who celebrated a harvest festival in the autumn of 1621 with the Wampanoag Indians, sharing turkey and gravy and that weird cranberry sauce in a can. Not quite—it's likely the menu was largely provided by the local Wampanoag people and consisted of venison, fish, eels, and vegetables. The first recorded celebration, however, was in 1578 in what is today Newfoundland in Canada; Canadian Thanksgiving is now celebrated on the second Monday in October, presumably because it's just too darned cold in November.

The first Congress asked President Washington to declare a day to give thanks for the adoption of the new Constitution in 1789, he obliged by naming November 26. He proclaimed another, several years later, on February 19, 1795, and John Adams named another on May 9, 1799. Jefferson refused to go along with a national day of prayer and fasting during his administration, fearing it would violate the First Amendment ban on state establishment of religion. Over the years, presidents made similar declarations, though the days and even months continued to vary considerably. Lincoln seems to have established it definitively in 1863 as the last Thursday in November.

Fast-forward 70 years, when Franklin Roosevelt begins his first term. As he sets forth on his ambitious agenda for the country, he starts to get letters from retailers in the fall of 1933, noting that Thanksgiving will fall as late as it can, on November 30. They are concerned that this will make for a very short shopping season and suggest that maybe, perhaps, FDR might do something to help them out by moving it back a week. This seems to be one of the earlier acknowledgments of the critical nature of what we all now know as Black Friday. Nothing

Eleanor Roosevelt watches as the president operates on the big turkey, setting in motion the annual Thanksgiving feast at Warm Springs, Georgia. Photo taken November 29, 1935. FDR Presidential Library & Museum.

happened that year, but in 1939 the same date loomed, so Roosevelt decided, in August, to nonchalantly mention in a news conference at his summer home on Campobello Island that he was going to reschedule Thanksgiving, emphasizing that there was nothing sacred about the date.

Today, we'd call this a wedge issue, and sides were chosen almost immediately. It made the front page of the next two days' *New York Times*, along with a story quoting the mayor of Plymouth, Massachusetts, as "heartily disapproving" of the change. The disapproval didn't end there, and got quite creatively snarky. A store in Kokomo, Indiana, put up a sign: "Do your shopping now. Who knows, tomorrow may be Christmas." New Hampshire Senator Henry Styles Bridges suggested that while he was at it, the president could abolish winter. *Newsweek* printed a petition from a man in South Dakota suggesting that the shopping season could be extended even further by celebrating Roosevelt's January 30 birthday instead of Christmas. And if you're a movie fan, remember that animated scene of the turkey jumping back and forth between Thursdays on the calendar in *Holiday Inn*. The mayor of Atlantic City coined the lovely term "Franksgiving" to cover the whole mess, which today would make a terrific hashtag.

A Gallup poll revealed that Democrats narrowly approved of the idea, while Republicans and independents didn't, and by the end, 21 states made the change, while 23 didn't. Even individual cities made their own decisions, although Ocala, Florida, nearly wound up with November 13 because of a typo in the mayor's proclamation. The governor of Texas, ever the statesman, declared that they would celebrate both days, which no doubt must have made everybody happy.

Somewhat more seriously, calendar makers, who printed months in advance, were left with a whole lot of incorrect calendars, except for the lucky Defiance Sales Corporation of New York, which had mistakenly printed and shipped 100,000 with the wrong—now right—date marked for the holiday.

In much of the press coverage from the time, one other source of concern features prominently, from a somewhat unexpected source: football. In a modern world, where a national college championship is held well after New Year's and the Super Bowl often drifts into February, it seems positively quaint to think that, in those days, the final rivalry games of the college football season were played on Thanksgiving. But that's how it was, so changing the calendar would mean last-minute rescheduling, not to mention the spectacle of students attending college forced to decide when to go home for a holiday that might now be a week earlier or later in their hometown.

The deed was done, though, and by means of a presidential proclamation. These are undefined in the Constitution or in statute, and they, along with executive orders, occupy a murky place in federal law, a so-called "zone of twilight," though generally they have been determined to be within the executive powers somewhat loosely laid out in Article II. Proclamations are now largely ceremonial in nature, like declaring National Forest Products Week in October or designating May as National Mental Health Awareness Month. To date, there have been something over 9,000 presidential proclamations and not quite 14,000 executive orders; FDR alone issued over 3,500, by far the most.

THANKSGIVING DAY—1939

BY THE PRESIDENT OF THE UNITED STATES OF AMERICA

A Proclamation

I, FRANKLIN D. ROOSEVELT, President of the United States of America, do hereby designate Thursday, the twenty-third of November 1939, as a day of general thanksgiving.

More than three centuries ago, at the season of the gathering in of the harvest, the Pilgrims humbly paused in their work and gave thanks to God for the preservation of their community and for the abundant yield of the soil. A century and a half later, after the new Nation had been formed, and the charter of government, the Constitution of the Republic, had received the assent of the States, President Washington and his successors invited the people of the Nation to lay down their tasks one day in the year and give thanks for the blessings that had been granted them by Divine Providence. It is fitting that we should continue this hallowed custom and select a day in 1939 to be dedicated to reverent thoughts of thanksgiving.

Our Nation has gone steadily forward in the application of democratic processes to economic and social problems. We have faced the specters of business depression, of unemployment, and of widespread agricultural distress, and our positive efforts to alleviate these conditions have met with heartening results. We have also been permitted to see the fruition of measures which we have undertaken in the realms of health, social welfare, and the conservation of resources. As a Nation we are deeply grateful that in a world of turmoil we are at peace with all countries, and we especially rejoice in the strengthened bonds of our friendship with the other peoples of the Western Hemisphere.

Let us, on the day set aside for this purpose, give thanks to the Ruler of the Universe for the strength which He has vouchsafed us to carry on our daily labors and for the hope that lives within us of the coming of a day when peace and the productive activities of peace shall reign on every continent.

IN WITNESS WHEREOF, I have hereunto set my hand and caused the seal of the United States of America to be affixed.

DONE at the City of Washington this 31st day of October, in the year of our Lord nineteen hundred and thirty-nine, and of the Independence of the [SEAL] United States of America the one hundred and sixty-fourth.

FRANKLIN D ROOSEVELT

By the President:

CORDELL HULL
    Secretary of State.

[No. 2373]

U. S. GOVERNMENT PRINTING OFFICE: 1939

Presidential Proclamation 2373, "Thanksgiving Day 1939." FDR Presidential Library & Museum.

It's quite extraordinary, today, to think that not only did all this go on, but that it went on at the same time that the whole world was going to hell. The *New York Times*' front page, two days after Roosevelt's press conference, revealed Germany's demand for the return of Danzig and resolution of the Polish Corridor question, and featured headlines such as "Italy Warns Poles Not to Fight Reich" and "Japanese Occupy Hong Kong Border." Within two weeks, the German Army had crossed the Polish border and Europe was at war. This also played out as speculation was rising that FDR would violate tradition and run for a third term in the 1940 election, which no doubt complicated the political aspects here.

This all went on until the spring of 1941, when Roosevelt admitted that the expected boom in holiday sales never materialized—actually, about 75 percent of stores in New York said it worked against them because of the differences between states—so he was going to shift back to the traditional date for 1942. Congress decided to make sure no further mischief was made, and the House passed a bill in October officially establishing Thanksgiving as a federal holiday for the first time, on the last Thursday of November. The Senate, however, amended the act to make it the *fourth* Thursday, as FDR had repositioned it. The fact that that amendment was passed two days after Pearl Harbor remains a bit of a head-scratcher.

Things remained stable until 1968 with the passage of the Monday Holiday Act, which formally established Columbus Day, and moved Memorial Day and Veteran's Day to Mondays along with Washington's Birthday (not President's Day—there is no such federal holiday), to create three-day weekends for federal employees; Veteran's Day reverted to the traditional November 11 in 1975. Martin Luther King Day was added, also on a Monday, in 1983. The government is careful to point out that "Federal holidays" are just that, for federal employees and the District of Columbia, and that states determine their own legal holidays.

OK, that's enough of that. Do yourself a favor, take a moment now to think of something or someone you're truly thankful for, and express that gratitude over a turkey sandwich, as I leave you with a few lines from 1939:

> Thirty days hath September,
> April, June, and November.
> All the rest have thirty-one
> Until we hear from Washington.

SOURCES

The American Presidency Project. Accessed October 30, 2015. http://www.presidency.ucsb.edu/
index.php.

Contrubis, John. *Executive Orders and Proclamations (No. 95-772 A)*. Congressional Research Service,
March 9, 1999. http://www.llsdc.org/assets/sourcebook/crs-exec-orders-procs.pdf.

Encyclopedia Britannica. "Thanksgiving Day." Last modified April 7, 2016. https://www.britannica
.com/topic/Thanksgiving-Day.

FDR Presidential Library and Museum. "Thanksgiving—in Roosevelt History." Accessed October 3,
2016. https://fdrlibrary.wordpress.com/tag/thanksgiving/.

———. "The Year We Had Two Thanksgivings." Accessed October 30, 2015. http://docs.fdrlibrary
.marist.edu/THANKSG.HTML.

MacPherson, Ryan C. "Our Thanksgiving Holiday in Historical Perspective." Accessed October 3,
2016. http://www.ryancmacpherson.com/hist-207/72-thanksgiving-in-historical-perspective
.html.

National Archives and Records Administration (NARA). "Congress Establishes Thanksgiving."
Accessed January 16, 2012. https://www.archives.gov/legislative/features/thanksgiving/.

New York Times. "Roosevelt to Move Thanksgiving; Retailers for It, Plymouth Is Not." August 15, 1939.

———. "Shift in Thanksgiving Date Arouses the Whole Country." August 16, 1939.

———. "Thanksgiving Goes Back to Old Date in '42; President Says Change Did Not Boom Trade."
May 21, 1942.

Newsweek. "Turkey Days: Whole United States Confused over Conflicting Thanksgivings."
(November 20, 1939).

Stathis, Stephen W. *Federal Holidays: Evolution and Application (No. 98-301 GOV)*. Congressional
Research Service, February 8, 1999. http://www.senate.gov/reference/resources/pdf/Federal
_Holidays.pdf.

31
"Letters of Transit"
fictional travel documents
invented for the play *Everybody Comes to Rick's* by Murray Burnett and Joan Alison
and incorporated into *Casablanca* by screenwriter Howard Koch
1942

Yes, *Casablanca*. It is nearly universally named as one of the greatest movies of all time: glamorous, star-crossed lovers, torn apart by the forces of war, thrown unexpectedly back together in a whirlwind of rekindled passion, jealousy, intrigue, and suspicion. The café, the piano, the champagne cocktails, the evening gowns and dinner jackets, the Nazis, the threats at every turn. Beautifully shot and lit, Ingrid Bergman's facial expressions alone as she enters Rick's for the first time or when Victor Laszlo strikes up La Marseillaise. Sigh.

Much as we all love this movie, though, there are parts that, frankly, don't make a great deal of sense. For example, why exactly is the runway wet in the climactic airport scene, when they're in the Moroccan desert? Not that anybody cares. And besides, these few problems don't amount to a hill of beans in this crazy mixed-up world, do they? One central error, though, three little words, conjures an idea so convincing and seductive that it forms the impetus and backbone for the entire story, and reinforces the ways in which words can support journeys of all kinds.

The quotation marks in the title here likely give it away. No, there are no such things as "letters of transit," though why let that get in the way of a good story? The idea of documents to facilitate travel goes back at least as far as Bible times; in the Old Testament, Nehemiah asks King Artaxerxes for permission to travel and is given a letter "to the governors beyond the river" requesting his safe passage. And 2,500 years later, the language in your passport is effectively the same thing, stated as a request to other countries to allow the bearer to pass "without delay or hindrance," though of course it is just that—a request, subject to the laws and occasional whims of whomever is on the other side of the river. It's a diplomatic nicety, part and parcel of a complex system of controlling the movement of people across, and occasionally within, borders.

For a long time, this was an informal, catch-as-catch-can system, not unlike Nehemiah. Nations were mostly kingdoms and domains, travel over great distances was uncommon and dangerous, and only the noteworthy needed to ask for permission. The King's License was required to enter or leave 11th-century England, though clause 50 of Magna Carta guaranteed the right to come and go in 1215. For several decades, individual American states issued passports, which must have caused occasional amusement around the world; it was only in 1856 that the State Department was given exclusive authority to issue American passports.

The entire worldwide passport system, somewhat surprisingly, fell into disuse in the latter half of the 19th century. The increasing volume and speed of travel, made possible by the development of railways, made the old system unworkable and untenable, and it was largely abandoned. Only the fear of espionage and the bonus opportunity to keep a closer eye on people brought it back during World War I, since which time it has remained firmly ensconced. The first international standards were established by a conference of the League of Nations in 1920, and photographs were added soon thereafter, replacing the somewhat comical practice of elaborate physical description for identification of the bearer.

The passport is proof of identity and citizenship (which is not, by the way, the same as nationality). It's one of a number of forms of travel documentation we now use, including the visa, an authorization to enter and stay for a given period of time and under certain circumstances. I've taught a couple of times in Canada and so was required to go through Immigration to get a work permit, which specified how long I could remain and what I could do. It was a curious experience standing in that line, as officials periodically came through looking for anyone who was requesting refugee status or asylum. There are specialized refugee travel documents, based on a 1951 international convention, which are issued by the state where a refugee is currently residing, allowing them to leave and return to that state. It looks like a passport but is marked "travel document" with two diagonal stripes on the upper left of the front cover.

Visas can be refused, for example, for people with a criminal record or disease, who are seen as a threat to national security, or who show no intent to return to where they came from. There are also specialized travel documents for stateless persons (people with no citizenship) as well as fake or fantasy ones; for a price, you too can have a passport from the World Government of World Citizens, for all the good it will do you. They cite Article 13(2) of the Universal Declaration of Human Rights: "Everyone has the right to leave any country, including his own, and to return to his country." True, though note that it says you have the right to leave and come back—but it doesn't say anybody else has to let you in, especially with a passport you bought on the Internet for a hundred bucks from a fake world government.

The closest genuine document to a "letter of transit" is probably a "laissez-passer," a safe conduct issued for one-way travel to the issuing country, sometimes for humanitarian reasons, but also to allow diplomats of newly enemy nations to leave after war is declared. But the actual letter of transit exists only in fiction, invented, seemingly quite casually, for the play and then adopted by Howard Koch in his mad scramble to concoct a coherent screenplay for *Casablanca*, writing pages nearly as fast as they could be filmed. As the Peter Lorre character says, these letters would get the bearers out of the country: "Cannot be rescinded, not even questioned." All well and good, but—he also says, in his exotic middle-European accent, that they're "signed by General de Gaulle." Why, we are left to wonder, would the occupying Germans or even the collaborationist Vichy government care in the slightest about papers signed by de Gaulle, who by late 1941 was in exile outside London? (The printed screenplay says he was supposed to say "Marshal Weygand," a Vichy official of the time, which I just don't hear, though trust me, there are staunch defenders who will tell you in no uncertain terms, that's what Lorre says.)

Documents of all kinds are interwoven into the fabric of the film. In the first line of spoken dialogue, the police dispatcher describes the murder of two German couriers carrying the letters of transit. The opening narration also highlights the importance of exit visas—which are uncommon but real, often used today by governments such as Saudi Arabia and Uzbekistan who fear emigration. In 1940s unoccupied France, exit visas were indeed difficult to acquire because nations such as Spain and especially Portugal were continually changing their requirements, opening and closing their borders, frustrating people who desperately wanted to flee to the promise of the New World. The first ten minutes of the film are filled with talk of exit visas, letters of transit, and the immortal "Can I see your papers?" leading to a man shot in the street rather than betray the Free France literature in his pocket.

The rest of the film is an increasingly intense search for those letters, against a backdrop of desperation; a line cut from the final version has a beautiful woman telling an older man, "It used to take a villa at Cannes, or the very least, a string of pearls. Now all I ask is an exit visa." We know, of course, that the letters are in Sam's piano as he plays "As Time Goes By," first for Ilsa and then for Rick, before they are ultimately used on that suspiciously rainy runway.

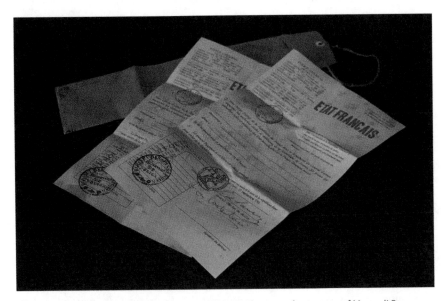

Image of *Casablanca* letters of transit (prop replica). Photograph courtesy of Magnoli Props (www.magnoliprops.com).

The play was written in 1940, the screenplay in 1942, and the film was released the following January, nominated for eight Academy Awards and winning for Best Picture, Director, and Adapted Screenplay. At that time, international travel had become difficult at best, dangerous or impossible or prohibited at worst, and which side of a shifting border you were on could be a life-or-death matter, so it's little wonder there's a fascination here with the idea of a magical document, a few words on the right paper that could mean escape, freedom, a new life.

Our first view of Rick is of his hand signing a credit note dated December 2, 1941, and the action takes place over the next 48 hours or so, just days before Pearl Harbor, in the last sliver of American innocence before the war comes. Now I think I understand why the movie is set then; after December 7, Rick will become a citizen of a belligerent country and his movements will be far more difficult.

So this is a story about words and movement: letters and visas, lies told and plans made on a tarmac, the end of regained love and the beginning of a beautiful friendship. Words written and spoken that help us to move, and that move us still.

SOURCES

Casablanca. Directed by Michael Curtiz. 1942. Burbank, CA: Warner Home Video, 1999.

Ebert, Roger. *Questions for the Movie Answer Man.* Kansas City, MO: Andrews McMeel Publishing, 1997.

Government of Canada. "History of Passports." Last modified April 10, 2014. http://www.cic.gc.ca/english/games/teachers-corner/history-passports.asp.

Koch, Howard, and Epstein, Julius J. *Casablanca; Script and Legend.* Woodstock, NY: Overlook Press, 1973.

Lloyd, Martin. *The Passport: The History of Man's Most Travelled Document.* Stroud, UK: Sutton, 2003.

Poznanski, Renée. *Jews in France during World War II.* Tauber Institute for the Study of European Jewry Series. Waltham, MA: Brandeis University Press in Association with the United States Holocaust Memorial Museum; University Press of New England, 2001.

Rick. "Everybody Comes to Rick's." *Rick on Theater* (blog), May 17, 2009. http://rickontheater.blogspot.com/2009/05/everybody-comes-to-ricks.html.

Sohn, Louis B., Thomas Buergenthal, and Joint Project on the Governing Rules of International Law. *The Movement of Persons across Borders.* Studies in Transnational Legal Policy; No. 23. Washington, DC: American Society of International Law, 1992.

United Nations. "Universal Declaration of Human Rights." Accessed October 14, 2016. http://www.un.org/en/universal-declaration-human-rights/.

World Government of World Citizens. "The World Passport." Accessed October 14, 2016. http://www.worldservice.org/docpass.html.

32
"We Can Do It!" Poster

a poster
designed by J. Howard Miller for Westinghouse Electric,
often mistakenly attributed as "Rosie the Riveter"

1943

When you think about World War II, lots of images come to mind, and it seems like most of them are in black and white: pictures of Roosevelt and Churchill or film of ships exploding at Pearl Harbor, the flag-raising at Iwo Jima, Nazi Party rallies, scrap drives and victory gardens, camps for concentration or internment, celebrating in Times Square on V-E Day, a mushroom cloud, the millions of dead and the ruins left behind by years of global warfare.

With the passing of the generations who lived and fought and died during that time, all we now have are the things they've left behind, many of which today evoke a sort of wistfulness about a nation united in a common purpose.

One image, however, blazing with color and energy, although intended to have the briefest of lives, has persisted, making its way through the cultural landscape of the last seven decades, its journey telling us as much about the world of its day as about our own, and almost never what it's been believed to be.

When we think today of the war years and particularly when we look at pictures or movies of the time, we do so with a sort of assured inevitability. We know how it all ended, that the villagers in *Mrs. Miniver* and the submariners in *Destination Tokyo* have more hardships to endure but they'll eventually win through in the end. That was by no means certain in early 1943, although the tide was just starting to turn in favor of the Allies after a very bad 1942.

The Casablanca Conference in January of '43 laid out the Allied philosophy and strategy, to seek nothing less than the unconditional surrender of the Axis. The gruesome Battle of Stalingrad was ending, the first land victory in

Asia came in Papua New Guinea, advances were being made in Guadalcanal and the Aleutians, and bombing was being intensified in Europe. But there is still a long, long way to go in the second half of February 1943.

During those two weeks, the Americans were engaged in back-and-forth combat with Rommel in Tunisia, the Russians were driven out of Kharkov in Ukraine, the Allies were bombing Sicily, and on the home front, Roosevelt warned the American people that victory is likely not just around the corner. A sampling of headlines from that period confirms they were jittery times: a move to consider raising the workweek from 48 to 52 hours, a delay in an Army plan to send troops to Arizona to pick cotton, an appeal from the governor of New York for people to volunteer to work on farms, and an article where a general described a wage dispute and three-hour work stoppage in two Boeing airplane factories as "treasonous."

To contemporary eyes, though, the most striking stories from that period deal with food rationing, which was about to ramp up, using a point system, starting on March 1. Ration books were being distributed in their millions, and a rush on canned goods was halted by a freeze on purchases a week beforehand. Under the new system, less than half the amount of food consumed in the previous year would be available in the civilian marketplace and extensive tables of point values were published to let people know what they were in for. A 15-ounce can of tomatoes was 13 points, peaches 11, applesauce or soup 8—and each individual was allotted 48 points a *month*. (Sauerkraut was only four points.)

It's against that backdrop that one of a series of posters designed by 24-year-old Pittsburgh artist J. Howard Miller, is put up in Westinghouse Electric company plants making helmet liners in Pennsylvania and the Midwest for only two weeks, from February 15th to the 28th; if you look carefully at an image of the original, you can see the posting dates in the lower-left corner.

The poster measures 17 x 22 inches, roughly four times the size of a sheet of letter-size paper, and was commissioned by Westinghouse's in-house War Production Coordinating Committee. Fewer than 1,800 copies were printed, and when the two weeks were up, so far as we can tell, she was taken down and largely forgotten.

Posters convey simple messages, with a dart-like sharpness and impact, and overall fall into a more general category known as ephemera—materials that are intended to be temporary, such as handbills, brochures, menus, and so on. When these things do last, they can often speak volumes about the life and times of the society that gave rise to them in ways that all the "official" sources and documents can't.

"We Can Do It!" poster, also known as Rosie the Riveter, created by the Office for Emergency Management, War Production Board. National Archives and Records Administration (NARA).

It's not clear who the woman in the poster is; there are at least a couple of claimants, including Geraldine Hoff, a Michigan teenager seen in a photograph working at a machine in a polka-dot headscarf, unaware of her possible fame until she saw the poster in a magazine article 40 years later. Some historians doubt it's her, as Miller typically used live models. What is certain is that she's a strong woman depicted in vibrant primary colors, a defiant look in her eye, rolling up her sleeves and ready for anything.

What's she not, though, is Rosie the Riveter. Rosie came to life in a 1942 hit song written by Redd Evans and John Jacob Loeb, containing lyrics like "Keeps a sharp lookout for sabotage / Sitting up there on the fuselage," and here again many potential inspirations for Rosie have emerged over the years. Then for the Memorial Day 1943 cover of the *Saturday Evening Post*, Norman Rockwell got into the act with a somewhat more zaftig Rosie, modeled by a Vermont telephone operator, munching on a sandwich, rivet gun in her lap, foot squarely on a copy of *Mein Kampf*, perhaps recreating the pose of the prophet Isaiah on the Sistine Chapel ceiling. This Rosie was much more famous in its day, donated to the government war bond effort, raffled off, sold and resold until fetching just under $5 million at auction from the daughter of the Wal-Mart founder and now residing in the Crystal Bridges Museum in Arkansas. Zealous copyright enforcement by the Rockwell estate means this image is considerably less well known today.

All the Rosies became a symbol and metaphor for the influx of women into the workforce, from 13 to 19 million between 1940 and '45, in large part to replace men who went into the military, and in many people's minds paving the way for their more widespread entry in the decades to come.

Evelyn T. Gray, riveter, and Pearlyne Smiley, bucker, completing a job on the center section of a bomber, photo c. 1942. National Archives and Records Administration (NARA).

Our poster, however, was not recruiting women to work; it was aimed squarely at those people already working, as part of a much larger strategy of propaganda, meant to mobilize a nation and link the military front to the home front, combining the techniques and power of art and advertising to enlarge people's views of their wartime responsibilities. Posters in runs of thousands or even millions, exhorting secrecy, thrift, and sacrifice, including buying war bonds, were commonplace in both public venues and the workplace. And those factories were no places of "Kumbaya" cooperation; the several years before Pearl Harbor were a time of considerable labor organization and unrest. The year 1941 alone saw 4,000 strikes involving two million workers, and an increase of 17 percent in union membership. In the face of war, to facilitate productivity, thousands of companies, including Westinghouse, encouraged by the federal War Production Board, formed labor-management committees, with largely minimal effect apart from bond drives and propaganda campaigns.

"We Can Do It" is fairly tame by comparison to many of these. (For the record, GM had a 1942 poster with the same slogan, showing two male arms symbolizing labor and management, with clenched fists and rolling sleeves, pointing downward.) The temperature was high enough that posters even frowned on long bathroom breaks; one said, "Killing time is killing men." Wow. Anything less than full commitment to work could mark someone as a potential traitor. So when our girl is saying "We can do it," she's not calling women to the factories—she's telling the people already there to stop looking at posters, work harder, and follow orders. What labor peace there was didn't last; 5,000 strikes occurred in 1946, involving over 10 percent of the work force.

It's not clear how this poster was rediscovered; it appeared in a 1982 *Washington Post Magazine* article and on the cover of *Smithsonian* magazine in 1994. Then there was a postage stamp in 1999, and the coffee mugs, and T-shirts, and bobble heads—the full treatment. It was adopted as an emblem (dare one say poster child?) of the feminist movement and of the rising presence and power of women in many areas of life, and at some point it became conflated with the Rosie the Riveter name and mythos of wartime unity and camaraderie. Even the logo for the Rosie the Riveter Trust, which supports the national park in California dedicated to the wartime home front, uses a stylized version of the poster image.

Actually, this might be less a "document that changed the world" than the other way around. She's not Rosie the Riveter, except now, she kinda is. Whoever the woman in the polka dot turban is, if anyone, as she rolls up her sleeve to get to work, she tells us her story—from industrial pacifier, to feminist touchstone, to home-front solidarity icon, to object of cultural nostalgia for a time that may not have ever been. She was never really any of these and yet is now somehow all of them. Never meant to survive, she has nonetheless endured, serially appropriated, serially evocative, showing us that how we see something is often at least as important as what's really there.

SOURCES

Bird, William L., and Rubenstein, Harry R. *Design for Victory: World War II Posters on the American Home Front*. New York: Princeton Architectural Press, 1998.

Doyle, Jack. "Rosie The Riveter, 1942–1945." *PopHistoryDig.com*. February 28, 2009. http://www.pophistorydig.com/topics/rosie-the- riveter-1941- 1945/.

Honey, Maureen. *Creating Rosie the Riveter: Class, Gender, and Propaganda during World War II*. Amherst: University of Massachusetts Press, 1984.

Kimble, James J., and Lester C. Olson. "Visual Rhetoric Representing Rosie the Riveter: Myth and Misconception in J. Howard Miller's 'We Can Do It!' Poster." *Rhetoric and Public Affairs* 9, no. 4 (2006): 533–69.

New York Times, February 15–28, 1943.

Rosie the Riveter Trust. "Home Page." Accessed October 2, 2016. http://www.rosietheriveter.org/.

Rupp, Leila J. *Mobilizing Women for War: German and American Propaganda, 1939–1945*. Princeton, NJ: Princeton University Press, 1978.

United States Bureau of the Census. *Statistical Abstract of the United States, 1947*. Washington, DC: US Government Printing Office,1947.

33

Joseph McCarthy's "List"

a purported list of names of Communists in the US State Department
probably described by Sen. Joseph McCarthy in a speech in Wheeling, West Virginia

1950

Has anybody seen my list? I'm a list maker, things to do, errands to run, groceries to buy, work to get through today. None of which guarantees that anything on said list will get accomplished, mind you, but there's comfort in the making and even more satisfaction in eventually crossing something off. I know I had it here a minute ago.

Lists are a tool for reminding, and for memorializing, ranking, or enumerating. It's also a way to categorize or group things or people; you're either on the list to get invited to the party, or you're not. Naturally, a list mostly helps if you can lay your hands on it; otherwise, what's the point? Although perhaps, not always. Maybe all that really matters is the idea of a list and how widely you wave it and how loud and often you yell about it. When the circumstances are right, what *isn't* there can be more formidable, and more believed, than what is.

No recording was made of Senator McCarthy's speech to about 275 people on the night of February 9 for Lincoln Day at the Ohio County Republican Women's Club in the Colonnade Room of the McClure Hotel, so reports differ on exactly what he said. At the time, he was very much under the radar and agreed to make five speeches that day to help pay his dues with the Republican Party, and apparently he didn't much care what he talked about since it wasn't going to get much attention anyway. It seemed he asked his congressional staff to put together a speech on housing, and turned to two reporters for a conservative Washington newspaper (one by mistake as a McCarthy staffer called George Waters instead of Jim Walters) to put together something on Communists in government. Did they ever. And furthered their own careers in the process; McCarthy hired Waters as his press secretary and his colleague Ed Nellor as his speechwriter, though he also stated later under oath that he wrote the speech himself.

So there was a prepared text, though at least some people said he spoke largely extemporaneously. News reports and personal accounts varied, but the version he later entered into the *Congressional Record* contained lines that have rung down the years: "In my opinion the State Department, which is one of the most important government departments, is thoroughly infested with Communists. I have in my hand fifty-seven cases of individuals who would appear to be either card carrying members or certainly loyal to the Communist Party, but who nevertheless are still helping to shape our foreign policy."

Well. First of all, that number. This version of the speech says 57, which he repeated in later interviews. It appears to have come from a 1947 report by staff of a Congressional subcommittee, who found 108 "incidents of inefficiencies"—but no Communists—in State Department loyalty files. Only 57 were still employed, of whom more than half had already been cleared by the FBI. Multiple reports from the speech, however, reported he actually said he had 205 names, which he later denied. That number sprouted from a 1946 letter from then Secretary of State James Francis Byrnes, replying to an inquiry about 4,000 or so employees who had been transferred to the State Department from other agencies. Of them, 285 had negative recommendations, 79 of whom had been "separated from the service," leaving 206, which mistakenly became 205. In later rants, the number bounced around between those, sometimes 81 for variety, and eventually 10 or maybe only 9 investigated by McCarthy's Senate committee.

Senator Joseph McCarthy standing at microphone with two other men, probably discussing the Senate Select Committee to Study Censure Charges (Watkins Committee) chaired by Senator Arthur V. Watkins. Library of Congress.

None of which mattered, since the seeds were sown, in ground that was made fertile by serious and possibly justified concerns about the growing influence and power of Communism on the world stage and perhaps at home as well. In early 1950, the Cold War was in full flower. The previous year saw the blockade of Berlin; the first Soviet atomic test; and the formation of East Germany, the People's Republic of China, and NATO. North Korean forces would invade the south later that June. McCarthy's speech came one day after the formation of the East German Stasi secret police and two days after the United States recognized anti-Communist governments in Vietnam, Laos, and Cambodia, the same week as the first Diner's Club payment and the publication of Kurt Vonnegut's first story.

McCarthy's activities were embraced by the far right, as well as what's been called a broader "coalition of the aggrieved"—people who were just unhappy, about the changing postwar world, about the UN, the ongoing programs from the New Deal, and for that matter water fluoridation, mental health programs, and even polio vaccinations, all of which could be, after all, Communist brainwashing or poisoning plots.

And for a while, this all worked. Hence, the blacklists—most infamously, perhaps, in the entertainment industry in the guise of *Red Channels*, published later in 1950 by a magazine called *Counterattack* and listing dozens of names of people with alleged, if in many cases very tenuous, Communist ties. Apparently, Gypsy Rose Lee spoke at a meeting of the Hollywood Anti-Nazi League and "entertained" at a dance of the New York Council of the Arts, Sciences and Professions. Being a stripper was OK, but these were beyond the pale, so off TV and radio she went. It was much more serious for many; one researcher has estimated several hundred people were imprisoned and perhaps 10,000 or more lost jobs, in some cases just for being subpoenaed by the House Un-American Activities Committee or pleading the Fifth.

This leads us to the $64,000 question. (The so-named TV game show, by the way, wouldn't premiere for another five years.) How did this happen? How could a little-known and less-regarded senator whip up all the frenzy he did with a list that likely didn't even exist? Let's start with Senator McCarthy's, shall we say, complicated relationship with the truth. A letter of commendation on his war record as a Marine corps tail gunner, purportedly signed by his commanding officer and Admiral Nimitz, turned out to have been written by McCarthy himself. His "war wound" came from a ceremony for sailors making their first crossing of the Equator, but in his Senate campaign, he went after the legendary sitting progressive senator Robert LaFollette Jr. for not enlisting and for war profiteering. The facts—that LaFollette was 46 on Pearl Harbor Day and that McCarthy himself made about as much in wartime investments—needn't have bothered anybody, right?

But again . . . why, and how? Why was he believed? Yes, there was a ready audience, and yes, an undercurrent of suspicion and fear of Communism was already at large; the House Un-American Activities Committee had been hard at work since 1938, with earlier investigations as far back as 1918. But still—and I can't emphasize this enough—*there was no list*. Or at least no actual list at the time of the speech or, in reality, in any meaningful way going forward.

This story, then, is of a document that never really was, which tells us that documents can have influence even when they don't exist. People invest "documents," or in this case pieces of paper (if there even was a piece of paper), that somebody says is a "document," with a number of properties. And if that somebody is a US senator, and if those people are ready to hear and to believe because they're more than a little scared already and looking for somebody to tell them what to do, all the better. "I have in my hand, a list" is potent stuff.

Documents, imaginary and real, get authority from circumstance and perception, as well as from what they really say and are. Their meaning and effect is grounded partly in their actual function, form, and content and partly in their social context. We, and our actions and reactions, do much of a document's work. And if McCarthy's list had been real, if that piece of paper had been a list of names and had survived and been preserved, it would have become an even more important document today—but less about potential Communist sympathizers in the State Department than a record of the event, of the time, and an object lesson about demagoguery and fear.

I'd be remiss if I didn't mention here that my own institution was subjected to a state legislative investigation/witch hunt, and dismissed three tenured faculty members in 1948, mostly for failing to cooperate. The firings of Herbert Phillips, Joe Butterworth, and Ralph Gundlach gave the University of Washington a black eye and eased the way for similar indignations elsewhere. It is a tender subject in some quarters to this day.

Of course, we're all smarter now, more experienced at critical thinking and separating truth from fiction. So it couldn't happen again. We've all learned from our mistakes, and know better than to trust any person, or organization, or government, that claims to have a list of bad people or bad ideas. If only.

It seems only fitting to give the last words to Edward R. Murrow, whose *See It Now* program in March 1954 dissected and furthered an already sliding opinion of McCarthy and his tactics. By November of that year, he'd be condemned by the Senate; that seemed to break him. By May 1957 he was dead, likely of alcoholism, aged 48. Murrow's broadcast ended thus: "The actions of the junior Senator from Wisconsin have caused alarm and dismay amongst our allies abroad, and given considerable comfort to our enemies. And whose fault is that? Not really his. He didn't create this situation of fear; he merely exploited it—and rather successfully. Cassius was right. 'The fault, dear Brutus, is not in our stars, but in ourselves.'"

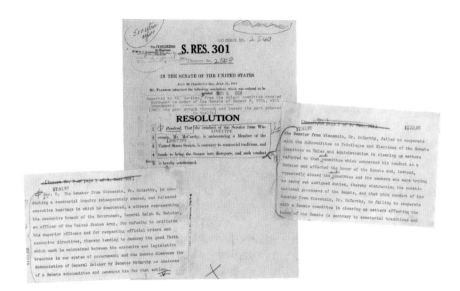

Senate Resolution 301: Censure of Senator Joseph McCarthy, December 2, 1954. National Archives and Records Administration (NARA).

SOURCES

American Business Consultants, and Counterattack. *Red Channels: The Report of Communist Influence in Radio and Television.* New York: American Business Consultants, 1950.

Fried, Albert. *McCarthyism: The Great American Red Scare: A Documentary History.* New York: Oxford University Press, 1997.

Herman, Arthur. *Joseph McCarthy: Reexamining the Life and Legacy of America's Most Hated Senator.* New York: Free Press, 2000.

Leviero, Anthony. "Final Vote Condemns McCarthy, 67–22, for Abusing Senate and Committee; Zwicker Count Eliminated in Debate." *New York Times,* December 3, 1954.

Reeves, Thomas C. *The Life and Times of Joe McCarthy: A Biography.* New York: Stein and Day, 1982.

Schrecker, Ellen. *The Age of McCarthyism: A Brief History with Documents.* Boston: Bedford Books of St. Martin's Press, 1994.

Wick, Nancy. "Seeing Red." *Columns* (December 1997). http://www.washington.edu/alumni/columns/dec97/red1.html.

Wikipedia. "Joseph McCarthy." Accessed June 20, 2014. http://en.wikipedia.org/w/index.php?title=Joseph_McCarthy&oldid=613344817.

———. "McCarthyism." Accessed June 19, 2014. http://en.wikipedia.org/w/index.php?title=McCarthyism&oldid=612963888.

34
Mental Disorder Diagnosis Manual

The *Diagnostic and Statistical Manual of Mental Disorders,*
better known as the DSM
published by the American Psychiatric Association

1952

"You've got to be crazy!" We all say things like that, usually in exasperation or disbelief. The word "crazy" entered English in the 16th century and originally meant cracked or flawed, like the crazing on the surface of pottery; it could also mean sickly or frail. It was another few years before it took on the connotation of "unsound mind" or "insane" or, of course, "nuts" (which originally meant "infatuated" in Britain; Americans made it mean "deranged").

No matter how that word is used, it's not in a clinical sense. It's a bit too colloquial for most professionals, I'm guessing, and anyway they have a far more sophisticated and extensive vocabulary and terminology to describe all our syndromes and conditions. That all started with a thin little spiral-bound volume, very technical and very dry, that has changed and grown several times and has fundamentally changed the way we think about, and talk about, our minds and selves.

1952 was a remarkable year: Elizabeth II takes the throne, the *Today* show premieres, the polio vaccine is introduced, Ralph Ellison publishes *Invisible Man.* You could make an argument that the publication of the DSM, and what came after it, is in that same league. Its roots go back over a century earlier, to the 1840 US Census, which was the first to try to determine the number of people who were "insane" or "idiotic." Controversy ensued when substantially larger proportions of blacks in free states were categorized that way, leading to claims that slavery was beneficial, and that the numbers were flawed.

From there, the process got more sophisticated, leading first to a manual for standardizing statistics for insane asylums in 1918. It reads as though it could just as easily be discussing hospital patients, prisoners, students, or even cars in a garage, down to suggestions for color coding cards for various record-keeping purposes and using black ink for men and red for women. Some of the 22 categories here sound familiar, like paranoia or psychosis; some don't, like "presbyophrenia," a chronic memory disorder; and many are things we now think of quite differently. The manual lists multiple sclerosis, epilepsy, and syphilis as "mental diseases" and includes some very peculiar language about racial categories. There's also the obligatory catch-all "undiagnosed psychoses" and number 22, "Not insane."

12

e. g., "1 yr." for 11 mos., 12½ mos., etc., and "1 mo." for 35 days, etc. Avoid "60 yrs." for 59 or 61 yrs.
  Avoid ambiguous abbreviations; as "lob. pneu." (lobar or lobular?), "par." (paranoic or paralytic?), etc., and use only standard abbreviations.
  If the place assigned to any caption of the schedule is too limited to enter all ascertained data, mark the blank "over", and enter the data on the back of the card.
  Entries on all cards should be typewritten. Designate items on the cards, by underscoring; as, single. Do not cross out items or use check marks.

CLASSIFICATION OF MENTAL DISEASES
Explanatory notes of the various groups and clinical types follow the classification.
1. **Traumatic psychoses**
    (a) Traumatic delirium
    (b) Traumatic constitution
    (c) Post-traumatic mental enfeeblement (dementia)
2. **Senile psychoses**
    (a) Simple deterioration
    (b) Presbyophrenic type
    (c) Delirious and confused types
    (d) Depressed and agitated states in addition to de-
        terioration
    (e) Paranoid types
    (f) Pre-senile types
3. **Psychoses with cerebral arteriosclerosis**
4. **General paralysis**
5. **Psychoses with cerebral syphilis**
6. **Psychoses with Huntington's chorea**
7. **Psychoses with brain tumor**
8. **Psychoses with other brain or nervous diseases**
The following are the more frequent affections and should be specified in the diagnosis.
    Cerebral embolism
    Paralysis agitans
    Meningitis, tubercular or other forms (to be specified)
    Multiple sclerosis
    Tabes
    Acute chorea
    Other conditions (to be specified)

Page 12 of the 1918 edition of the *Statistical Manual for the Use of Institutions for the Insane*, showing the classification of mental diseases. University of Michigan via HathiTrust (accessed at https://babel.hathitrust.org/cgi/pt?id=mdp.39015069449968).

During and following World War II, the War Department got into the act with the somewhat sinister-sounding "Medical 203," a technical bulletin that really first attempted to seriously tackle diagnostic nomenclature and treatment options and, in the process, help to build up psychiatry as a profession to be taken more seriously. In its few pages, it lays out a number of "psychiatric disorders and reactions" that involve personality, character and behavior, affect, and psychoses, and combat exhaustion is included. All of this is an important contribution, as this is also among the earliest portrayals of mental disorder as the result of external stimuli rather than being just inherent.

Then the fun begins. Other attempts, including international ones, were undertaken, and in the early 1950s the American Psychiatric Association merged several of them, with Medical 203 at the center, in the publication of the *Diagnostic and Statistical Manual of Mental Disorders* (DSM-I) in 1952. In its 130 pages or so, we find just over a hundred diagnoses with explanatory material, code numbers, and standard forms, all very official and impressive. (Though the copy I've got is printed badly in places, with pages obviously not from clean rolls of paper.)

The manual has since been revised several times. The second was done quietly and became known as DSM-II. Apparently nobody liked it, although it was the first specifically to include discussion of children. Subsequent versions were published increasingly publicly and loudly, each one largely repudiating the bases of the previous one, all emerging from a complex stew of forces—scientific, economic, social and cultural, political—that act on it.

Some documents are comparatively simple—Lincoln writes and edits the Gettysburg Address and reads it. Others are tortuously complex; the DSM-5 took 14 years to work through, and there's still great unhappiness about it. Lots of controversies, about distinctions made too fine and not fine enough, reliance on symptoms rather than causes, cultural bias, financial conflicts of interest with the pharmaceutical industry, and of course the big one: What exactly is a mental disorder? One source laying out a research agenda for the newest version confides that "[t]he most contentious issue is whether *disease*, *illness*, and *disorder* are scientific biomedical terms or are sociopolitical terms that necessarily involve a value judgment."

Many stories can be found regarding the controversies around revisions. In DSM-5, approved in 2012, Asperger's syndrome was dropped as a separate category and posttraumatic stress disorder has substantially changed, both of which have agitated lots of people. The classic story, though, is homosexuality, which somehow slipped into DSM-II (code 302.0) as one of several otherwise undefined "sexual deviations" along with pedophilia, transvestism, and voyeurism, nestled snugly between "inadequate personality" and "alcoholism" in the nonpsychotic mental disorders. Many years of struggle, activism, and debate led it to be dropped in the third edition, which meant, in effect, that homosexuality was a mental disorder for a few years and then it wasn't, because that's what the book said.

The DSM, like many systems, creates its own reality. I'm not saying that mental illness isn't real, far from it, but this manual prescribes, literally, a way of thinking about, classifying, and discussing it, with all the ramifications and consequences that follow, intended and otherwise. Its definitions effectively create the disorders: no definition, no disorder, no diagnosis, no treatment, no insurance. And it makes a few million dollars a year for the APA in the process, not to mention the whole secondary structure of training programs, guidebooks, software, and so on, to help people use the thing correctly.

It's telling that the DSM's roots go back to the census and record-keeping. Those early efforts were more about "how many" than "what." But then you eventually get to "what" because once you start counting, you want to make the counting better and more precise. Statistics beget analysis, which begets more statistics, and so on; witness for example the recent proliferation of ever more exotic sports statistics in an era of analytics. Once you have the data, the analysis techniques can be oh so tempting. The diagnostic component here is not so much an afterthought as a largely inevitable consequence.

John William Waterhouse's 1903 painting *Echo and Narcissus*. Walker Art Gallery, Liverpool, via Wikimedia Commons (accessed at https://commons.wikimedia.org/wiki/File:John_William_Waterhouse_-_Echo_and_Narcissus_-_Google_Art_Project.jpg).

A diagnosis, especially in this realm, can be comforting, even empowering, as well as lead to treatment and therapeutic regimes. Having a name for something, knowing that you're not just . . . crazy . . . can be a huge relief. Of course, the opposite is true, as well; there is the potential for stigmatization in the way you're perceived by others or yourself, or even treatment for the "wrong" thing.

So, names have power, at least the power we give them. If it feels like everybody's got a syndrome these days, there might be a reason for that. From those 22 categories in 1918, the DSM-5 now has 20 *chapters*, the rate of mental disorder diagnoses continues to rise, and many of these have entered the popular lexicon: How often do you hear *bipolar, narcissism, OCD,* and *ADHD* thrown around casually? More names, more sophisticated names, more use of those names, more power, and on and on.

As I was researching the DSM, I remembered a quote from one of the 20th century's great philosophers, Douglas Adams, who said in the *Hitchhiker's Guide to the Galaxy* that the best way not to be unhappy is not to have a word for it. Food for thought in an ever-more-diagnosed and diagnosing world.

SOURCES

American Psychiatric Association. "Timeline." DSM-5 Development. Accessed August 7, 2013. http://www.dsm5.org/about/Pages/Timeline.aspx.

American Psychiatric Association Committee on Nomenclature Statistics. *Diagnostic and Statistical Manual: Mental Disorders.* 1st ed. Washington, DC: American Psychiatric Assn., Mental Hospital Service, 1952.

American Psychiatric Association and National Committee for Mental Hygiene. Bureau of Statistics. *Statistical Manual for the Use of Institutions for the Insane.* New York: National Committee for Mental Hygiene, 1918.

Clegg, Joshua W. "Teaching about Mental Health and Illness through the History of the DSM." *History of Psychology* 15, no. 4 (November 2012): 364–70.

Grob, Gerald N. "Origins of DSM-I: A Study in Appearance and Reality." *American Journal of Psychiatry* 148, no. 4 (May 1991): 421–31.

Houts, Arthur C. "Fifty Years of Psychiatric Nomenclature: Reflections on the 1943 War Department Technical Bulletin, Medical 203." *Journal of Clinical Psychology* 56, no. 7 (June 9, 2000): 935–67.

Kupfer, David J., Michael B. First, and Darrel A. Regier. *A Research Agenda for DSM-V.* Washington, DC: American Psychiatric Association, 2002.

Kutchins, Herb, and Stuart A. Kirk. *Making Us Crazy: DSM: The Psychiatric Bible and the Creation of Mental Disorders.* London: Constable, 1999.

Litwack, Leon F. "The Federal Government and the Free Negro, 1790–1860." *Journal of Negro History* 43, no. 4 (October 1958): 261. doi:10.2307/2716144.

Office of the Surgeon General, Army Service Forces. "Nomenclature of Psychiatric Disorders and Reactions." War Department Technical Bulletin, Medical 203. 1946. *Journal of Clinical Psychology* 56, no. 7 (June 9, 2000): 925–34.

35
Airplane "Black Box"
a prototype flight data recorder
developed by David Warren of the Aeronautical Research Laboratory
in Melbourne, Australia
1958

Somehow, I'm not surprised that there's a name for words that have two contradictory meanings. There are several, for that matter, to describe words like "cleave," which can mean to separate or to cling together, "oversight," to look for a mistake or to miss one, or "sanction," to condone or to punish. These are sometimes called auto-antonyms or self-antonyms; contranyms; or my favorite, antagonyms. These must be a nightmare for learners of English; think about the two meanings of "inflammable," which can either mean something that won't burn or something that will, which is about as contranymy as you can get.

Now imagine a document, itself intended to be inflammable, that embodies contradictions of its own: an aftereffect of tragedy meant to help understand and to prevent further ones, and something you very much want to be there, constantly doing its job, and which nobody ever wants to be needed or read.

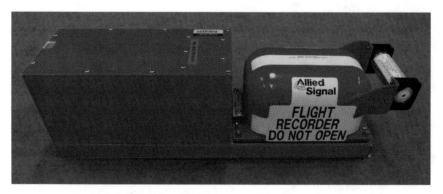

An example of a flight recorder. Australian Transport Safety Bureau.

As with other important innovations, there's no clear, single inventor of what we now know as the flight data recorder. Several simultaneous and separate streams of work were going on as far back as the late 1930s in France and continuing throughout World War II, including the "Mata Hari," used in test flights in Finland in 1942. Charles Lindbergh used a device to track and record altitude on a rotating spool for his 1927 transatlantic flight. Many sources, however, point to the seminal work of David Warren, a chemist working on fuel combustion, who, while sitting in a meeting discussing potential explanations for the crash of an early jet called the Comet, let his mind wander toward an early wire recorder he'd seen and how valuable that might be as a means for logging sounds and voices in cockpits. Warren, whose father died in an air crash in 1934, appears to have written about the idea in 1954. There then followed a long and onerous odyssey, beset with indifference and bureaucracy (including being referred to as a solution looking for a problem), strongly flavored with gumption and stick-to-it-iveness, that yielded a prototype system in 1958. It incorporated many elements that are now familiar: ways of recording both voices and data about the flight in a housing meant to survive the extreme circumstances of an airplane crash and explosion. Warren later recounted a moment of breakthrough when, unbeknownst to him, the secretary of the UK's Air Registration Board was brought to his office by the head of the laboratory and said, in a line straight from a B movie, "I say, old chap, that's a damn good idea. Put that lad on the next Courier and we'll show them in London." And off he went.

There's also no single explanation for why flight recorders are often called black boxes: perhaps because early ones needed to be black to prevent exposure of photographic film used inside as a recording medium, or perhaps because when recovered they were so often charred and burned black. In any event, they're now bright orange, and labeled FLIGHT RECORDER DO NOT OPEN in English and French.

Most people hear, and think, about flight recorders only after a crash, and they're usually put in the back of the plane since, as somebody once said, planes rarely back into mountains. The data can also, though, be downloaded for ongoing monitoring purposes, to check on fuel usage, for example. Not long after Warren's prototype was constructed, a 1960 crash inquiry led to Australia being the first country to mandate their use, in 1963; the United States followed a year later. They're now commonplace in cars, ships, and trains as well.

Flight recorders today use solid-state memory, replacing prior systems that used magnetic tape, and are able to store 2 hours of audio data (the last 2 hours, constantly overwriting) and 25 hours of flight data. US federal regulations require 88 parameters to be recorded, though the Boeing 787 can record nearly 150,000, requiring sophisticated analysis software. Time, altitude, airspeed, acceleration, heading, positions of controls, fuel flow, and more are constantly being recorded in a device that is tested to survive 3,400 Gs, 5,000 pounds per square inch of pressure, 2,000°F for an hour, submersion in salt water for 30 days, and having a 500-pound weight with a quarter-inch spike dropped on it from ten feet. If it makes contact with water, an underwater locator beacon is activated, inaudible to humans, pulsing at 37.5 KHz once a second for about a month until it loses power. Data is retrieved via means familiar to many of us: a USB or Ethernet port.

No matter how durable they're designed to be, they don't always survive and they're not always found. A number of recorders are still unrecovered, going as far back as a United Airlines plane that crashed in Lake Michigan in 250 feet of water in 1965. There are others presumed to be in the Persian Gulf or the Andaman Sea or 16,000 feet deep in the Indian Ocean—from a 1987 South African Airways crash near Mauritius. Sometimes they get found long after the fact: It took 31 years, but two men found the remains of the cockpit voice recorder from Eastern Airlines flight 980, which crashed in the Andes near La Paz, Bolivia, in 1985. Only one device survived from any of the hijacked planes on 9/11: the cockpit voice recorder from United Flight 93, which crashed in Pennsylvania. Most famous as this is being written is the still-missing Malaysian Airlines flight 370, likely somewhere in the vast expanses of the southern Indian Ocean, waiting to deliver its secrets.

When one is found, the National Transportation Safety Board has a highly structured 12-page protocol for its recovery, encompassing many procedures and safeguards about custody, authority, preservation, and especially the flow of information about the data itself and its interpretation—to whom, how, and when, in minute, even picayune detail, perhaps betraying an overly sensitive and bureaucratic mind-set or the product of unfortunate experience, or both. One learns here to pack it in bubble wrap and seal it inside a plastic beverage container; if it's in water, keep it in water, and ship it via commercial airliner. (No comment.) Data briefings must be done over landlines and not cell phones, premature release of information is grounds for disciplinary action, and foreign investigations with NTSB help are exempt from Freedom of Information Act requests for two years.

As a documentary form, flight recorders bear strong similarities to a couple of familiar parallels: the ship's log, historically meant to record the distance and time traveled and other important milestones of a maritime journey, and, weirdly, the eight-track tape cartridge of the 1960s and '70s, which was a single

Navy Lieutenant Jason S. Hall (right) watches as FBI Agent Duback tags the cockpit voice recorder from EgyptAir Flight 990 on the deck of the USS *Grapple* on November 13, 1999. The flight crashed into the Atlantic Ocean on October 31, 1999. US Department of Defense photo by Isaac D. Merriman, US Navy (accessed at http://archive.defense.gov/photos/newsphoto. aspx?newsphotoid=2575).

eternal loop of magnetic tape that could play, say, Jethro Tull's album *Aqualung* over and over, incessantly, until your roommate finally turned it off. But I digress.

The whole black box idea betrays a static mind-set: plane takes off, things happen, they get recorded, and, if something really bad happens, find box and examine data. Today, that's not the only way it could go. Much if not all of this data could be streamed and collected in real time; one computer scientist has proposed metaphorical "glass boxes" to highlight the transparency, ubiquity, and invulnerability they would provide. Opposition to this idea has come from a source that has dogged the flight recording process from the get-go, namely pilots. The Australian pilots' union was cautious about the very first systems, fearing Big Brother-like surveillance of their actions; similar objections have been raised about introducing cockpit cameras.

Warren and his colleagues named their invention the "Flight Memory," and though generally credited with most of the important ideas and innovations we now know, they were never able to patent them or realize much monetary benefit from them. An English-made device based on their design survived a 1965 crash in London, which must have been vindication of a sort. Warren went back to his laboratory until his retirement in 1985; when he died in 2010, somebody thoughtfully attached a whimsical label to his coffin: FLIGHT DATA RECORDER INVENTOR: DO NOT OPEN.

Let me point out one final contradiction here—and that's the name "black box." Another contranym. There are other uses of that phrase: a plain, blank theater space, a serious warning on a pharmaceutical label, a nickname for the president's "nuclear football," and even a mutant in the Marvel Comics universe who can telepathically extract information from any electronic device. Often, however, a "black box" is something opaque and impenetrable, a process or system of unknown operation that just works, sort of in the "don't ask any questions and nobody gets hurt" kind of way. Here it's just the opposite, a device nobody wants to be opened, but when it is, it's meant to reveal, to provide answers. The vast majority of them are never really used for their full purpose, but when one is, everybody knows.

SOURCES

Bonsor, Kevin, and Nathan Chandler. "How Black Boxes Work." *HowStuffWorks*, June 13, 2001. Accessed April 23, 2014. http://science.howstuffworks.com/transport/flight/modern/black -box.htm.

Crotty, David. "ARL Flight Memory Recorder" *Museum Victoria Collections*. Last modified 2010. Accessed April 23, 2014. http://collections.museumvictoria.com.au/articles/3720.

Encyclopedia Britannica. "Flight Recorder: Recording Instrument." Accessed April 23, 2014. https://www.britannica.com/technology/flight-recorder.

Executive Order 13228 of October 8, 2001, Establishing the Office of Homeland Security and the Homeland Security Council. Code of Federal Regulations, title 3 (2001): 796–802. http://www .gpo.gov/fdsys/pkg/CFR-2002-title3-vol1/pdf/CFR-2002-title3-vol1-eo13228.pdf.

Kavi, Krishna M. "Beyond the Black Box." *IEEE Spectrum*. Published June 30, 2010. Accessed April 23, 2014. http://spectrum.ieee.org/aerospace/aviation/beyond-the-black-box.

National Archives and Records Administration's Office of the Federal Register (OFR) and Government Publishing Office. Flight Data Recorders: Filtered Data. 14 CFR §121.346 (2010). http://www .ecfr.gov/cgi-bin/text-idx?SID=1048d68c0a677298828a48b3d04fcbfb&mc=true&node=se14 .3.121_1346&rgn=div8.

National Commission on Terrorist Attacks upon the United States. *The 9/11 Commission Report: Final Report of the National Commission on Terrorist Attacks upon the United States: Official Government Edition*. Official Government ed. Washington, DC: US Government Printing Office, 2004.

National Transportation Safety Board, Vehicle Recorder Division. *Flight Data Recorder Handbook for Aviation Accident Investigations*. Accessed October 31, 2016. http://www.ntsb.gov/investiga tions/process/Documents/FDR_Handbook.pdf.

Sear, Jeremy. "The ARL 'Black Box' Flight Recorder—Invention and Memory." Bachelor's thesis, Department of History, The University of Melbourne, Australia, 2001. Accessed October 31, 2016. http://kenblackbox.com/documents/The_ARL_Black_Box_Flight_Recorder.pdf.

Webb, Sam. "Mystery of Andes Plane Crash That Killed 29 May Finally Be Solved—Thanks to Two Ordinary Guys." *Daily Mirror* (London). June 5, 2016. http://www.mirror.co.uk/news/world-news/mystery-andes-plane-crash-killed-8117278.

Wikipedia. "David Warren (inventor)." Accessed April 21, 2014. http://en.wikipedia.org/w/index.php?title=David_Warren_(inventor)&oldid=604833514.

———. "Flight recorder." Accessed April 23, 2014. http://en.wikipedia.org/w/index.php?title=Flight_recorder&oldid=604984665.

———. "List of Unrecovered Flight Recorders." Accessed April 15, 2014. https://en.wikipedia.org/w/index.php?title=List_of_unrecovered_flight_recorders&oldid=603527998.

36
Space Needle "Sketch"
**a purported sketch of a structure that would
eventually become the Space Needle**
created by Edward Carlson, perhaps in Stuttgart, Germany
current location unknown, perhaps lost

1959

It's so frustrating when you get that great idea, but you're just not in the right place for it. You know the drill: you're driving in the car, or taking a walk, or in the shower, or in a bar, and it strikes—the answer to world peace or the next great hit song or just the right words to finally break off that problematic relationship. But how to get it down? You desperately reach for whatever's handy, furiously scribble something down, and then you can relax, secure in the knowledge that your deathless prose or monumental design is now safe and preserved for the ages.

Lots of ideas get no further than that. In the cold light of day, once the mojito has worn off or the steam from the shower has subsided, inspiration can often dissipate too. Now and then, though, a great idea, no matter how modest its beginnings, can survive and endure and even point the way to the future.

The Space Needle. iStock.

202

I'm giving away a little bit with the word "purported," but not everything; there's more to this story, and the story of this story, than just that. The Space Needle is about as iconic as it gets for Seattle; every conference and meeting in the city has the Needle somehow worked in as part of its logo; it's become what the Golden Gate Bridge is for San Francisco, the Gateway Arch is for St. Louis, or palm trees and starving screenwriters are for Los Angeles. It forms the backdrop, the spine if you will, for *Sleepless in Seattle*, taking the place of the Empire State Building in relocating *An Affair to Remember*, and it featured prominently for many years viewed from the elegant high-rise window in *Frasier*, even if there's no place in town you could actually get that view from that angle.

It doesn't take long living in Seattle before the story is heard. How Edward Carlson, universally known as Eddie, civic leader, self-made man, president of Western Hotels and chairman of the 1962 World's Fair Commission, travels to Europe in 1959, perhaps with friends picking up a car in Stuttgart. A local there tells him if he only has one night in town that he must eat in the TV tower that offers a spectacular view of the countryside. He's struck by the idea of it, a restaurant in the sky . . . and here is where the story starts to diverge. At breakfast the next morning, on a placemat, he doodles a picture of a spire with a flying saucer at the top; at least this is the story he tells in his memoir and that is recounted in the official history of the fair. Or at a souvenir stand he picks up a postcard of the tower, scribbles a drawing on the other side, and sends it back to Seattle. Or he brings the postcard back with him. Or, as Carlson himself recounted in a 1981 interview, it's on a napkin, a story that gains ground after a television interview a few years later in which he helpfully redrew it; and that recreated image is apparently the one most often found in histories of the event. But, no matter how detailed or colorful or entertaining the story, no such original drawing has surfaced.

The fact that there isn't a definitive version of this, that no museum or family member claims the "official" original sketch, doesn't seem to bother anybody. Yet the stories persist, largely because it feels like there ought to have been something of that sort. There's always a starting point for an idea or innovation, and the cocktail napkin is a common and convenient trope, shorthand for the haphazard beginning of the creative process. The bolt from the blue, offhand, momentary happenstance, when one reaches out to grab whatever's at hand.

Image of the Space Needle sketch, re-created by Edward Carlson in 1987.
Space Needle LLC.

Stories are also told, as true today as they ever were, of other great notions that started unpretentiously. In 1957, Richard Berry hears a song he likes, goes to the men's room to grab, um, what's available and writes the lyrics to "Louie, Louie." Francis Scott Key, temporarily held by the British during the 1814 bombardment of Fort McHenry, composes the lyrics to what would become the Star-Spangled Banner on the only paper he has, the back of a letter (see chapter 11). On his way to commemorate the Battle of Gettysburg, Abraham Lincoln makes a few notes on the back of an envelope. And the perfectly aptly named Arthur Laffer, out for drinks with Donald Rumsfeld of an evening in 1974, draws a simple graph on, yes, a cocktail napkin under his wine glass, and the Laffer Curve, and trickle-down economics, is unleashed on an unsuspecting world.

Why do we sketch, or jot, or dash off ideas? (And why are so many of those words so short?) To have a record, or more precisely to have something to record our ideas on, to give them tangible form, to have something to show, demonstrate, or remember. This protects the idea, including legally, as intellectual property; you can't copyright an idea, but you can when it's on a placemat, and there are more than a few people who claim their share of credit for the Needle's ultimate design. Doing that on the proverbial cocktail napkin adds to the mystique—the grand idea emerging from humble beginnings. Recording it also freezes it, gives it form and boundaries and, often, a sense of incompleteness, when you can't quite get it right—also a frequent companion in the creative process.

You could also, for that matter, think of the Needle itself as a document—a record of the aspirations and desires of that time and of the process by which the people who imagined and carried out the World's Fair did what they did. Furthermore, it's part of Seattle's expression of itself, the kind of mid-century Jet Set image that set the pattern for how the city and the region saw itself and came to be known. The theme of that fair was Century 21, and its proto-space-age outlook inspired many, not least the design team of *The Jetsons*, who took the Needle as inspiration for their sky-high apartment buildings.

And then there's the story of the story. This is how myths, in the colloquial sense, get started; some simple act or sketch that, over the decades, becomes layered over with gauzy half-memory. Lincoln didn't write the Gettysburg Address on an envelope; several drafts have been found, including one on official stationery. But it makes a terrific story, the great man drafting a few scattered notes to deliver one of the greatest, most eloquent statements in the English language. Which he no doubt did, just not quite that way.

So this is, perhaps, the story of the story of a document that never existed, or more likely one that's lost. At some point, though, there had to be something. No project that complex and involved could even remotely begin, let alone be completed, without plans and records and documents of all kinds, from drawings to budgets to schedules. The urge to "get it down," to begin and to foster the process of creation by somehow recording your ideas, endures, whether that's on a cocktail napkin or a whiteboard or an iPad.

Digital scribblings have their attractive qualities, too; they're much easier to share and perhaps to manipulate and collaborate around, if less romantic. Given the modern proliferation and proximity to mobile information devices, the likelihood of being without a handy way to record the next great idea is pretty low; one wonders what the tablet version of a cocktail napkin would be. Actually, one doesn't have to wonder; among the wide variety of sketching and doodling apps there are several that use the napkin as a metaphor, proving once again that a good idea is a good idea, regardless of the medium.

SOURCES

Berger, Knute. *Space Needle: The Spirit of Seattle*. Seattle, WA: Documentary Media, 2012.

Cameron, Richard, Harold Mansfield, Cameron Film Productions, and Space Needle Corporation. *The Space Needle Story: A 1962 Chronicle of the Construction of Seattle's Landmark*. Seattle, WA: Space Needle, 2006.

Hill, John Gordon, and KCTS. *When Seattle Invented the Future: The 1962 World's Fair*. Seattle: KCTS9, 2012.

Mansfield, Harold. *The Space Needle Story*. Mercer Island, WA: Writing Works, 1976.

Morgan, Murray. *Century 21: The Story of the Seattle World's Fair, 1962*. Seattle: Acme Press; Distributed by University of Washington Press, 1963.

37
Obama Birth Certificate
a Certificate of Live Birth in the name of Barack Hussein Obama II
issued by the State of Hawaii Department of Health
1961

Everybody's got them—that set of papers that record things we've done, like diplomas or awards; things we're allowed to do by licenses; or that mark milestones in our lives, such as marriage certificates. These are among the sorts of things you keep, and keep safe, some for sentimental purposes, others because they might be needed someday.

But they're not, by and large, things anybody generally looks at either frequently or very closely. Maybe your driver's license gets a once-over now and then at a traffic stop or a bar; border agents seem to have more intrusive ways of poring over passports. Maybe you swap looks at office ID cards for fun. But who ever looks really hard at, say, your birth certificate? If I hadn't been writing this book, I wouldn't have looked at mine in years, and yet I'm still me, so far as I know.

There are circumstances, of course, when otherwise unexamined documents get scrutinized much more closely—like checking a college transcript when being hired for a new job, for example. Once in a great while, though, typically when the potential stakes are very high, that scrutiny can be very public, very uncomfortable, and not always completely conclusive.

Births have been recorded for a very long time, back into ancient times, often for taxation and military service purposes. English church registers give us rudimentary records back to the 16th century, and the colonies of Virginia and Massachusetts were establishing record-keeping requirements and guidelines as early as the 1630s. Beyond the bare facts of names, dates, and places of births, information was also gathered about parents, and then increasingly on demographic and health-related matters.

A birth certificate is what it says, a certification of the circumstances of the birth of a baby. (Many certificates, as does the Obama one, specify "live birth," to distinguish it from a fetal death certificate.) This one has the sorts of details you'd expect to find, especially in that era: baby's name; date, time and place of birth; parents' names, occupations, and races; signature of the attending physician; and so on. The 2003 US Standard Certificate of Live Birth is two dense pages with lots of check boxes about the circumstances of birth and also the education and race of the parents, many questions about prenatal care, and greatly detailed questions about medical information for the mother and child and the nature of the delivery.

It's one of the most personal documents we have, actually the first one we get (if you don't count fetal sonograms, I suppose). It's the only one that follows us through our entire life, cradle to grave, when it's inevitably joined by a death certificate. It allows people to prove parentage, inheritance rights, and citizenship and to apply for a driver's license, register to vote, obtain a passport, and receive Social Security. It's the initial link in a chain of documents that establish our identity and status; without that chain, in important legal and societal ways, you don't exist, and hence the origin of the term "undocumented." It's not just a good and helpful idea—it's essential to establishing a way of life and legal persona, and moreover a requirement of the international Convention on the Rights of the Child, ratified by 191 countries and in force since 1990, which states that all children have the right to a name, to acquire a nationality, and to preserve their identity, even though it's been estimated that two-fifths of all children are still not registered at birth.

It also has to be right. Instructions for filling out birth certificates stress the importance of care; if "Billy" is entered, then "Billy" is your name, not "William," and it takes legal action to change that, or for that matter to change the gender listed. Misspellings also may lead to misfiling, which can render a document unfindable. A 1967 handbook from the US government gives several pages of detailed guidelines and standards: Use a good typewriter ribbon, don't erase, complete every item, don't abbreviate. For children conceived or born out of wedlock, make no entry for the father's name. And if the child is born on a moving conveyance, register them as if the birth occurred in the place where they were first removed from the conveyance. Much of this is to assist the compilation of vital statistics, which are of great use to demographers, planners, researchers, public health officials, and the like. Like any form, it's also meant to ensure the certificate's accuracy, quality, consistency, and reliability, making life easier for people who have to work with them down the line.

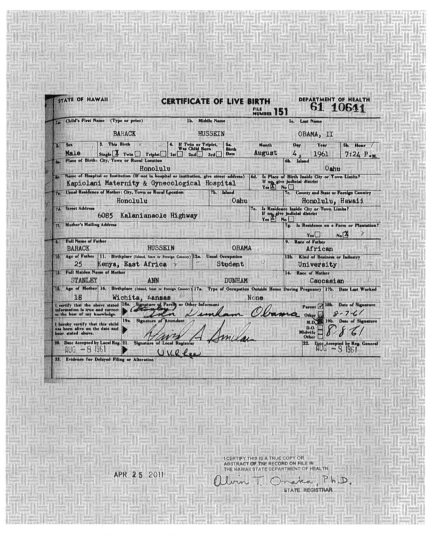

The birth certificate of President Barack Obama. Whitehouse.gov.

Though states and, eventually, the federal government (first the Census Bureau and now the National Center for Health Statistics) began to systematically collect vital statistics, registration is and has always been a local phenomenon and activity, and what "standards" there are have not always been universally or systematically applied. A 1988 report from the Inspector General of the US Department of Health and Human Services estimated that there were some 10,000 valid certificate forms, official seals, and signatures, making the detection of fraudulent, counterfeit, or imposter certificates "extremely difficult." Moreover, "such certificates can then be used as 'breeder' documents to obtain driver's licenses, passports, Social Security cards or other documents with which to create a false identity," costing society billions of dollars annually.

The 9/11 Commission also recommended federal standards for identity documents, and the 2004 Intelligence Reform and Terrorism Prevention Act mandated minimum standards for birth certificates, including safety paper or other security measures to prevent tampering, counterfeiting, or duplication. Congress stopped short of requiring a single national design or form, though it did impose some vague controls on getting a copy of somebody else's. That's understandable, though it might unintentionally complicate the work of future genealogists and historians.

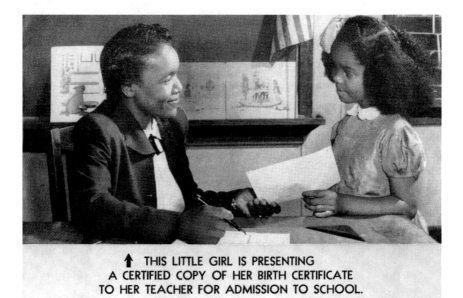

↑ THIS LITTLE GIRL IS PRESENTING
A CERTIFIED COPY OF HER BIRTH CERTIFICATE
TO HER TEACHER FOR ADMISSION TO SCHOOL.

A page from *A Birth Certificate for Baby,* published in 1948 by the US Public Health Service. University of Washington Libraries.

To be clear, I'm not a lawyer or forensic expert, so I have no way of independently knowing whether the image on my computer screen, from the state of Hawaii's website, represents an authentic birth certificate for Barack Obama or not. Which is more or less the point. Over the years and years of questions, discussion, debate, and supporting evidence about it, knowledgeable people, including the relevant state officials, have consistently affirmed its authenticity. And yet, still not everybody's convinced; polls have routinely shown that 20–30 percent of Americans think it's a fake—bearing in mind, however, that 79 percent also think that the government is keeping UFO secrets from us. There are also, seriously, people who will lay out for you, in great detail, the ways in which the PDF version is faked, and of course the long-reputed phony "Kenyan" birth certificate in Obama's name, which is really a modification of a 1959 South Australian certificate grabbed off the Internet belonging to one David Bomford. And so it goes.

For any such "official" document, the intention is to *document* something, and its authority comes from where and how it was issued. Most of us have no way of independently authenticating a birth certificate or most other kinds of documents; in the vast majority of cases unless you see something obviously wrong, like a college transcript with white-out on it, you take them at face value, and when there is a question, you ask the people in a position to know whether it's right or not, and that's that.

The authenticity and trustworthiness of these documents is partially a matter of look and feel—you expect higher-quality paper, professional-looking printing, maybe chips or holograms or other physical devices. All of which can be forged or faked with various levels of difficulty. It also comes from the chain of people and processes by which a document is produced and maintained; the more secure those are, the better you feel.

On a more personal level, this leads to a most intriguing question. My birth certificate gives all the right information: date, parents, place, and so on. Or at least I think it does. It shows no fingerprints, no photograph, no DNA. I've always believed all of that was correct and records my birth, but apart from my family's say-so, I have no other independent evidence to that effect. So how do I know for sure it's mine? And, for that matter, how do you know yours is yours?

A number of kinds of legal documents are becoming natively digital. Many court systems, for example, encourage or require digital submission of filings, and electronic signatures are increasingly commonplace. Lots of other familiar printed forms—newspapers, magazines, checks—have already ventured down that road. Some documents, though, seem to have a more personal or legal connection, like a will or a mortgage, or seem somehow more important. For those, it feels just better, more secure, to have something tangible to hold on to, so digital versions of those seem less likely to be embraced quickly. Several states have begun the process of experimenting with a driver's license app, though progress has been slower than expected, at least so far. It may well be, then, that this first and most basic document we get will be one of the last pieces of paper that future generations have.

SOURCES

Brumberg, H. L., D. Dozor, and S. G. Golombek. "History of the Birth Certificate: From Inception to the Future of Electronic Data." *Journal of Perinatology* 32, no. 6 (June 2012): 407–11. doi:10.1038/jp.2012.3.

Mikkelson, David. "Birth Certificate: Is Barack Obama's Birth Certificate a Forgery?" *Snopes.com*. Last modified February 21, 2014. http://www.snopes.com/politics/obama/birthers/birthcertificate.asp.

Morrison, Chloé. "Driver's License on Your Phone? App Adds ID to Virtual Wallet Trend." *Nooga.com*. June 4, 2015. http://nooga.com/170134/drivers-license-on-your-phone-app-adds-id-to-virtual-wallet-trend/.

Mundy, Liza. "The Strange History of the Birth Certificate." *New Republic* (February 13, 2013). https://newrepublic.com/article/112375/birth-certificates-age-adoption-and-egg-donation.

National Center for Health Statistics. *Hospital Handbook on Birth and Fetal Death Registration.* Public Health Service Publication; No. 593A. Washington, DC: U.S. Government Printing Office, 1967.

Office of the United Nations High Commissioner for Human Rights. "Convention on the Rights of the Child," Accessed September 28, 2016. http://www.ohchr.org/en/professionalinterest/pages/crc.aspx.

Patane, Matthew. "Where Are Iowa's Digital Driver's Licenses?" *Des Moines Register*, July 29, 2016. http://www.desmoinesregister.com/story/tech/2016/07/29/where-iowas-digital-drivers-licenses/87524766/.

Pfeiffer, Dan. "President Obama's Long Form Birth Certificate." Whitehouse.gov. April 27, 2011. https://www.whitehouse.gov/blog/2011/04/27/president-obamas-long-form-birth-certificate.

Tatelman, Todd B. "Intelligence Reform and Terrorism Prevention Act of 2004: National Standards for Drivers' Licenses, Social Security Cards, and Birth Certificates." Congressional Research Service. January 6, 2005.

United States National Office of Vital Statistics. *First Things and Last: The Story of Birth and Death Certificates.* Public Health Service Publication; No. 724. Washington, DC: U.S. Dept. of Health, Education and Welfare, Public Health Service, National Office of Vital Statistics, 1960.

Washington State Department of Health. "Birth, Death, Marriage and Divorce Certificates." Accessed September 28, 2016. http://www.doh.wa.gov/LicensesPermitsandCertificates/BirthDeathMarriageandDivorce.

Whitney, Lance. "The Driver's License of the Future Is Coming to Your Smartphone." *CNET*, March 21, 2015. https://www.cnet.com/news/your-future-drivers-license-could-go-digital/.

38
Zapruder Film
a film of the assassination of President John Kennedy
taken by Abraham Zapruder in Dallas, Texas,
now housed in the National Archives, copyright held by the Sixth Floor Museum
1963

Every generation seems to have their version of "Where were you when you first heard?" Where were you when men walked on the moon? Or when the space shuttle *Challenger* exploded? Or on 9/11? Those moments not only bring us back to a specific time and place, they're also inscribed on our minds as they were recorded and repeatedly seen: an orange flash in the distant sky, the impossible plane impossibly flying horizontally into the perfectly vertical building, Armstrong and Aldrin bouncing like marionettes.

For many people, though, that question can mean only one event, one year, one day. Even many decades on, it resonates, saddens, infuriates, and confuses. And while there are many accounts and images from that day, and myriad explanations and theories about what those accounts and images mean, one stands out. A film that's silent yet has spoken to so many, recording the moment at which an era ended, a reservoir of memory and lodestone of controversy, to this very day.

It almost didn't happen. Abraham Zapruder, Russian immigrant, Kennedy fan, and owner of Jennifer Juniors, a dressmaking business in Dallas, left his movie camera at home that November morning. The day dawned cloudy and it looked like a bad day for filming, but then it cleared, so he went home to get it. And since the view from his office window was poor, he went outside, trying several angles before perching himself and his Bell and Howell 8 mm Model 414 PD camera, serial number AS 13486, on a concrete block, about 65 feet from the middle of Elm Street, his secretary steadying him from behind because of his vertigo. Then, at 12:30 p.m., the motorcade came by, and then ...

It's little surprise that we know all these minor details about the Zapruder film; if it's not the most scrutinized motion picture ever, it must have the greatest ratio of eyeballs to frames of all time. In reality, it's barely a "film" at all: only 486 frames, not counting the family scenes and test shots at the beginning,

The Abraham Zapruder camera. National Archives and Records Administration (NARA).

covering just 26.6 seconds. Assuming, that is, that you believe the "official" timing based on analysis of the camera speed, one of hundreds of details that at least somebody disputes about every aspect of the Kennedy assassination investigations. Researching this is an exercise in "know your sources"; lots of seemingly responsible-looking works turn out to be deeply conspiratorial at heart, and almost anything here will get you an argument.

Zapruder witnessed the assassination through his viewfinder, in fact magnified by a telephoto lens, and his film is the only known complete recording of it. He was so shaken by what he saw that he started screaming, and then wandered, dazed, around the plaza for a few minutes. Thus began an odyssey for the rest of that afternoon and into the night, featuring a number of reporters, police, FBI, Secret Service, photographic lab technicians, his office staff and family and more. By the end of that day, he's been interviewed on television and shepherded all over town to get the film developed and printed. Three copies are made with varying processing settings, getting notarized affidavits of authenticity from technicians along the way. The film gets its first two showings, in the Dallas Kodak lab to his business partner and a newspaper reporter, and at home to his wife and son-in-law that night. The next day, he sells the print rights to *Life* magazine for $50,000 (to be followed by an additional $100,000 two days later for all additional rights, which is at least $1 million in current dollars).

By all accounts, the most shocking part, the image that symbolizes the whole day, is what's now known as Frame 313. This is the frame that shows the bullet striking the president's head and pulverizing his skull, a chunk of which flies off. It's a yellowish, reddish burst on the top of his head, obscuring Jackie's face, though her iconic pink jacket and pillbox hat are instantly recognizable behind the gore. It's hard to look at still, and was seen as so shocking at the time that everybody agreed, from Zapruder to *Life* magazine's publishers, that it shouldn't be seen, on the grounds of dignity and good taste, with seemingly almost no concern at the time for the public's right to know. It wouldn't be widely seen until the first nationwide television airing of the film by Geraldo Rivera in 1975.

Frame 313 of the Zapruder film. Zapruder film © 1967 (renewed 1995), the Sixth Floor Museum at Dealey Plaza.

That was only the beginning. Over the years, the saga continued, as numerous copies and copies of copies and copies of copies of copies were made, and the originals made their way from hand to hand, from the Secret Service to the FBI, to the Warren Commission, to the National Archives for safekeeping. Time, Inc., the parent of *Life*, sold the rights back to the family for $1 to settle a copyright suit based on the Rivera program. Oliver Stone paid $85,000 to use it in *J.F.K.*, one year before an act of Congress declared the film and other materials as "assassination records" and thus official property of the government. The family fights back, but it's seized under eminent domain in 1998, and the family is paid $16 million in compensation. They retained the copyright, however, which they donated to The Sixth Floor Museum, located in the Texas School Book Depository, in 1999. The government copies reside in the National Archives, and the film was placed on the National Film Registry by the Library of Congress in 1994, the same year as *Invasion of the Body Snatchers, The Manchurian Candidate,* and *The African Queen.*

All of this raises a couple of document-y questions. With all that copying going on, of a celluloid film, perhaps transferred to video, each successive copy will get more and more degraded, so at what point would an nth-generation copy no longer be "the" Zapruder film? If it were natively digital, this wouldn't be an issue, since any digital copies would presumably be perfect, but it might also be susceptible to even more claims of subtle and undetectable manipulation. And—when does an artifact, of any description, become so important, so historically relevant, that private ownership is beyond the pale? If a new "original" manuscript version of the Bill of Rights or John Wilkes Booth's diary surfaced, would those get seized too?

There are other films and images of the assassination, though none as complete, and more might yet still emerge. According to some sources, at least 32 photographers were taking images around that time (one film surfaced in 2007); The Sixth Floor Museum says that at least three remain unidentified, their pictures as yet unseen.

And despite—or perhaps because of—all the scrutiny and examination of the Zapruder film, it's a source of controversy itself. The full gamut of opinions is in play here, ranging from how it conclusively proves that Oswald acted alone, to how it conclusive proves exactly the opposite, with, naturally, a few who believe the film itself has been tampered with, manipulated, or even completely faked. It's evidence of something, to everybody, just not necessarily the same thing. Just consider, too: If we didn't have it, if it were never taken—would we be better or worse off?

Only two days later, Oswald's shooting on live television by Jack Ruby provided another image that is still debated. Since then, more have joined it, from the Rodney King beating to the emergency plane landing on the Hudson River to police body cam recordings to . . . something that happened yesterday, no doubt. The ubiquity of recording devices today and, crucially, the availability of instant sharing mean that fewer and fewer phenomena now will go unrecorded. Cell phone videos of plane crashes, tornadoes, explosions, and the like are routine. This is largely to the good, providing evidence and documentation of important events. But it also means that new versions of Frame 313, once too appalling to be shown, will become more and more commonplace, and likely more disputed, in the days and years to come.

SOURCES

Beaujon, Andrew. "Rodney King, Dead at 47, Sparked Citizen Journalism That's Now Commonplace." *Poynter* (June 18, 2012). http://www.poynter.org/latest-news/mediawire/177521/rodney-king -dead-at-47-sparked-citizen-journalism-thats-now-commonplace/.

CBS News. "The Man Who Shot the Zapruder Film." Last modified October 21, 2013. http://www .cbsnews.com/news/the-man-who-shot-the-zapruder-film-57607086/.

Fetzer, James H. *The Great Zapruder Film Hoax: Deceit and Deception in the Death of JFK*. Chicago: Catfeet Press, 2003.

The Sixth Floor Museum at Dealey Plaza. "Frequently Asked Questions." Accessed December 5, 2016. http://www.jfk.org/the-museum/faq/.

———. "Zapruder Film Timeline." Accessed December 5, 2012. http://www.jfk.org/the-collections/ abraham-zapruder-film/abraham-zapruder-film-timeline/.

Vågnes, Øyvind. *Zaprudered: The Kennedy Assassination Film in Visual Culture*. Austin: University of Texas Press, 2011.

Wikipedia. "Zapruder film." Last modified November 9, 2013. http://en.wikipedia.org/w/index .php?title=Zapruder_film&oldid=580534015.

Wrone, David R. *The Zapruder Film: Reframing JFK's Assassination*. Lawrence: University Press of Kansas, 2003.

39
Quotations of Chairman Mao

also known as the "Little Red Book"

compiled and published by the General Political Department
of the People's Liberation Army

1965

"There's nothing certain in life but death and taxes." Truer words were never spoken, and everybody knows that wry little quote and it can easily be found in lots of writings and speeches; there's also a movie with that title, an LA rock band, even a brand of black beer. Chief Justice Roberts used it in his noteworthy 2012 majority decision upholding the Affordable Care Act, citing, as most people do, Benjamin Franklin as the author, in a 1789 letter to Jean-Baptiste Le Roy. Dig a little deeper, though, and you'll find that the first known usage is in a play by Christopher Bullock called *The Cobbler of Preston* from 1716, almost 75 years before Franklin. This sort of thing happens all the time—if you're stuck, cite Mark Twain, Shakespeare, the Bible, Oscar Wilde, or *Casablanca* for that matter; they're all good for a snappy one-liner.

Quotations are used often in wedding toasts, graduation speeches, epigraphs; they're usually employed to add a bit of panache, or oomph—if Dorothy Parker said this, it must be worthwhile, so there. And there are lots of sources, good, bad, and indifferent, that are designed to help find just the right one for just the right occasion. For about a generation, though, in the most populous nation on Earth, there was only one source of quotations that mattered, because the words of only one person mattered—until they didn't.

It is indeed a little red book, an unimposing little thing, barely five inches long, bound in red vinyl; it sits very comfortably in your hand. What it lacks in size, it more than made up for in sheer numbers. There's no way to know how many copies were printed, since the work was done in multiple places; a more or less official count puts the total number at just over a billion, including multiple editions in Chinese, in dozens of other languages, in recordings, even in Braille. The first American-printed edition came out in 1967 from Bantam as a paperback. It is undoubtedly one of the most printed and widely distributed books of all time. It contains 427 quotations in 33 chapters, covering such broad

Quotations of Chairman Mao, chapter 6, titled "Imperialism and all reactionaries are paper tigers." University of Washington Libraries.

topics as "War and Peace," "Unity," "Discipline," "Criticism and Self-Criticism," along with old favorites like "Imperialism and All Reactionaries are Paper Tigers" and "Correcting Mistaken Ideas."

Mao didn't write this book per se; rather, it's a compilation of quotations drawn from his writings and speeches over almost 40 years, reaching back to 1926, conceived by Defense Minister General Lin Biao and emerging from a daily feature in the People's Liberation Army newspaper. There were precursor works, including several apparently unauthorized and sloppy editions of Mao's writings printed in the mid-1940s, a situation that prompted the Communist Party to decide to publish an authentic version, proofread and organized by Mao, which began appearing in 1951. By the mid-1960s, those four volumes were the most important reading material in China, widely, almost universally reproduced even on ceramics and porcelain figures, as well as daily reading in the military, and those excerpts formed the foundation for what would become the *Quotations.*

It went through a number of editions and versions; the closest thing to a "definitive" version would be the third edition, published in August 1965, on which all other later ones are based. That's the same month as the first American ground offensive in South Vietnam, the signing of the Voting Rights Act and the Watts Riots; it's also the year of the first commercial communication satellite, Ralph Nader's *Unsafe at Any Speed*, Medicare, and the murder of Malcolm X.

Lin Biao wrote an endorsement, in calligraphy, exhorting the people to "study Chairman Mao's writings, follow his teachings and act according to his instructions." Promoting the Little Red Book added to his luster and prestige, and by 1969 he was named Mao's successor. Then the rumors and character assassination started, and by 1971 he was dead in a mysterious plane crash, disgraced, and the people were instructed to tear out his endorsement page from all copies. Today, in an odd twist of fate, intact and undefaced copies can fetch many thousands of dollars on the collectibles market.

The goal was for 99 percent of the population of China to read it; it was an unofficial requirement to own, read, and carry it at all times during the Cultural Revolution. It was often given as a gift on auspicious occasions. Studying the *Quotations* was required in schools and workplaces; it was also used as a reading tool in the army, and a simpler, primer form was also printed. It had a cachet among American audiences as well, at least of a sort; as one importer recalled, it was a "status symbol for anybody opposing bureaucratic authority. Waving it was evidence that whoever owned a copy was at least a rebel." He initially ordered 25,000, which were gobbled up within a month, eventually selling more than a million copies in the United States over 15 years.

The production of this work on such a massive scale was an enormous undertaking; hundreds of new printing houses had to be built specifically for this purpose and sufficient resources and printing presses had to be procured. This pushed the limits of the Chinese printing industry, disrupting plans for other ideological works. By one estimate, over 650,000 tons of paper was used to print this one work over a five-year period.

One of the most widely known and cited quotations, "Let a hundred flowers bloom," is, as is so often the case with quotations, imprecise. In a 1957 speech, Mao said, "Letting a hundred flowers blossom and a hundred schools of thought contend is the policy for promoting progress in the arts and the sciences and a flourishing socialist culture in our land." It isn't entirely clear whether or not that was intended to encourage dissenting heads to pop up, so they could be more easily lopped off, but within just a few weeks Mao changed course and many people paid the price for speaking their minds.

Mao died in September 1976, and by the late '70s the Cultural Revolution was ending. The Little Red Book fell out of favor; the government discouraged it, ceasing printing in 1979; and millions were later destroyed, though printing did resume in 1993 for the centennial of Mao's birth. Today, it's more an object of nostalgia and mild curiosity, certainly no longer the force it once was.

The point of all of this, it seems obvious, was indoctrination and control. If everybody in your country is, literally, reading from the same page, then managing what and how they think is made considerably easier, and for about a decade or so, that worked. Although this is one of the clearest examples of the use of a text to reinforce an authoritarian regime, it's by no means the only one; *Mein Kampf* was distributed free to all newlywed couples and soldiers on the front during the Nazi government years.

Now, of course, things are more complicated. What's a tyrannical government to do if they want to control what their people read and think? Would Mao have a Twitter feed or Instagram account? There are parts of the *Quotations* that read that way, though many go on at considerably greater length. The one-way world of publication and distribution has yielded to a more complicated, two-way world of social networking, which fosters and prizes participation, discussion, engagement, and sharing rather than consistency, enforcement, and control.

Unless, that is, you control the pipelines. Social networking only works if you've got access to a network to be social on, and are free to use it as you want. A number of governments have decided their best option is to keep a firm hand on the tap and restrict what the Internet is within their borders. A 2015 report lists over a dozen countries where the Internet is "Not Free," including Saudi Arabia, Iran, Cuba, Belarus, and Myanmar along with, of course, China. While it's understandably difficult to know the exact extent of their grip on Internet use, which they refer to as "Internet sovereignty," it's likely there are many thousands of people employing techniques such as blocking specific Internet addresses or Web pages; scanning discussion groups, blogs, e-mail, and so on for forbidden topics; and filtering results on search engines in response to certain query words, accompanied by directives given to a variety of online companies on what should and should not be allowed to be published or searched. A robust and innovative set of tactics to circumvent these measures goes on, leading to a cat-and-mouse game of intellectual freedom and repression and what's been termed a parallel Internet universe within China.

Compared to this Great Firewall of China, as it's popularly known, the Little Red Book seems somehow quaint and toothless. The resolute and forthright people clutching and brandishing them proudly in propaganda posters of the time would have had no idea that within 50 years their revolutionary handiwork would evolve from turning the pages of a book to tapping on a computer mouse, clicking away freedom of expression for over a billion people.

从政治上思想上理论上彻底批倒批臭中国的赫鲁晓夫

A propaganda poster from November 1967, translated in the IISH catalog as "Fully criticize the Chinese Khrushchev from a political, ideological and theoretical perspective." Stefan Landsberger Visual Documents Collection, International Institute of Social History, Amsterdam.

SOURCES

Chao, Eveline. "A Week Behind the Great Firewall of China." *Fast Company*, April 8, 2016. https://www.fastcompany.com/3056721/most-innovative-companies/a-week-behind-the-great-firewall-of-china.

Denyer, Simon. "China's Scary Lesson to the World: Censoring the Internet Works." *Washington Post*, May 23, 2016. https://www.washingtonpost.com/world/asia_pacific/chinas-scary-lesson-to-the-world-censoring-the-internet-works/2016/05/23/413afe78-fff3-11e5-8bb1-f124a43f84dc_story.html.

Freedom House. "Freedom on the Net 2015." https://freedomhouse.org/report/freedom-net/freedom-net-2015.

GreatFire.org. "Home Page—English." Accessed September 21, 2016. https://en.greatfire.org/.

Jiao Guobiao. "How Much Did Mao Zedong, Deng Xiaoping, and Jiang Zemin Get Paid for Their Publications?" *Chinascope*, December 31, 2007. Accessed August 25, 2016. http://chinascope.org/main/content/view/413/131.

National Federation of Independent Business v. Sebelius, Secretary of Health and Human Services, 648 F. 3d 1235 (2012). https://www.law.cornell.edu/supremecourt/text/11-393.

Noyes, Henry. "China Syndrome (II)." *China Today* (April 1997).

Oliver, Lei Han. "Sources and Early Printing History of Chairman Mao's 'Quotations.'" The Bibliographical Society of America. Last modified January, 10, 2004. http://www.bibsocamer.org/bibsite/han/index.html.

Shapiro, Fred R. "Quote . . . Misquote." *New York Times Magazine* (July 21, 2008). Accessed October 20, 2016. http://www.nytimes.com/2008/07/21/magazine/27wwwl-guestsafire-t.html.

Wikipedia. "Quotations from Chairman Mao Tse-tung." Last modified October 6, 2016. https://en.wikipedia.org/wiki/Quotations_from_Chairman_Mao_Tse-tung.

Xinhuanet.com. "'Quotations from Chairman Mao' Has Become Popular Collectibles." Translated by Google Translate. Last modified July 13, 2004. http://news.xinhuanet.com/collection/2004-07/13/content_1595108.htm.

The 18½-Minute Gap

a magnetic tape of a conversation between
Richard Nixon and H. R. Haldeman
specifically an 18½-minute interruption
recorded in the Executive Office Building in Washington, D.C.,
now in the Nixon Presidential Library

1972

Everybody loves a good mystery. At the end of a Miss Marple novel or an episode of a police procedural, all is revealed, the guilty are exposed, and justice and harmony reign. Unsolved mysteries, though, are a good deal less fulfilling; untied loose ends are rarely appreciated. That's why people continue to puzzle over what happened to Amelia Earhart, who Jack the Ripper really was, and why Ryan Seacrest is so popular.

To people of a certain age, one mystery, now a bit forgotten in the mists of time, brings back floods of memories, reminding us of once-novel and colorful phrases like "expletive deleted," "dirty tricks," and "unindicted co-conspirator." If you're too young to remember the Saturday Night Massacre or the "smoking gun," you missed one of the most turbulent times in the nation's history, when the resilience of the Constitution was seriously in question, and the question of the time was "What did the president know, and when did he know it?" which, sadly, we've heard a few more times since then.

For a time, a great deal of attention focused on one strip of magnetic tape, about 90 feet worth, with an unexplained buzz where there should have been conversation between two of the most powerful men in the country. Its mere existence contributed to a growing sense of cynicism and further undermined people's trust of the government and other institutions. The mysteries locked up in that tape and what is, and isn't, there transfixed the nation at the time, and still today the desire to know, to figure it out, goes on.

I know you're not supposed to do this with a mystery, but I'll give away the ending here—we don't know what's in the 18½-minute gap, though that's not for lack of trying to find out. The conversation in question between Nixon and Haldeman took place at a meeting on June 20, 1972, starting at 11:30 a.m. June 20 is three days after the Watergate break-in on the 17th, and, entertainingly, one day after a unanimous Supreme Court ruled that the government had no authority to spy on private citizens without warrants. Those were the days. It's also, sadly, the day Howard Johnson went to that big HoJo's in the sky.

Nixon wasn't the first president with a penchant for recording; FDR, JFK, and LBJ indulged as well, though not with nearly such thoroughness or enthusiasm. Microphones were also installed in the Oval Office and Cabinet Room and even at Camp David, including phone lines. In total, about 3,500 hours of recordings were made, now housed in the National Archives and the Nixon Presidential Library, after a string of legal battles lasting 25 years over disputes on executive privilege and national security.

The recording itself is hard to understand; the voices are faint, there's an odd frequent burping noise from the voice-activated recorder starting and stopping, and mostly, it's deadly, deadly dull. Imagine sitting in on somebody else's meeting that you have no interest in—and bring a pillow. They talk about the weather, the president's schedule, magazine coverage, a woman from Michigan running for Congress, and the recent flooding in Rapid City, South Dakota. In the middle of discussing sending Mrs. Nixon to visit the flood area (she went), the voices stop abruptly, seven minutes and twelve seconds into the tape, and a penetrating and persistent buzz begins. This lasts for the now-infamous 18½ minutes, before stopping just as abruptly, when they're discussing the upcoming Democratic convention, before turning to weightier matters like Haldeman's opinion of the movie *The Hot Rock*.

That's it. Recording went on for another year or so, until the existence of the tapes, a closely held secret, was revealed as part of the Watergate hearings. Keep in mind that the "gap" conversation is held just three days before the so-called "smoking gun" taped conversations in which it is made painfully clear that Nixon knew, and was directing, what was going on. Transcripts of those were finally released on August 5, 1974, and within a week, Nixon had resigned, ending what his successor, Gerald Ford, engraved in our memories as "our long national nightmare."

Spare a thought now for Rose Mary Woods, a footnote to history, and no doubt a woman of integrity and trust, Richard Nixon's loyal secretary since 1951. In transcribing tapes, she discovered to her horror, so she said, the gap. She took the fall, for a few minutes' worth, thinking that maybe she had kept her foot on a pedal control while reaching for a phone call and mistakenly hitting the record button rather than the stop. This "Rose Mary Stretch" didn't really convince anybody, and besides, there's another 14 minutes to account for.

Rose Mary Woods, President Richard Nixon's secretary, shown at her White House desk in 1973 demonstrating the "Rose Mary Stretch" that could have resulted in the erasure of part of the Watergate tapes. Associated Press.

There have been numerous dogged attempts to unearth what was there and what happened. A special investigative panel of forensic audio experts went at it at the time; they were able to find that there were actually between five and nine segments to the buzz corresponding to different electrical outlets the recorder had been plugged into at various times, that it was done by hand, that speech had been there, but that despite trying a variety of highly specialized techniques they couldn't recover it. Later investigations, as recently as 2009, have examined the tape as well as Haldeman's somewhat suspicious hand-written notes from the meeting, which may or may not have been fiddled with. Hyperspectral imaging, video spectral comparison and electrostatic detection analysis were used, and the results? Bupkus. It's a buzz, a few buzzes in fact, and at least for now, unexplained buzzes they will remain. Theories continue to abound—that Rose Mary Woods did more damage than she thought; that shadowy "White House lawyers" got to the tape; or, as Alexander Haig once suggested, that Nixon himself, through technological ineptitude, had a hand in it. Or there's the simple explanation that when Elvis and the aliens showed up, their magnetic fields wiped the tapes.

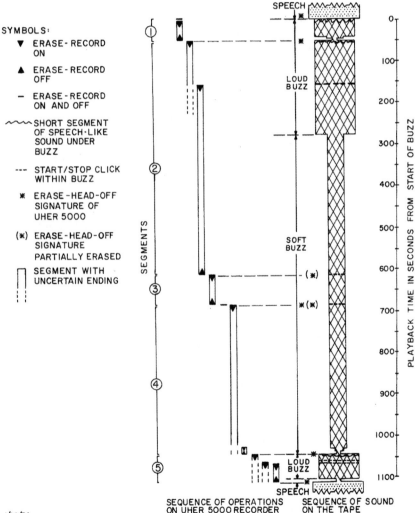

KEY TO BUZZ SECTION IN WHITE HOUSE TAPE OF JUNE 20, 1972

Schematic of the buzzing section of the tape, from page D.14 of a 1974 report on the results of a technical investigation of the 18.5-minute gap. Advisory Panel on White House Tapes.

And yet, there's the tantalizing hope that someday, some new technique will come along, like fingerprints and DNA did for criminal investigations, that will let us hear beneath the buzzes and, finally, know. Because we do always want to know.

I've used this example in teaching a few times, and the question always arises, among people whose parents are young enough not to have first-hand knowledge of those days: Why? Why did this all happen, why was the Constitution put in jeopardy by Nixon's actions, and most excruciatingly, *why didn't he burn the tapes?* Herein lies the mystery within the mystery, a question likely never answerable and yet still worth asking and exploring.

Thinking about the gap initially put me in mind of the famous piece by the pianist John Cage, called *4'33"*, which consists of 3 movements of musicians doing nothing. Silence. Except it isn't silence—Cage wanted listeners to focus on the sounds of the environment and fill the space from within. Like the gap, also not silence as I had originally thought, it's a void, a hole, into which we can pour our doubts and suspicions, and perhaps hear what we want to hear.

That wanting to know was more than just strictly political in this case. The techniques that were used in the original forensic audio investigation broke new ground and became a textbook for future work, eventually forming part of the standards for verifying authenticity of tape recordings. Demonstrating once again that much as we love a mystery, we'll keep digging until we figure out a way to figure it out, and in the process sometimes push forward the boundaries of our knowledge.

SOURCES

Advisory Panel on White House Tapes. *The EOB Tape of June 20, 1972: Report on a Technical Investigation Conducted for the U.S. District Court for the District of Columbia by the Advisory Panel on White House Tapes.* May 31, 1974. Accessed August 16, 2016. http://www.aes.org/aeshc/docs/forensic.audio/watergate.tapes.report.pdf.

Corn, David. "CSI: Watergate." *Mother Jones* (July 28, 2009). Accessed July 20, 2016. http://www.motherjones.com/politics/2009/09/csi-watergate.

Kopel, David. "The Missing 18 1/2 Minutes: Presidential Destruction of Incriminating Evidence." *Washington Post,* June 16, 2014. Accessed July 20, 2016. https://www.washingtonpost.com/news/volokh-conspiracy/wp/2014/06/16/the-missing-18-12-minutes-presidential-destruction-of-incriminating-evidence/.

Lardner, George Jr. "Haig Tells of Theories on Erasure." *Washington Post,* December 7, 1973.

McKnight, John G., and Mark R. Weiss. "'Watergate' and Forensic Audio Engineering." Audio Engineering Society. November 14, 2005. Accessed July 20, 2016. http://www.aes.org/aeshc/docs/forensic.audio/watergate.tapes.introduction.html.

Mellinger, Philip T. "Cracking Watergate's Infamous 18 1/2 Minute Gap." *Forensic Magazine* (February 17, 2011). Accessed July 20, 2016. http://www.forensicmag.com/article/2011/02/cracking-watergates-infamous-18-12-minute-gap.

————. "The Deep Throat Operation and the '18 1/2-Minute Gap.'" *Washingtonian* (November 16, 2011). Accessed August 16, 2016. https://www.washingtonian.com/2011/11/16/the -deep-throat-operation-and-the-18-minute-gap/.

nixontapes.org. "New Theories Related to Watergate Continue to Capture Public Imagination." November 18, 2009. Accessed July 20, 2016. http://www.nixontapes.org/mellinger.html.

————. "Transcript of Recording, June 20, 1972 Meeting between President Nixon and H. R. Haldeman." N.d. http://nixontapes.org/watergate/342-016.pdf.

Nixon Presidential Library and Museum. "How the Tapes Are Preserved." Accessed July 20, 2016. https://www.nixonlibrary.gov/forresearchers/find/tapes/processing/preservation.php.

Paynter, David G., and Margaret Ann T. Kelly. "Examination of H. R. Haldeman Notes." National Archives. June 8, 2011. Accessed July 20, 2016. http://www.archives.gov/research/investiga tions/watergate/haldeman-notes.html.

Shenon, Philip. "Rose Mary Woods, 87, Nixon Loyalist for Decades, Dies." *New York Times*, January 24, 2005. Accessed August 16, 2016. http://www.nytimes.com/2005/01/24/politics/rose-mary -woods-87-nixon-loyalist-for-decades-dies.html.

Washington Post. "The Watergate Story: Timeline." Accessed July 20, 2016. http://www.washington post.com/wp-srv/politics/special/watergate/timeline.html.

Wikipedia. "June 1972." August 15, 2016. https://en.wikipedia.org/w/index.php?title=June_1972 &oldid=734599697.

Internet Protocol

RFC 791, "DARPA Internet Program Protocol Specification"
a standard edited by Jon Postel, based on the work of Robert Kahn and Vinton Cerf
and approved by the Internet Engineering Task Force

1981

What makes the Internet work? Most of us have a vague sense, if that, of what goes on behind the curtain or under the hood—bits and bytes whooshing around, somewhere, like in an IBM commercial, or maybe *Tron*. There must be cables, right? And racks of black boxes with lots of blinking lights or streaming shadowy green digits cascading on a screen, like *The Matrix*—that's what they show on the news when there's been a major hacking incident or some other new cyber development.

Yes, there are cables and boxes (and lights), but those are just tools. The reality of what makes it happen isn't all that complicated, an example of elegant simplicity and minimalism, crafted and honed by pioneering and forward-thinking technical experts in T-shirts and sandals. Like a lot of infrastructure, its workings are largely hidden beneath the surface and thus easily taken for granted. The plumbing works, the lights go on, and the cat video streamed, so I'm good.

The foundation for all that, what makes it possible, has its roots in a 30-year-old document that specifies a lightweight but powerful regime that laid the seeds for a radical transformation of many aspects of contemporary life.

Many news stories have been written about the anniversaries of the first e-mail and of the World Wide Web, but somehow this consistently gets missed. I can guess why—it's very technical and makes pretty turgid reading. Much of its 45 pages is the equivalent of typewriter art diagrams specifying how the guts of the Internet work. True, in October 1969 the first message of sorts went from one computer to another via a network, and yes, there are other milestones and standards you could point to as important, but TCP/IP gives it structure and makes it work, and that started here.

TCP/IP stands for the Transfer Control Protocol/Internet Protocol, and its roots go back to those early days and the search for a way to link computers to share data. Initially that was intended for things like moving files around and

Internet Protocol

APPENDIX A: Examples & Scenarios

Example 1:

   This is an example of the minimal data carrying internet datagram:

```
 0                   1                   2                   3
 0 1 2 3 4 5 6 7 8 9 0 1 2 3 4 5 6 7 8 9 0 1 2 3 4 5 6 7 8 9 0 1
+-+-+-+-+-+-+-+-+-+-+-+-+-+-+-+-+-+-+-+-+-+-+-+-+-+-+-+-+-+-+-+-+
|Ver= 4 |IHL= 5 |Type of Service|        Total Length = 21      |
+-+-+-+-+-+-+-+-+-+-+-+-+-+-+-+-+-+-+-+-+-+-+-+-+-+-+-+-+-+-+-+-+
|         Identification = 111   |Flg=0|   Fragment Offset = 0  |
+-+-+-+-+-+-+-+-+-+-+-+-+-+-+-+-+-+-+-+-+-+-+-+-+-+-+-+-+-+-+-+-+
|   Time = 123  |  Protocol = 1  |       header checksum         |
+-+-+-+-+-+-+-+-+-+-+-+-+-+-+-+-+-+-+-+-+-+-+-+-+-+-+-+-+-+-+-+-+
|                       source address                          |
+-+-+-+-+-+-+-+-+-+-+-+-+-+-+-+-+-+-+-+-+-+-+-+-+-+-+-+-+-+-+-+-+
|                     destination address                       |
+-+-+-+-+-+-+-+-+-+-+-+-+-+-+-+-+-+-+-+-+-+-+-+-+-+-+-+-+-+-+-+-+
|     data      |
+-+-+-+-+-+-+-+-+
```

Example Internet Datagram

Figure 5.

Note that each tick mark represents one bit position.

This is a internet datagram in version 4 of internet protocol; the
internet header consists of five 32 bit words, and the total length of
the datagram is 21 octets.   This datagram is a complete datagram (not
a fragment).

Page 34 of RFC 791: *Internet Protocol*, edited by Jon Postel and published in September 1981, which specifies the Department of Defense Standard Internet Protocol. This particular page shows an example of a minimal-data-carrying Internet datagram. Internet Engineering Task Force (IETF).

logging in to computers remotely to make using them more efficient, back when computing power and time were precious commodities.

Using these protocols, the "Internet" is a network, connecting a number of networks together, and it alone does very little, except pass digital stuff around, unchanged and unexamined. That's the genius of this—that the Internet does about as little as possible, and there's no specific hardware or software required to be a part of it. This simplicity makes it easy to implement, subscribe to, and maintain, which is part of its incredible success.

What it does is called packet switching. When any file or message is sent across the Internet, it's divided up into lots of smaller chunks or packets, each of which can take separate paths to the destination, where they're reassembled. Each of those chunks takes the most efficient path at that instant, which means it could go anywhere in the network. That improves performance and speed. It doesn't matter what the sender or receiver are, where they are, or who they are. So long as they both subscribe to the TCP/IP protocols, the message will go through and everybody's happy.

Once you have this base layer of networking where stuff moves around, lots of much more interesting things can use it, taking all that for granted. Things like e-mail, for example, or timekeeping, or the maintenance of the domain name service that lets everything be found. Oh yeah, and the Web; it's one of a bunch of applications that ride on top of TCP/IP like a Honda on an interstate without the slightest care what goes into keeping the road working. That's why a full Web address includes that "http://" business; http stands for the Hypertext Transfer Protocol, one of a number of protocols that work atop TCP/IP.

This document itself is one of a long series of several thousand "RFCs," short for "requests for comment," which tells us something about the people and processes involved: collaborative, open, often operating by consensus, coming to a shared understanding and agreement. There is a formal approval process, described in something called the Tao of IETF, which also helpfully lays out the preferred meeting dress code of T-shirts and sandals. It's both charming and only a little icky that Jon Postel, the longtime editor, had his obituary sent out as RFC 2468.

A great deal of networking effort in those days was government/Defense Department stuff; the Defense Advanced Research Projects Agency approved this as the military network standard in 1982, which really gets things rolling. However, the migration to this standard wasn't seamless or easy. In fact, a couple of tart e-mails from Jon Postel point to this; to nudge network administrators along, the powers that be turned off a previous protocol for a few days, and even then, it took three months for everybody to get on board when the switchover finally happened.

This Internet thing seems likely to be around for a while, and has affected most parts of daily life. It's gotten so common, so fully ingrained, that it's in the process of losing its capital I; soon it appears it will no longer be a proper noun. Strictly speaking, any network of networks is *an* internet; what we have come to think of as *the* Internet is just the global version of that.

Let me focus on one aftereffect you might not have thought about: disintermediation. Remember Napster? Copyright infringement notwithstanding, it's a great example of a peer-to-peer system; anybody could download music files from anybody on the network. Handy, and you don't need a recording company or record store to make that work. Which is great, unless you're a recording company or record store. Substitute "movie" or "book" or any other format in there and you see what happens. In a peer-to-peer world, like the Internet, what's the middle for? For that matter, what's the middle?

And yet. The world has gotten tough for booksellers and record stores but Amazon and iTunes are thriving. So are the App Store, Google Play, Netflix, Spotify, Expedia, Pandora, and a range of other intermediaries and advice-givers ready and willing to help out in the networked age, so it seems that even if you cut out the middleman, that middle keeps reemerging.

One more curiosity about the RFC document itself: it betrays the technology of its time in its formatting. It's laid out in pages, explicitly trying to replicate the look and feel of the typed pages of the early days, spaced out with blank lines between page numbers, not all that unlike the Gutenberg indulgence. It seems strange, even retrograde, to 21st-century eyes, used to PDF documents or Web pages that don't rely on, well, pages. Meanwhile, the technology it laid out has liberated information of all types from its containers, potentially forever.

SOURCES

IETF Trust. "The Tao of IETF: A Novice's Guide to the Internet Engineering Task Force." Last modified November 2, 2012. http://www.ietf.org/tao.html.

Living Internet. "TCP/IP Internet Protocol." Accessed August 7, 2012. http://www.livinginternet.com/i/ii_tcpip.htm.

Postel, Jon. "Internet Protocol." RFC 791. September 1981. Accessed August 7, 2012. http://datatracker.ietf.org/doc/rfc791/.

Oliver, Mike. "TCP/IP Frequently Asked Questions." Accessed August 7, 2012. http://www.itprc.com/tcpipfaq/.

Wikipedia. "Internet protocol suite." Last modified December 3, 2016. https://en.wikipedia.org/wiki/Internet_protocol_suite.

42
Vietnam Veterans Memorial
designed by Maya Ying Lin
constructed on the National Mall in Washington, D.C.
1982

How do you help yourself to remember something? I've found that the string-around-the-finger trick is not only cliché, it's also unhelpful and potentially cuts off your circulation. I'm an inveterate note maker—lists, Post-its, and scraps of paper everywhere. I've also been known to put things in the wrong pocket to jog my memory, and my friend Diane taught me the trick of throwing a book from the nightstand when something occurs to me just when dropping off to sleep, which is quite effective, assuming you can recall why there's a book in the middle of the bedroom floor in the morning.

Remembrances of a person are often easier: photographs, mementos, letters, diaries; there's a wide range of objects of all kinds that help to evoke and jog memories. Often these are private, or shared among family or a few friends. At times, though, circumstances dictate larger, broader, collective remembering, and untold numbers of memorials of all shapes and sizes have been erected over the millennia. One of these, of an unconventional and originally contentious design, tried to capture the complexity of a decades-long conflict in a simple, stark, elegant, and ultimately beautiful way—and along the way showed us more about ourselves and how we remember than anyone would have imagined.

———

Any story of the Vietnam memorial has to begin with Jan Scruggs, a volunteer infantryman who was wounded by a rocket-propelled grenade in his first tour of duty at age 19 and saw 12 men die in a mortar accident in his second. An alcohol-fueled flashback of that incident, 10 years later while watching *The Deer Hunter*, inspired him to envision a memorial to the men who died in Vietnam, one that would symbolize national reconciliation for a war that had riven the country, take no government money, and be a "delayed victory

235

parade" for those who served. No small order, particularly when, after the first splashy news conference, exactly $144.50 had come in. That embarrassment fueled him and his organization, which maneuvered the twists and turns of official Washington, bureaucracy, doubt, and scorn, and eventually marshaled the resources to build a monument on the National Mall, often called the nation's front yard, nearly in the shadow of the Lincoln Memorial. But what should it be? After extensive discussion and rigmarole, a call went out for a competition in 1980, seeking a design that would "recognize and honor those who served and died" and acknowledge their "courage, sacrifice and devotion to duty. [It] will make no political statement regarding the war or its conduct. It will transcend those issues. The hope is that the creation of the memorial will begin a healing process."

It didn't quite work out that way, at least at first. A total of 1,421 entries came in, anonymously, with names in sealed envelopes taped on the back. An expert jury cut them to 232, then 39, then 3. Their unanimous choice was number 1026, engendering comments on its simplicity, eloquence, power, challenge, experience, reflectiveness, and reverence. The one-page submission depicted the memorial as "a rift in the earth"; later, it would be called a "black gash of shame," but that lay in the future. We all now know envelope number 1026 held the name of Maya Ying Lin, a Yale architecture student who entered as a class project—for which she received a B.

One of Maya Ying Lin's architectural drawings submitted in the 1981 competition for the Vietnam Veterans Memorial. Library of Congress.

In an essay she wrote at the time but didn't publish for nearly 20 years, Lin comes across as naïve on the ways of politics though fierce in defense of her artistic vision. She said she designed it for herself, what she believed it should be, not in an attempt to second-guess the jury. Exploring the nature of memorials and their functions, she notes that until World War I, individual lives, and names, were rarely dealt with. A war memorial at Yale was being updated at the time with names from Vietnam and that process struck her: the power of a name, let alone more than 50,000. She traveled to Washington to see the site and had the "impulse to cut into the earth . . . opening it up, an initial violence and pain that in time would heal." Her initial sketch seemed too simple, she thought, so she tried adding elements, but less turned out to be more, and her original vision, incorporating chronological names, became her submission.

After she won, the trouble began. Her Asian heritage, the black color of the wall, its simplicity, the lack of a heroic statue—all were criticized and worse. It's hard to read accounts of the multiple controversies and near-deaths of the project, fueled by many quarters including original supporter Ross Perot and the odious Interior Secretary James Watt, without a smug hindsight. Yes, eventually a statue was added, as was a memorial to women who served and a plaque honoring those who died other than in combat, but today we know it would be built, and embraced, even in spite of such intense scrutiny and even hatred.

It is, formally, a list, of 58,272 names extracted from a database of "combat zone casualties" and based on criteria, specifying dates and geographic areas, from a 1965 executive order, in chronological order by date of casualty or date reported missing. Those missing are designated with plus signs, which can be converted to the diamonds next to the dead when their deaths are confirmed, or encircled if they come back alive, though none have as yet. As of 2011, 229 names have been added as the list is updated; no civilians are listed, nor are those who died from indirect causes, such as cancer from Agent Orange exposure or suicide from posttraumatic stress disorder. It's estimated those names would require two additional walls.

The names are engraved in black granite from India (neither Canadian nor Swedish granite was deemed acceptable, as they had shielded draft evaders), in the Optima typeface. The sequence begins with 1959 at the top of panel 1E, the first on the East arm, and continues to its end 246 feet away, then loops back to the extreme western end with names from May 25, 1968, concluding at the bottom of panel 70W with men killed during the Mayaguez incident in 1975. All names are indexed by panel and line number and can be searched online. Getting everything right is a tough process, and it's not perfect. The first two men listed, Dale Buis and Chester Ovnand, were killed by guerillas while watching a movie; Ovnand's name was one of a few dozen misspelled (as Ovnard), because of conflicting records, and was eventually fixed and relocated; Sgt. Richard Fitzgibbon Jr. was murdered by another airman in June 1956 and after years of lobbying was added in 1999 to panel 52E.

The memorial was dedicated on November 13, 1982, at the end of a week-long tribute to Vietnam veterans, weeks after EPCOT Center opened and the Tylenol murders, and two weeks before the release of *Thriller*. Almost immediately and simultaneously, two extraordinary phenomena surfaced: visitors reached out to touch the names, and eventually to make rubbings of them as mementos, as one might of a headstone. Then there were the offerings, which actually began, if the story is to be believed, with a naval officer who threw his brother's Purple Heart medal into the trench where the concrete was being poured during construction. Tens of thousands of objects of all kinds have been left; flowers are not preserved, flags without messages are given to scouting groups, drugs are confiscated, but everything else is kept and preserved by the Museum and Archaeological Regional Storage facility in Maryland. Many come without explanation or names attached, so we are left to wonder. They all mean something to somebody, though without context or purpose, they're adrift in our collective consciousness.

A photo of the Vietnam Veterans Memorial, taken September 26, 2014. Austin Kirk (flickr user: aukirk).

If you've been to the wall, you know—you're immediately struck by the surface, black and polished. You can see yourself, reflected in, surrounded by, the dead and the missing. Name after name, row after row, panel after panel. We see ourselves as we see them. The memorial is, clearly, a document, straightforwardly recording names and sequence; it also memorializes the war in general, our experience of it, and our coming to terms with it. You could also argue that each offering is also a document, though often uncertain, unknown, private, even secret, of a person, an act, a relationship, a regret.

I would go further. I would say that all of it, together, the totality of the wall, the additions, the tortuous processes, the objects individually and collectively: *that*, all of it, is the document. When you think of a war memorial, you think of marble columns, bronze men in heroic poses on bronze horses, or at least you used to. A memorial speaks, too, about its society and context when it's built, and as it evolves over time; it's as much about the remembering as the remembered. The story told here isn't grand or exalted, not about generals or victory; it's about people and a war and a time not all that long ago that still requires healing, and reconciliation, and remembrance, one name at a time.

SOURCES

Druzin, Heath. "Jan Scruggs, Legacy Etched in the Stone of Vietnam Wall, Ready to Retire." *Stars and Stripes*. June 29, 2015. Accessed July 1, 2015. http://www.stripes.com/news/special-reports/vietnam-at-50/jan-scruggs-legacy-etched-in-the-stone-of-vietnam-wall-ready-to-retire-1.355373.

Hass, Kristin Ann. *Carried to the Wall: American Memory and the Vietnam Veterans Memorial*. Berkeley: University of California Press, 1998.

Inskeep, Steve. "Vietnam Veterans' Memorial Founder: Monument Almost Never Got Built." *NPR*, April 30, 2015. Accessed July 1, 2015. http://www.npr.org/2015/04/30/403034599/vietnam-veterans-memorial-founder-monument-almost-never-got-built.

Kino, Carol. "Once Inspired by a War, Now by the Land." *New York Times*, November 7, 2008. http://www.nytimes.com/2008/11/09/arts/design/09kino.html.

Lin, Maya. "Making the Memorial." *New York Review of Books* (November 2, 2000). http://www.nybooks.com/articles/2000/11/02/making-the-memorial/.

National Park Service. "Vietnam Veterans Memorial Collection." Accessed July 1, 2015. http://www.nps.gov/orgs/1802/vive.htm.

National Public Radio. "Vietnam Memorial Has Spelling Errors Set in Stone." February 24, 2012. Accessed July 3, 2015. http://www.npr.org/2012/02/24/147367962/correcting-a-national-record-literally-set-in-stone.

Scruggs, Jan C., and Joel L. Swerdlow. *To Heal a Nation: The Vietnam Veterans Memorial*. New York: Harper & Row, 1985.

Turner Publishing, Inc. *Offerings at the Wall: Artifacts from the Vietnam Veterans Memorial Collection*. Atlanta, GA: Turner Pub.; Kansas City, MO: Andrews and McMeel, 1995.

U.S. Department of Defense. "Name of Technical Sergeant Richard B. Fitzgibbon to Be Added to the Vietnam Veterans Memorial." November 6, 1998. Accessed July 3, 2015. http://www.defense.gov/releases/release.aspx?releaseid=1902.

The Wall-USA. "The Vietnam Veterans Memorial Wall Page." Accessed July 1, 2015. http://thewall-usa.com/index.asp.

Wikipedia. "Vietnam Veterans Memorial." Last updated June 30, 2015. https://en.wikipedia.org/w/index.php?title=Vietnam_Veterans_Memorial&oldid=669325862.

Wikisource. "Maya Lin's Original Competition Submission for the Vietnam Veterans Memorial." Last modified February 2, 2013. Accessed July 1, 2015. https://en.wikisource.org/wiki/Maya_Lin%27s_original_competition_submission_for_the_Vietnam_Veterans_Memorial.

43
AIDS Quilt

the NAMES Project AIDS Memorial Quilt
conceived and started by Cleve Jones in San Francisco
now housed at the NAMES Project Foundation in Atlanta

1987

Remember when it was fun to be sick? As an adult, it's a lot less enjoyable, but as a kid, you could stay home from school, get spoiled, have grilled cheese sandwiches and tomato soup, and be tucked in all warm and cozy; maybe if you were lucky you might even get a story read to you.

Stories are important—that's why there are so many kinds and so many ways of telling them, including through documents. Some do this in a straightforward way, like the Declaration of Independence. Others tell us about their creators and their rationales, their subjects and contexts, in a more incidental fashion. Consider the wanted poster for John Wilkes Booth, intended at the time to help track down the most notorious fugitive in the nation's history, and coincidentally one of the first wanted posters to feature a photographic image, his theatrical publicity photo. Today you could argue that that poster tells a long and unpleasant story drawing a direct if convoluted line back to the Declaration and its shortcomings.

Documents come in lots of shapes and sizes and forms. Reports, charts, maps, statistics, they all have their purposes and intents, can all be useful individually or together to describe, for example, the adoption of a new teaching method or the spread of a new virus.

What about a quilt? Can a quilt be a document? Sure it can. They often record and tell the stories of individuals, families, communities, events, and histories. By their very nature, they're an assembly of various materials. And it's a very old form; the earliest known patchwork textiles go back at least 5,000 years and the use of "patchwork" as a metaphor at least 400.

One quilt, the largest of its kind—in fact, so large it will likely never again be intact—has documented its subject in a way so vivid, so undeniable, so real, it helped to change the way many people perceived an unknown and frightening disease.

A section of panel 04445 of the AIDS Memorial Quilt. DB King (flickr user: bootbearwdc).

It isn't entirely clear when HIV first made its way to humans; there is some evidence it could have been as early as the late 19th century, though documented individual cases of deaths seem to first appear around 1959. Public attention wasn't focused until larger numbers of cases occurred in urban areas, and the name "AIDS" wasn't officially put into use by the CDC until 1982.

Once it hit the popular consciousness, however, it cut a huge swath, particularly since so little was known about it and because the earliest largest concentrations of cases were found in specific, often marginalized populations: Haitian immigrants, hemophiliacs, intravenous drug users, and gay men. At a candlelight vigil honoring the memory of assassinated city supervisor Harvey Milk and mayor George Moscone in San Francisco in 1985—by that time already the site of hundreds of deaths—names of victims were carried on placards and then assembled on a wall, bringing to mind a patchwork quilt. And thus, in a moment, the idea was born. Cleve Jones, a longtime activist, Milk assistant, and march organizer, made the first panel for his friend Marvin Feldman in 1986, and the idea rapidly spread. The first display of forty panels took place at the San Francisco City Hall in June of 1987, roughly two weeks after President Reagan dramatically spoke in front of the Berlin Wall, calling on Mikhail Gorbachev to tear it down. An organization was formed and by October of 1987, nearly 2,000 panels were displayed on the National Mall in Washington, where it was viewed by half a million people.

A news article from that display calls out some of the famous names already there—Rock Hudson, Roy Cohn, Michael Bennett, and Liberace with his gold lamé and rhinestone panel—and draws the contrast between the colorful quilt and the granite of the nearby and still-new Vietnam Veterans Memorial. As one contributor said, "This is our wall. This will remind people that there's a war going on now." It also tells the stories of people, people who concealed their diagnosis and disease and even their identity, such as an anonymous retired military officer who created a panel for his deceased lover who chose landscape architecture over interior design because it was "less stereotypically homo-sexual," and the dying man who made his own panel.

The NAMES Project AIDS Memorial Quilt on display at the National Mall. US National Library of Medicine.

The quilt continues to grow, now comprising over 49,000 panels repre-senting more than 94,000 names. Each panel is three by six feet, roughly the size of a grave; if assembled it would cover over 1.3 million square feet and weigh 54 tons. In 1989, the project was nominated for the Nobel Peace Prize, the same year the film *Common Threads: Stories from the Quilt* won the Academy Award for Best Documentary Feature. You know you've arrived when Miss America accompanies you down Pennsylvania Avenue in a presidential inau-gural parade, for Bill Clinton's first inaugural in 1993.

As new panels are submitted to the Foundation, they are now photographed and a database of those along with additional materials such as letters, photographs, and biographies is also maintained. This leads to the inevitable challenge of description and organization; each panel receives a unique code number, but given the multiple varieties of interest (art historians, quilters, researchers, and students, not to mention people just looking for a name), there will have to be considerable attention paid to appropriate metadata to facilitate search. There's also a significant need for conservation efforts; as panels are moved and displayed, often out of doors, they're exposed to light, heat, moisture, dirt, bugs, and who knows what else, not to mention being handled, and the materials themselves have special needs. Consider how you might keep all of the following safe and intact: every kind of fabric and textile you can imagine, from lace to mink to suede to bubble wrap and metal, gems, clothing, hair, wedding rings, cremation ashes, jockstraps, condoms, bowling balls, and the inevitable feathers and sequins. Contributors are advised to use stitching rather than glue for durability, textile paint or dye, and iron-on transfers for photographs or letters.

The goals of the project include remembrance, awareness, education, and fundraising, most of which are inherently difficult to assess, though its scale and reach are clear. It has inspired other similar memorials, for those killed in action in Iraq, victims of the 9/11 attacks, other diseases, even virtual memorial quilts. It's inevitably political—it started in a time of growing and evolving activism, often confrontational in nature, and people in some quarters have criticized the quilt project as not provocative enough.

The quilt has several intriguing features as a document. It may never be finished, and if it was, how and when would we know? It also has no single, inherent structure or order; the blocks of panels could be connected in any number of ways, each equally effective and authentic. As it almost certainly will never be fully assembled again, it exists only, exclusively in fragmentary, federated form—a collective enterprise not only in construction and maintenance but also in configuration. You might even say it now functions more as a collection than a single item—never intact, though bounded and defined and distributed, increasing the possibility for interaction and impact.

Perhaps, though, the most satisfying and genuine explanation of its power is the simplest. It's a *quilt*. The individual panels are objects of love, loss, pain, remembrance, and hope, and like any quilt, it's a symbol of comfort and warmth and home—for those who have gone and for those who remain.

SOURCES

Biggs, John. "The AIDS Quilt, Digitized: Microsoft and the NAMES Project Team Up to Bring Remembrance Project into the 21st Century." *TechCrunch*, July 24, 2012. Accessed August 30, 2016. http://techcrunch.com/2012/07/24/the-aids-quilt-digitized-microsoft-and-the-names -project-team-up-to-bring-remembrance-project-into-the-21st-century/.

Boodman, Sandra G. "Giant Quilt Names 1,920 AIDS Victims; Memorial Will Be Unfurled on Mall." *Washington Post*, October 10, 1987.

Capozzola, Christopher. "AIDS Memorial Quilt—Names Project." In *Encyclopedia of Lesbian, Gay, Bisexual, and Transgender History in America*, edited by Mark Stein, 39–40. New York: Charles Scribner's Sons, 2004.

Kaiser Family Foundation. "Global HIV/AIDS Timeline." July 2, 2015. http://www.kff.org/hivaids/ timeline/hivtimeline.cfm.

Kulpa, Robert. "Names Project AIDS Memorial Quilt." In *LGBTQ America Today*, edited by John C. Hawley, 783–88. Westport, CT: Greenwood Press, 2010.

The Names Project Foundation. "The Names Project—AIDS Memorial Quilt." Accessed August 30, 2016. http://www.aidsquilt.org/.

Rosen, Rebecca J. "A Map of Loss: The AIDS Quilt Goes Online." *Atlantic* (July 24, 2012). Accessed August 30, 2016. http://www.theatlantic.com/technology/archive/2012/07/a-map-of-loss -the-aids-quilt-goes-online/260188/.

Wikipedia. "NAMES Project AIDS Memorial Quilt." Last modified July 12, 2016. Accessed August 30, 2016. https://en.wikipedia.org/w/index.php?title=NAMES_Project_AIDS_Mem orial_Quilt&oldid=729516099.

44
Nupedia

a Web-based encyclopedia project
cocreated by Larry Sanger and Jimmy Wales
now largely defunct, discontinued in 2003 though fragments
and newer versions can be found online

2000

There are lots of ways we "know" things: the results of scientific experimenta-tion or mathematical proof, experience, deduction, induction, rumor, a trusted source or authority, tradition, belief. Each has its strengths and weaknesses; each can work, or let you down.

The desire to know, and moreover to collect what's known or what's worth knowing, in a tidy yet all-encompassing package, is ancient. Pliny the Elder gets credit for the first attempt we know of, the *Historia Naturalis*, finished just a couple of years before he gave his life exploring intriguing clouds over what turned out to be Mt. Vesuvius, proving this work is riskier than it looks. Hundreds, thousands more, in untold forms and languages—Francis Bacon, Diderot, the *Britannica*, and on and on—have followed down the centuries.

As we all know, encyclopedias aren't what they used to be, and likely never will be again. That's due to Wikipedia, sure, but the real story goes a bit further back, only a few months earlier, with the launch of an online effort that, although it didn't quite work out the way it was intended, did pave the way for that other one, and posed an age-old challenge for a new millennium: knowing how we know what we know.

That's "Nupedia" as in N-U-pedia; N-E-W-pedia is an obvious way to spell it even though that's not how it was named. The "pedia" part is a borrowing, from the early 16th-century word "encyclopedia," which itself comes from "*enykylios paideia*," erroneous Greek for "general education," what a learned person should know.

This particular pedia emerged from the early, heady days of the Web as well as the open-source movement, dedicated to fostering freely shared soft-ware and other intellectual works, including the GNU operating system (often pronounced with a hard *g* as in "guh-new"), which Nupedia might have

been sort of named after. It was the joint brainchild of two outsize figures of the Internet age: Jimmy Wales, the former options trader who carefully pasted updates into his *World Book* encyclopedia as a child, and Larry Sanger, a doctoral student in epistemology who was casting around for something to do post-Y2K.

It's difficult to separate their various roles and contributions, not to mention separate versions of events, and stronger people than I have gone mad trying, but here's a thumbnail. Larry was hoping to build a "highly reliable, peer-reviewed resource that fully appreciated and employed the efforts of subject area experts, as well as the general public." Jimmy wanted to build something that would take advantage of the aspects of the Internet he thought most valuable and salient: freedom, interactivity, the power of the open-source movement, and even fun, to "distribute a free encyclopedia to every single person on the planet in their own language."

They were probably doomed from the start. Nupedia had worthy aims, and in many ways tried to replicate the authority structures and systems that print encyclopedias and other "respectable" sources use, including an advisory board and a core set of experts and editors with appropriate backgrounds and pedigrees, a seven-step peer-review and editing system, and so on.

Photo of Larry Sanger.   Photo of Jimmy Wales. Joi Ito (flickr user: joi).

They connected online via their mutual interest in philosophy, particu-larly Ayn Rand's objectivism, which tells us "facts are facts, independent of any consciousness. No amount of passionate wishing, desperate longing or hopeful pleading can alter the facts." This gets reflected in early Nupedia rules insisting on integrating multiple viewpoints to achieve a lack of bias or perspective.

Larry established and promulgated those initial rules in early 2000, with the website going live on March 9; the *New York Times* main headline that day read, with considerable unintended understatement: "Gore and Bush Set for a Fiery Race That Starts Now."

It generated considerable interest and participation; the first article to be completed, on "atonality," complete with 14 footnotes, 27 references, and a discography, was finalized that September. It was, though, an excruciatingly slow and laborious process, which produced a grand total of fewer than two dozen entries in that first year. Jimmy tried to write one, on a topic he knew well, options-pricing theory, and said it felt like homework. Not a good sign.

Somewhere around New Year's Day of 2001—and here stories diverge again—one of them got the idea of using a wiki, essentially a website that could be edited by anybody, as a way to kick-start the slow pace and improve workflow and efficiency. Larry sends out an e-mail to the mailing list with the now-famous subject line "Let's make a wiki" and calling it "an idea to add a little feature to Nupedia." If only he suspected. Initial reaction was lukewarm, as the Nupedia faithful felt it was a bit too informal and unstructured, but nonetheless Wikipedia.com (the .org came later) was launched on January 15, 2001. Within a day the first article, on the letter U, was up; within two weeks there were 600 articles, then more than 1,000 by mid-February, and more than 20,000 within the year. Wikipedia is a classic example of unforeseen consequences.

Obviously, Wikipedia quickly overshadowed its ancestor; Nupedia was effectively shut down by 2003, Larry had been laid off by Jimmy's company the year before, though Larry's personal vision of a reliable, contributory online encyclopedia persisted, launching the infelicitously named Citizendium project in 2007, which met a similar fate. Jimmy of course became the world-famous if occasionally uncomfortable god-king of Wikipedia, and their messy breakup has been sport for Internet historians and gossipmongers ever since. Reading the articles about the Nupedia in the Wikipedia (or the *Britannica* for that matter) has a strange, down-the-rabbit-hole feeling to it, and occasionally it's downright snide. The Wikipedia article (at least today) includes this little zinger: "The Nupedia website at nupedia.com was shut down on September 26, 2003.[*citation needed*] Nupedia's encyclopedic content, which was often described as limited, has since been assimilated into Wikipedia." Ouch. Resistance is futile.

If not for the Nupedia—and moreover, the creatively volatile combo that was Larry and Jimbo—it seems likely something like Wikipedia would have developed, but how big, how popular, how transformative, we shall never know. Traditional encyclopedias have relied on long publishing histories, established track records, and authors with impressive credentials chosen by thoughtful editors attempting to assemble and shape a coherent package representing the state of our knowledge. Wikipedia goes exactly the opposite way; let everybody have a crack at it, and what emerges is what "we" "know." The increasing calcification and bureaucracy that Wikipedia has suffered in the last several years aren't surprising; bottom-up work isn't as easy or as easy to manage as it sounds.

Print encyclopedias are stable; what's on page 976 of Volume IX will be there tomorrow as it was yesterday, which is reassuring, if problematic in a world that changes all the time. With Wikipedia, it's never quite so sure—you can't access the same Wikipedia twice, not only because the reality it's trying to represent is changing, but because *it's* changing as well. It's one thing to know that the world changes; it's another not to be able to find the same fact again, maybe because it's not a fact any more, or because some editor or committee or flame warrior decided it shouldn't be there anymore. And don't even get me started on their preference for verifiability over truth or accuracy.

This seems somehow more arbitrary than the top-down approach, or perhaps just differently arbitrary; it's either one expert's judgment, bias, and prejudice, with an editorial infrastructure to catch or to reinforce it, or it's lots of people with varying judgments and biases and axes to grind, who somehow have to come to consensus on what's what.

Which of course, 'twas ever thus, and also true for all the other encyclopedias ever created. Knowledge is socially constructed, and comforting as it might be to believe that facts are facts, it's not that simple, not by a long shot. No fact exists in a vacuum. Never has; never will. Yesterday's "fact" can be today's misunderstanding and tomorrow's superstition, or vice versa. If you "know" that witches cause disease or famine, then executing them to purify and safeguard your community makes perfect sense. On the other hand, if you "know" that tiny invisible bugs cause disease, spending large amounts of money and time to cure and prevent them makes sense. At least until some new "knowledge" comes along.

There have been imagined visions of similar tools or projects; in the 1930s, H. G. Wells saw his "World Brain" idea as a means of forestalling totalitarianism by promoting universal understanding. The *Encyclopedia Galactica* features in Isaac Asimov's *Foundation* series as well as in Carl Sagan's *Cosmos*, and a work by that same name is the stodgy foil to the much hipper *Hitchhiker's Guide to the Galaxy*, about which it is said, "though it cannot hope to be useful or informative on all matters, it does make the reassuring claim that where it is inaccurate, it is at least definitively inaccurate. In cases of major discrepancy it was always reality that's got it wrong."

It's possible to view the Nupedia as the last gasp of authority in the face of knowledge-by-"community" but the jury might still be out on that, given Wikipedia's various plateaus. It's hard to deny, though, that what "we" "know" depends strongly on the "we" and on how we process, record, and use that knowledge. With a different set of assumptions, rules, and structures, and a different community that responds, reacts, and eventually changes those, you get a different Wikipedia, and thus a different "knowledge."

Like it or not, there's nothing new here, and it's true for each of us and for all of us. We construct knowledge, individually and societally, in a messy, bumpy, uneven, imperfect, ever-changing process, and ultimately that knowledge changes us as well. As it's always been, who gets to say, and how and why we say it, profoundly matters.

SOURCES

Adams, Douglas. *The Hitchhiker's Guide to the Galaxy: The Original Radio Scripts*. London: Pan, 1985.

Ayn Rand Institute. "Ayn Rand's Philosophy of Objectivism." Accessed August 31, 2016. https://www.aynrand.org/ideas/philosophy.

Chozick, Amy. "Jimmy Wales Is Not an Internet Billionaire." *New York Times*, June 27, 2013. http://www.nytimes.com/2013/06/30/magazine/jimmy-wales-is-not-an-internet-billionaire.html.

Gnu. *The Gnu Operating System and the Free Software Movement*. Last modified June 19, 2016. https://www.gnu.org/.

Greenwald, Ted. "How Jimmy Wales' Wikipedia Harnessed the Web as a Force for Good." *Wired* (March 19, 2013). Accessed August 31, 2016. http://www.wired.com/2013/03/jimmy-wales-wikipedia/.

Lih, Andrew. *The Wikipedia Revolution: How a Bunch of Nobodies Created the World's Greatest Encyclopedia*. New York: Hyperion, 2009.

Nupedia.com. "Nu Pedia." Accessed August 31, 2016. http://c2.com/cgi/wiki?NuPedia.

Nupedia Wiki. Accessed August 31, 2016. http://nupedia.wikia.com/wiki/Category:Nupedia.

Slashdot. "The Early History of Nupedia and Wikipedia: A Memoir." Accessed August 31, 2016. http://features.slashdot.org/story/05/04/18/164213/the-early-history-of-nupedia-and-wikipedia-a-memoir.

Wikipedia. "History of Wikipedia." Accessed August 31, 2016. https://en.wikipedia.org/w/index.php?title=History_of_Wikipedia&oldid=736791308.

———. "Larry Sanger." Accessed August 31, 2016. https://en.wikipedia.org/wiki/Larry_Sanger.

———. "Nupedia." *Wikipedia*. Accessed August 31, 2016. https://en.wikipedia.org/wiki/Nupedia.

Palm Beach County "Butterfly" Ballot

a ballot and instructions used in the presidential election
in Palm Beach County, Florida
now known as the "Butterfly Ballot"

2000

For years, I've taught courses in quantitative research methods, which includes how to construct and administer surveys. You hear about these all the time, including the ubiquitous polls that build to a fever pitch with the approach of any election, and the techniques involved have become increasingly complicated and sophisticated over the last several decades.

However, as I always tell my students, when you're doing this sort of work, people are a problem. It's very easy for somebody to answer a telephone poll or click a box on a survey form that says they're going to vote for X or believe Y or think we ought to do Z, but it's quite another to know, really know, really really know, what's going on in somebody's head. It takes hard work to put together instruments and instructions to do the best possible job of discerning just that.

Electorally, the only poll that matters is the last one—actually casting a vote, which seems comparatively straightforward. You vote for the person you want, somebody in charge counts them all up, and then we find out the winner. And more often than not that's how it goes. This is a story we all know the end of, and sort of know how we got to the end of, like it or not. But how we got to having to get to that end, an end that reverberates several elections on, is not so well understood.

There are lots of stories to be told about the 2000 election, including legal, constitutional, moral, judicial, social, political—and probably a marine biology or art history angle I haven't run across, but I'll let other people tell those. Here we are concerned with a document, actually two documents working together, that had a joint purpose and function, and how that worked, or didn't. A "ballot," which we borrowed from the Italian for the "little balls" used in elections in the Venetian Republic, is intended to allow someone to cast a vote so that those votes can be counted and a democratic decision can be made. So, like any document, it must be designed to appropriately fulfill those functions.

This brings us to Theresa LePore, who began as a file clerk in the Palm Beach County Supervisor of Elections office in 1971, age 16. By 2000 she had been elected supervisor, and thus it fell to her, as it did in every other county in Florida, to decide on the design for the ballot for the upcoming election. About a quarter of Palm Beach County residents then were over 65, and she had been involved with a federal task force on voters with visual impairments and disabilities, so she felt it was important to be sure candidates' names would be clearly visible. Since there were so many candidates for president and vice president (10 each), listing them on only one side of their Votomatic punch-card ballot instructions would make the print really small. (Imagine these instructions like the pages of an open book.) So she decides to use larger print and both pages astride the narrow exposed column of the actual voting card, with numbered arrows pointing from candidates' names to the appropriate holes to punch to vote for them. To be clear, the punch card was the actual ballot; she designed the instructions, and the combination had to work together to be used properly.

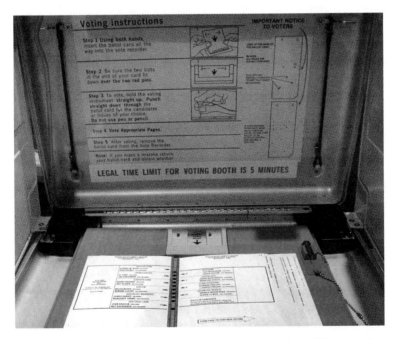

A Votomatic machine from Palm Beach County, Florida, part of an exhibit on voting that opened Friday, July 16, 2004, at the National Museum of American History. Associated Press/Adele Starr.

In a 2001 interview, she describes her hazy memories of that election day, arriving at the office at 4:00 a.m. to deal with the usual hectic pace. A couple of elderly gentlemen come by the elections office mid-morning to complain that they were confused, but it's only as the day progresses and more calls come in, followed by agitated visits from elected officials, particularly Democratic ones, that she starts to realize there's a substantial problem. In her desire for readability, she sacrificed—almost everybody believes inadvertently—another key design principle: usability. It's not hard to see the word "Democratic" listed second on the left (because the Democratic candidate had placed second in the most recent gubernatorial election, to Jeb Bush) and then follow along to punch the hole immediately to the right, the second in the column, which is really for Pat Buchanan, listed and with an arrow on the other side, who ran on the Reform Party line. Whoops.

Later analysis would suggest that between 2,000 and 3,000 people in Palm Beach County voted for Buchanan by making that mistake, along with uncommonly large numbers—thousands—of other problems: overvotes (people voting for more than one candidate for the same office, such as both Buchanan and Gore or punching the space for Gore and also writing him in), undervotes (people who voted for other offices but not for president), and what we all later learned way too much about, problems with chads.

Remember chads? The word itself, of uncertain origin, traces back to the late 1950s and refers to the little bits that got punched out of early computer storage technologies like cards and paper tape. Basically confetti. The first computer I ever laid hands on, when I was in high school way back in the 1970s, was an old teletype machine connected to a timesharing mainframe. It had a paper tape punch and reader as a storage mechanism, and much fun could be had with the bin full of chads it produced, at least until it had to get cleaned up.

With a good solid punch, the hole is made, the chad falls away, everybody's happy, and the ballot can be counted by detecting a light that would shine through a good clear hole. But a half-hearted, uncertain, hurried, indifferent punch can get you one of no less than six different kinds of problematic chad: dangling, dimpled, hanging, pierced, pregnant, and swinging. Which, if this weren't so serious, would sound like outcomes of some late-1960s suburban pool party.

People make errors when they vote all the time, and not just of the buyers' remorse variety. With any system, whether you touch a screen, pull a lever, fill in a bubble, whatever, you can get it wrong through inattention, carelessness, or what have you. But here's the thing—how would anybody else know? Buchanan got way more votes in Palm Beach County than would have normally been expected. Let's stipulate for the sake of argument that a confusing ballot caused that. How many? Which ones? How do you really know what's in somebody's mind at the fateful moment? The endless discussion in the weeks of haggling over all this afterward focused in no small part on "voter intent," which is next to impossible to discern, even by examining hanging chads, by hand, one by one, using magnifying glasses (one of which is now in the Smithsonian), as eventually happened.

The chad situation is largely separate, an artifact of using a punch card system. It underscores, though, the difficulties inherent in the simple counting of large numbers of things. Ask ten people each to count a stack of a few dozen pieces of paper, and they'll likely all come up with the same number, maybe a stray one or two here or there. Make it a few million, and watch the fun. Machines are better, though issues of maintenance, manufacture, programming, improper feeding or training can intrude here as well. As a county judge on the canvassing board said, when tested seven times on preprogrammed ballots, the machines had 100 percent accuracy every time; in a manual recount "no two people get the same results." For that matter, it appears that most of the increase Gore saw in a machine recount was because some chads were knocked loose by being fed through a second time.

Distressing as it may sound, as I also tell my students, just about every vote total that you've ever heard, of any magnitude, is wrong. It almost has to be, simply because of the myriad factors involved in counting a large number of anything. In a not-close election, these kinds of issues about design, error, inattention, and lots of others have marginal impacts. Decidedly not the case in 2000, hence all the legal and political wrangling that went on all the way to the doors of the US Supreme Court weeks later as the world waited. In the larger context, this is all complicated by the highly decentralized patchwork American electoral system, where critical decisions are made at the state and county level, to which almost nobody pays any attention unless something goes terrifyingly astray and then people freak out until they forget all about it again.

Broward County canvassing board member Judge Robert Rosenberg uses a magnifying glass to examine a disputed ballot Friday, Nov. 24, 2000, at the Broward County Courthouse in Fort Lauderdale, Florida. Associated Press/Alan Diaz.

The butterfly ballot has taken its place in the Awful Design Hall of Fame, along with the Three Mile Island control system and the O-rings on the *Challenger* space shuttle. The National Institute of Standards strongly recommended the elimination of Votomatic systems as far back as 1988. "Design" is something lots of people do, and digital tools have made it more commonplace; think of all the miserable PowerPoint slides and resumes and invitations you've ever seen. It's a common activity, and like many common activities, to do it well takes time; experience; training; talent; and, critically, testing and iteration to make sure the end product does what you want it to do and not something else. The sample ballot had been sent to the candidates, party chairs, and all 655,000 registered voters, and no complaints were raised. It wasn't until people tried to actually vote, to actually punch holes, that it all started to go so badly wrong.

It seems only fair to give the last word to Theresa LePore, who left the elections office in 2005, followed by many years of service to a number of volunteer and community organizations. When asked in 2001, "Who do you believe won Florida?" she said, simply but damningly, "I don't know. Too many variables. Too many factors."

SOURCES

ABC News. "Butterfly Ballot Designer Speaks Out." Published December 21, 2001. http://abcnews
.go.com/Politics/story?id=122175&page=1.

Berke, Richard L. "Gore and Bush Set for a Fiery Race That Starts Now." *New York Times*. March 9, 2000.
http://www.nytimes.com/2000/03/09/us/gore-and-bush-set-for-a-fiery-race-that-starts-now
.html.

DeHaven-Smith, Lance, ed. *The Battle for Florida: An Annotated Compendium of Materials from the
2000 Presidential Election*. Gainesville: University Press of Florida, 2005.

Palm Beach Post, "Theresa LePore, Full-Time Volunteer." September 10, 2010. Accessed February
11, 2016. http://www.palmbeachpost.com/news/news/theresa-lepore-full-time-volunteer/
nL9wJ/.

Pleasants, Julian M. *Hanging Chads: The Inside Story of the 2000 Presidential Recount in Florida*. New
York: Palgrave Macmillan, 2004.

"Theresa LePore." *LinkedIn*. Accessed February 11, 2016. https://www.linkedin.com/in/theresa
-lepore-91b71610.

Tognazzini, Bruce. "The Butterfly Ballot: Anatomy of a Disaster." *askTog*, January 2001. Accessed
February 11, 2016. http://www.asktog.com/columns/042ButterflyBallot.html.

Watson, Robert P., ed. *Counting Votes: Lessons from the 2000 Presidential Election in Florida*.
Gainesville: University Press of Florida, 2004.

Pope Benedict XVI's Resignation

the text of a resignation announcement
written and delivered by Pope Benedict XVI in Rome
now presumably housed in the Vatican Archives

2013

We've all had those days when we just wanted to pack it all in. Too many e-mails, yet another pointless meeting, life just getting you down. Most of us know, however trying things get, that the prospect of retirement is always there, and some day we can put down our work, put up our feet, and spend our final years doing whatever we want.

Not everybody is so lucky, particularly if you're a hereditary monarch, ruthless despot, or superhero. Age and infirmity don't matter, you're the job and the job is you. It takes a special sort of person to decide to buck that system and declare they're just not up to it any more, an act of finality and definition that also tells us something about authority and legitimacy and how we record those.

Pope Benedict XVI standing on the balcony of the Apostolic Palace in Castel Gandolfo, Italy, February 28, 2013, his last day as pope. Associated Press/Michael Kappeler.

There have been scattered prior papal resignations, most of which are a bit sketchy because of the passage of so much time—which is what you get with an organization that's been around for two millennia or so—reaching all the way back to Pontianus in 235 and Marcellinus in 304, through to Benedict IX, who somehow managed to become pope three times, might have sold the papacy to his godfather, and resigned once or twice in the 1040s. Better known is the case of Celestine V, almost universally described as "a very holy hermit"—which seems to be a euphemism for "oblivious to the real world"—who lived in a small wooden cell, largely refused to see his cardinals or do much of anything, and gave up after five months in 1294. A story, likely apocryphal, nonetheless survives, that one Cardinal Caetani had a small speaking tube inserted into the cell so that the "voice of the Holy Spirit" could encourage Celestine in the dead of night to retire or face the fires of hell, and who helpfully drafted the document for him.

Then there's the much-discussed saga of Gregory XII, one of many, many popes and people who claimed to be pope in the early 15th century, in a time now referred to as the Great Western Schism. This was a period of much to-ing and fro-ing, back and forth, with rival popes, colleges of cardinals, councils, and courts. Trying to sort this out involved a lot of "I'll quit if he does, *I'll* quit if *he* does, let's quit together, I don't want to quit." Gregory and another claimant, Benedict XIII, now referred to as an antipope, had both actually already been declared deposed by one church council at Pisa in 1409, although that didn't take; the crux of the matter there was that without agreement as to who is official, it's hard to officiate with any finality. They took documents seriously in those days; this Benedict, after having his money cut off, excommunicated pretty much everybody, including Charles VI, the king of France, but the Rector of the University of Paris publicly shredded the proclamation. So there.

Another council was finally called for the German city of Constance in 1415. More chicanery, intrigue, and yet another antipope briefly escaping while everybody was outside watching a tournament; it must have been quite a scene. A deal was finally struck, and after a few last attempts at delay, Gregory's protector, the unfortunately named Lord Carlo Malatesta, read out and submitted what one source calls Gregory's "document of cession," which the council quickly accepted, and the deed was done, just two days before the same council condemned and burned the Czech reformer Jan Hus for heresy, and only a few months before the Battle of Agincourt.

In a situation like this there has to be a document, or at least it feels as though there has to be, to make it feel official, final, no take backs. Canon Law 332 says "it is required for validity that the resignation is made freely and properly manifested," presumably meaning that it be somehow announced and made known, though not necessarily recorded or published. It then goes on to say "but not that it is accepted by anyone." True, although Benedict's announcement on February 11, 2013, was delivered to his colleague cardinals as "dear brothers" and also fixed a specific time and hour, at 8 p.m. on the 28th, when his resignation would take effect.

This isn't unlike Edward VIII's 1936 instrument of abdication, somewhat ignominiously typed on a sheet of letterhead, signed by everybody in sight, and addressed to no one in particular. Contrast this to Richard Nixon's one-sentence 1974 resignation letter, addressed and delivered to Secretary of State Kissinger.

There have been hints and suggestions that other popes have made provisions for a resignation but never acted on them. Pius VII thought he might not be allowed to leave France after presiding over Napoleon's imperial coronation in 1804, though Napoleon spared him the trouble by plunking the crown on his own head instead. Pius XII is said to have prepared a document declaring himself resigned if the Nazis took him prisoner, and even the indefatigable John Paul II wrote a letter of resignation as early as 1989 to be used if he became incapacitated physically or mentally. Naturally, there have also been the drearily predictable conspiracy theories, including that Benedict XVI was the victim of notoriously internecine Vatican politics and knew he couldn't win.

This question of disability is an important, if unpleasant, one. The US Constitution deals with this in the 25th Amendment so memorably trampled by Alexander Haig in the wake of President Reagan's shooting in 1981. The amendment requires a president to declare, in writing, that he's going to be unable to serve, as President George W. Bush did twice, for a couple of hours each time, for colonoscopies; Dick Cheney was acting president in both circumstances until President Bush woke up and signed another document reclaiming his authority. There's also a provision, not yet invoked, that the vice president and a majority of the cabinet could declare the president incapacitated, again in writing, with a convoluted process of resolution thereafter.

It's hard to ease out the boss, especially if he's got more titles than you have fingers, supreme dominion over the earthly and eternal church, not to mention God as a direct report. Unlike democracies or hereditary monarchies, there's no vice pope or heir apparent; it's almost more like a board of directors having to choose a new CEO. Canon law says that "special laws" are to be followed when the Roman See is "entirely impeded," also taken to mean exile or imprisonment, which is a great idea except that apparently no such laws exist.

An article written before Benedict's resignation describes a medieval theory that a mentally incapacitated pope wouldn't be able to carry out his duties and thus should be treated as though he were dead and a new pope elected, which seems a bit harsh. It raises this far more intriguing question, though: If a pope today was cognitively "impeded," could he resign, since Canon Law 187 says that only someone in their right mind can resign an ecclesiastical office?

THE WHITE HOUSE

WASHINGTON

August 9, 1974

Dear Mr. Secretary:

I hereby resign the Office of President of the
United States.

Sincerely,

The Honorable Henry A. Kissinger
The Secretary of State
Washington, D. C. 20520

Richard M. Nixon's resignation letter, dated August 9, 1974. National Archives and Records Administration (NARA).

And it's not as though the pope just has to nip down to Human Resources to fill out form PR-001. One imagines calligraphy in circumlocutory Latin, a seal, gold leaf, perhaps some tasteful illumination to reflect the dignity, gravity, and solemnity of the occasion and also to have something to stick in the archives for centuries to come. It may well be the case that such a document, or even something more prosaic, is indeed now housed in the Archivum Secretum Apostolicum Vaticanum. It is not at all clear, however, what, if any, documentation was involved. Benedict read out what's referred to on the Vatican website as a "declaratio," in which he announced his intention to resign, but I can find no evidence of anything more formal than that, which is an interesting story in itself. The canon law provision says that any resignation has to be "properly manifested," without specifying how, so perhaps his word was all it took.

Benedict's successor, Francis, has gone on to lead the church in his own way, as will his successor and the one after that, and thus it will continue to change in ways large and small. In addition, Benedict's act opens the door for future popes to more seriously consider resignation or retirement as an option, which has long been seen as anathema. It might also recalibrate the calculus for elections and church administration going forward; lots of things might be seen in new light when death is no longer the only viable means of a change at the top.

In Gregory's case, it likely took a long time for word to spread across the Christian world; in Benedict's case, the world knew within minutes. He didn't tweet it personally via the @pontifex Twitter handle. Vatican Radio did report that one of the first reactions to their Facebook posting of the news was "Hacked??"—the 21st-century equivalent, I suppose, of questioning whether a proclamation read out at Mass or posted on the church door was authentic, which is what gave rise to the use of seals on documents.

And ultimately that's what all this is about. All these various forms and kinds of documents serve as definite end points. One moment you're the pope or president or king, and at the next you're not. So such documents are markers of legitimacy, authority, and continuity, tangible evidence, public and verified, to record what was said and intended, marking the end of one era and the unquestioned beginning of the next.

SOURCES

Benedictus PP XVI. "Declaratio." *Libreria Editrice Vaticana.* Accessed October 25, 2016. http:// w2.vatican.va/content/benedict-xvi/en/speeches/2013/february/documents/hf_ben-xvi _spe_20130211_declaratio.html.

Chandler, Adam. "The Pope Benedict Conspiracy Theories." *The Atlantic* (February 13, 2015). http://www.theatlantic.com/international/archive/2015/02/Pope-Benedict-XVI-resignation -forced-conspiracy-theory/385462/.

Colbert, E. P., and B. Tierney. "Constance, Council of." In *New Catholic Encyclopedia*, edited by Thomas Carson, 168–73. Detroit: Thomson/Gale, in Association with the Catholic University of America, 2003.

Creighton, M. *A History of the Papacy from the Great Schism to the Sack of Rome.* New ed. London: Longmans, Green, and Co., 1897.

Elliott-Binns, Leonard Elliott. *The History of the Decline and Fall of the Medieval Papacy.* London: Methuen, 1934.

Norwich, John Julius. *Absolute Monarchs: A History of the Papacy.* New York: Random House, 2011.

Papal Encyclicals Online. "Council of Constance 1414–18." Accessed October 25, 2016. http://www .papalencyclicals.net/Councils/ecum16.htm.

Provost, James H. "What If the Pope Became Disabled?" *America Magazine* (September 30, 2000). http://americamagazine.org/issue/382/article/what-if-pope-became-disabled.

Smith, John Holland. *The Great Schism, 1378.* Turning Points in History. London: Hamilton, 1970.

Soenen, Micheline. "Gregory XII." In *The Papacy: An Encyclopedia*, ed. Philippe Levillain. New York: Routledge, 2002.

Vatican Radio. "Facebook Reaction to Pope Benedict XVI Plan to Resign Papacy." February 2, 2013. Accessed February 14, 2013. http://en.radiovaticana.va/articolo.asp?c=663859.

CONCLUSION: THE NEXT DOCUMENT?

Ah yes, the next one. Some document of great historic or cultural importance that will take its place with those here and the myriad others going back centuries and millennia. It might be, as we've seen, anything from anywhere for any purpose from any time. As such, there isn't a great deal we can say about it. It might be some traditional form or genre, like a contract or a treaty or a license, or one not even conceived yet. Its impact might be intentional or accidental or unintended. It might already have been created and is simply not yet known or discovered—moldering away in an archive or library or attic somewhere—or it may not yet be born.

There are a few things, though, that I'd suggest we do know, or at least suspect, about the "next" important document. It will likely be created to achieve some objective, to make something happen, or to record something for its creator or for a more general posterity. If it's yet to be created, it will also quite likely be born natively digital, perhaps never reaching any analog or tangible form, always and forever streaming or cloud-based, and perhaps not even able to be represented tangibly.

It's also just possible that it won't be something created by a person. So much that records or documents our lives today is done automatically or algorithmically, so it seems almost inevitable that sooner or later some object that is not the direct product of human hands and minds will have a profound effect on a par with those we're already familiar with.

About the only thing we can be fairly certain about is that there will be another, and another, and another, and that those will have multiple, not always obvious, stories behind their creation, use, lives, preservation, and impacts. Our history, as individuals and as societies and cultures, is inextricably and seemingly necessarily intertwined with these documenting things. They provide order and structure to lots of everyday and mundane parts of our lives, and in a few cases they take on great significance and meaning for generations on end.

And even though there is an increasing presence and number of technologies in play, let's not forget the people who lie behind these stories. It's extraordinary enough that we know Enheduanna's name from her writings; it's even more extraordinary to contemplate, more than a million and a half nights later, what she would make of that. The creators of the Rosetta Stone, on the other hand, were likely convinced that it would survive this long, though they could not have begun to imagine the journey it has taken and what it has become. We've run across a handful of popes, a few presidents, a senator, other people of great historical note like Einstein and Jefferson and Gutenberg and Susan B. Anthony and Mao.

In the main, though, we have men and women, represented here as the creators or objects of these documents, who otherwise would not have been widely known. Leonardo of Pisa explaining a novel system of counting and figuring. The Abbé Sieyès asking simple questions and helping to nudge France toward revolution. Larry Sanger and Jimmy Wales, so often at odds but united in an effort to revolutionize how we know what we know. So many people trying to bring order and structure to a corner of the world: Henry Martyn Robert, Fannie Farmer, Ebenezer Cobb Morley, Sir Ronald Fisher, Alfred Binet, the creators of the Internet Protocol and the DSM and the *Philosophical Transactions*. There is evil here, too, lurking forever in the shadows of the *Protocols of the Elders of Zion* and Joseph McCarthy's list, and loss, as memorialized in the AIDS Quilt and the Vietnam Veterans Memorial, and hope for the future in Alfred Nobel's will and the Alaska check and the 19th Amendment. And representing the ordinary people doing ordinary things that were unknowingly poised to be extraordinary, we have Abraham Zapruder starting his movie camera, Catherine Brewer about to receive her diploma, Francis Scott Key scratching out lyrics, Rose Mary Woods transcribing a tape recording, J. Howard Miller designing a poster he'll never know will be reproduced around the world decades later, Theresa LePore trying to make sure her older voters can clearly see what they're voting for.

While the forms and purposes and functions of these things will evolve, we will nonetheless still have them, and have to have them. They fulfill vital functions in our world, mostly unremarked and unremarkable, though they all have stories, and like these documents, those stories will go on as well.

ABOUT THE AUTHOR

Joseph Janes is associate professor at the University of Washington Information School. A frequent speaker in the United States and abroad, he is the author of several books on librarianship, technology, and their relationship, including *Library 2020*, and has written a monthly column for *American Libraries* magazine since 2002. He is the creator and host of *Documents That Changed the World*, a popular podcast series on the cultural impact of historic documents. He holds the MLS and PhD from Syracuse University and has taught at the University of Michigan, University of Toronto, University of North Carolina at Chapel Hill, and State University of New York at Albany as well as Syracuse and Washington.